Robert Williams Buchanan

The Land of Lorne

Or, a poet's adventures in the Scottish Hebrides

Robert Williams Buchanan

The Land of Lorne
Or, a poet's adventures in the Scottish Hebrides

ISBN/EAN: 9783337319403

Printed in Europe, USA, Canada, Australia, Japan

Cover: Foto ©Andreas Hilbeck / pixelio.de

More available books at **www.hansebooks.com**

THE LAND OF LORNE;

OR,

A POET'S ADVENTURES IN THE SCOTTISH HEBRIDES,

INCLUDING

THE CRUISE OF THE "TERN" TO THE OUTER HEBRIDES.

BY

ROBERT BUCHANAN.

TWO VOLUMES IN ONE.

———•———

NEW YORK:
FRANCIS B. FELT & CO., 91 MERCER STREET.
1871.

TO

Her Royal Highness

THE PRINCESS LOUISE

THESE PICTURES OF HER FUTURE HOME

IN THE HEBRIDES

ARE

(WITH HER ROYAL HIGHNESS' EXPRESS PERMISSION)

INSCRIBED,

ON THE OCCASION OF HER MARRIAGE,

BY THE AUTHOR.

January, 1871.

THE LAND OF LORNE.

"A LAND of rainbows spanning glens whose walls,
 Rock-built, are hung with many-colored mists;
 Of far-stretched meres, whose salt flood never rests—
 Of tuneful caves and playful waterfalls—
 Of mountains varying momently their crests.
 Proud be this land! whose poorest huts are halls
 Where Fancy entertains becoming guests,
 While native song the heroic past recalls."

WORDSWORTH.

PREFATORY NOTE.

A SMALL portion of the "Cruise of the *Tern*" has appeared in print before, though in a very imperfect shape; all the rest of the present work is now published for the first time. The pictures of life and scenery, such as they are, speak for themselves, and appeal more or less to everybody; but the narrative of the *Tern's* cruise may have a special interest for yachtsmen, as showing what a very small craft can do with proper management. The *Tern*, I believe, was the smallest craft of the kind that ever ventured round the point of Ardnamurchan, and thence to Ultima Thule, or the Outer Hebrides; but there is no reason whatever why other tiny yachts should not follow suit, and venture out to the wilds. To any sportsman desirous of such an expedition, and able to stand rough accommodation and wild weather, I can promise glorious amusement, just faintly spiced with a delightful sense of danger, sometimes more fanciful than real, frequently much more real than fanciful.

R. B.

CONTENTS.

PICTURES OF LORNE AND THE ISLES.

CHAPTER I.

FIRST GLIMPSE OF LORNE.

PAGE.

The White House on the Hill—The Land of Lorne—First Impressions of Oban—The Celtic Workmen—Maclean, Mactavish, and Duncan of the Pipes—The Lords of Lorne and their Descendants—Battle between Bruce and John of Lorne—Dunollie Castle—Glorification of Mist and Rain—An Autumn Afternoon—Old Castles—Dunstaffnage, ... 17

CHAPTER II.

PICTURES INLAND.

The Seasons—Cuckoos—Summer Days—Autumn—Winter—Moorland Lochs—The Fir Wood—The Moors and the Sea—Farm-houses and Crofters' Huts—Traces of former Cultivation on the Hills—The Ruined Sacters—Graveyard at Dunstaffnage—The Island of Inishail, ... 46

1*

CHAPTER III.

THE HEART OF LORNE.

PAGE.

Loch Awe and its Ancient Legend—Summer Days on the Lake—The Legend of Fraoch Eilan—Kilchurn Castle—Effects of Moonlight and of Storm—View from Glenara—The Pools of Cladich—Duncan Ban of the Songs—His Coire Cheathaich—His Mairi Ban Og, and Last Adieu to the Hills—Songs of the Children of the Mist—The Pass of Awe—The Ascent of Ben Cruachan, ... 53

CHAPTER IV.

SPORTS ON THE MOORS AND LOCHS.

Grouse and Black-game Shooting—A September Day on the Moors—The Grouse-Shooter—Peat-Bogs—Arrival of Snipe and Woodcock—Mountain Lochs and other Haunts of Wild Fowl—False and True Sportsmen, ... 79

CHAPTER V.

THE FIRTH OF LORNE.

The *Ocean Queen*, or *Coffin*—Shon Macnab's Race with "the Barber"—Lachlan Finlay—From Crinan to the Dorus Mhor—Hebridean Tides—Scarba—The Gulf of Corryvreckan—Its Horrors and Perils—Luing and the Small Isles—The Open Firth—Easdale and its Quarriers—Tombs at the Door—Miseries of Calm—Gylen Castle and the Island of Kerrera—King Haco's Invasion of the Hebrides—A Puff from the Southeast—The Island of Mull—Johnson and Boswell in the Hebrides—A Run to Tobermory—Loch Sunart—A Rainy Day—Ardtornish Castle—Anchored between Wind and Tide—Night on the Firth—Troubles of Darkness—Farewell to the *Ocean Queen*—Arrival of the *Tern*, ... 89

CHAPTER VI.

THE "TERN'S" FIRST FLIGHT.

PAGE.

The *Tern* Afloat—Off Ardnamurchan—First Glimpses of the Isles— The Cuchullin Hills—General Reflections—Flashing Forward—The Party on Board—The Scaur of Eig—Rum—Birds of the Ocean— Muck—Sunset on the Waters—Loch Scresort, Rum—The Gaelic Skipper—The Widow—A Climb among the Peaks—View of the Western Ocean from Rum—The *Tern* Weighing Anchor—Kilmory Bay—First View of Canna—At Anchor, ... 121

CHAPTER VII.

CANNA AND ITS PEOPLE.

The Laird of Canna—His Kingly Power—Prosperity of the State— The Island—The Old Tower—Canna in Storm and in Calm—The Milking—Twilight—A Poem by David Gray—Haunts of the Ocean Birds—Whispers from the Sea—The Canna People—The Quiet Life —The Graveyard on the Hill-side, ... 139

CHAPTER VIII.

EIRADH OF CANNA, ... 155

THE CRUISE OF THE "TERN."

CHAPTER IX.

NIGHT ON THE MINCH.

PAGE

Gloomy Prophecies—Terrors of the Minch—The Viking—Hamish Shaw, the Pilot—Leaving Canna Harbor—Pictures of Skye and the Cuchullins—Remarks on Sir Walter Scott and his Poems—Afloat on the Minch—the Far-off Isles—Twilight—Hamish Shaw at the Helm—Summer Night—Talk about Ghosts and Superstitions—The Evil Eye—The Death-Cry—Wind Rising—Wind and Mist—Water Snakes—Midnight—The Strange Ship—Peep o' Day—The Red Buoy—Anchorage in Loch Boisdale, ... 189

CHAPTER X.

THE FISHERS OF THE LONG ISLAND.

Loch Boisdale—The *Tern* at Anchor—The Inn and the Population—Rain—Boisdale in the Herring Season—Fishing-boats and Camps—A Night in a West-Country Smack—Herring-gutters—Habits of East-Country Fishermen, ... 219

CHAPTER XI.

GLIMPSES OF THE OUTER HEBRIDES.

PAGE.

First Glimpse—The Uists and Benbecula—Their Miserable Aspects
—Hamish Shaw—Solemnity of the People—Brighter Glimpses—
The Western Coast of the Island—Winter Storm—The Sound of
Harris—The Norwegian Skipper—The Fjords—Kelp-burners—View
from Kenneth Hill, Loch Boisdale—A Sunset—The Lagoons—
Characteristics of the People—Civilized and Uncivilized—Miserable
Dwellings—Comfortable Attire—Their Superstitions and Deep Spiritual Life, ... 229

CHAPTER XII.

SPORT IN THE WILDS.

The Sportsmen and their Dogs—The Hunter's Badge—The Weapons—Shooting in the Fjords—Eiders, Cormorants, Curlews—Duck-shooting near Loch Boisdale—The *Tern* at Anchor in Loch Huport
—Starvation—Wild-Goose Shooting on Loch Bee—The Shepherd's
Gifts—Goose Shooting on Loch Phlogibeg—The Melancholy Loch
—Breeding Places of the Wild Fowl—Rain-Storm—" Bonnie Kilmeny"—Short Rations—The Passing Ship—Red Deer, Salmon, and
Eagles—Corbies and Ravens—Seal Shooting in the Maddy Fjords
—Reflection on Wild Sports in General, ... 252

CHAPTER XIII.

COASTING SKYE.

Effects of Cruising on Yacht and Voyagers—Recrossing the Minch—
Northwest Coast of Skye—Becalmed off Loch Suizort—Midnight—
Lights of Heaven and Ocean—Dawn—Columns of the North Coast
—The Quirang—Scenery of the Northeast Coast—The Storm—
Portree Harbor, ... 291

CHAPTER XIV.

THE SAGA OF HACO THE KING.

I.—KING ALEXANDER'S DREAM AND DEATH, . . . 306
II.—KING HACO GATHERS HIS HOST, ... 303
III.—SAILING OF THE GREAT FLEET, ... 310
IV.—KING HACO'S SAILING SOUTHWARD, ... 312
V.—THE KING'S FLEET MEETS WITH A GREAT STORM, . 314
VI.—THE BATTLE OF LARGS, ... 316
VII.—KING HACO SAILS NORTHWARD, ... 319
VIII.—KING HACO'S SICKNESS, ... 322
IX.—KING HACO'S DEATH AND BURIAL, ... 324

CHAPTER XV.

GLEN SLIGACHAN AND THE CUCHULLINS.

Sconser and Sligachan—Party and Guide—Dawn on the Cuchullins—
Scuir-na-Gillean—A Rhapsody on Geology—Fire and Ice—The
Path along the Glen—Hart-o'-Corry—Ben Blaven—A Monologue
on Ossian—Schneider and the Red Deer—First Glimpse of the
"Corry of the Water"—Lochan Dhu, ... 327

CHAPTER XVI.

CORRUISK; OR, THE CORRY OF THE WATER.

The Lone Water—The Region of Twilight—*Blocs Perches*—Hamish Shaw's Views—The Cave of the Ghost—The Dunvegan Pilot's Story—Echoes, Mists and Shadows—Squalls in Loch Scavaig—A Highlander's Ideas of Beauty—Camping out in the Corry—A Stormy Dawn—The Fishermen and the Strange Harbor—Loch Scavaig—The Spar Cave—Camasunary, ... 354

CHAPTER XVII.

Epilogue; The "Tern's" Last Flight, ... 382

THE LAND OF LORNE.

CHAPTER I.

FIRST GLIMPSE OF LORNE.

The White House on the Hill—The Land of Lorne—First Impressions of Oban—The Celtic Workmen—Maclean, Mactavish, and Duncan of the Pipes—The Lords of Lorne and their Descendants—Battle between Bruce and John of Lorne—Dunollie Castle—Glorification of Mist and Rain—An Autumn Afternoon—Old Castles—Dunstaffnage.

WHEN the Wanderer (as the writer purposes to call himself in these pages, in order to get rid of the perkish and impertinent first person singular) first came to dwell in Lorne, and roamed, as is his wont, up hill and down dale from dawn to sunset, he soon grew weary of a landscape which seemed tame and colorless, of hills that, with one or two magnificent exceptions, seemed cold and unpicturesque. It was the springtime, moreover, and such a springtime! Day after day the rain descended, sometimes in a dreary "smurr," at others in a moaning torrent, and when the clouds did part, the sun looked through with a dismal and fitful stare, like a face swollen with weeping. The conies were frisking everywhere, fancying it always twilight. The mountain loch overflowed its banks, while far beneath the surface the buds of the yellow lily were wildly struggling upward, and the overfed burns roared day and night. Wherever one went, the farmer scowled, and the gamekeeper shook his head. Lorne seemed as weary as the Uists, *weary* but not *eerie*, and so without fascination. In a kind of dovecote perched on a hill, far from human habitation, the Wanderer dwelt and watched, while the gloomy gillie came and went, and the dogs howled from the rain-drenched kennel. The weasel bred at the very door, in some obscure corner of a drain, and the young weasels used to come fearlessly out on Sunday morning and play in the rain. Two hundred yards above the house was a mountain tarn, on the shores of which a desolate couple of teal were trying hard to hatch a brood ; and all around the miserable grouse and grayhens were sitting like stones, drenched on their eggs, hoping against hope. In the far distance, over a dreary sweep of marshes and pools, lay the little town of Oban, looking, when the mists cleared away a little, exactly like the wood-cuts of the City of Destruction in popular editions of the "Pilgrim's Progress." Now and then, too, the figure of a certain genial Edinburgh Professor, with long white hair and flowing plaid, might be seen toiling upward to Doubting Castle, exactly like Christian on his pilgrimage, but carrying, instead of a bundle on his back, the whole of Homer's hexameters in his brain, set to such popular tunes as "John Brown," and "Are ye sleepin', Maggie?" Few others had courage to climb so high, in weather so inclement; and, wonderful to add, the professor did not in the least share the new-comer's melancholy, but roundly vowed in good Doric that there was no sweeter spot in all the world than the "bonnie land of Lorne."

The Wanderer was for a time skeptical; but, as the days lengthened, and his eyes accommodated themselves to the new prospect, his skepticism changed into faith, his faith into enthusiasm, his enthusiasm into perfect love and passionate enjoyment.

The truth is, that Lorne, even in the summer season, does not captivate at first sight, does not galvanize the senses with beauty and brightly stimulate the imagination. Glencoe lies beyond it, and Morven just skirts it, and the only great mountain is Cruachan. There is no portion of the landscape which may be described as " grand," in the same sense that Glen Sligachan and Glencoe are grand; no sheet of water solemnly beautiful as Corruisk; no strange lagoons like those of the sea-surrounded Uist and Benbecula; for Lorne is fair and gentle, a green pastoral land, where the sheep bleat from a thousand hills, and the gray homestead stands in the midst of its own green fields, and the snug macadamized roads ramify in all directions to and from the tiny capital on the seaside, with the country carts bearing produce, the drouthy farmer trotting home at all hours on his sure-footed nag, and the stage-coach, swift and gay, wakening up the echoes in summer-time with the guard's cheery horn. There is greenness everywhere, even where the scenery is most wild—fine slopes of pasture alternating with the heather; and, though want and squalor and uncleanness are to be found here, as in all other parts of the Highlands, comfortable houses abound. Standing on one of the high hills above Oban, you see unfolded before you, as in a map, the whole of Lorne proper, with Ben Cruachan in the far distance, closing the scene to the eastward, towering over the whole prospect in supreme height and beauty, and cutting the gray sky with his two red and rocky cones. At his feet, but invisible to you, sleeps Loch Awe, a mighty fresh-water lake, communicating, through a turbulent river, with the sea. Looking northward, taking the beautifully-wooded promontory of Dunollie for a foreground, you behold the great firth of Lorne, with the green flat island of Lismore extended at the feet of the mountain region of Morven, and the waters creeping inland, southward of the Glencoe range, to form, first, the long, narrow arm of Loch Etive, which stretches many miles inland close past the base of Cruachan; and, second, the winding basin of Loch Creran, which separates Lorne from Glencoe. Yonder, to the west, straight across the firth, lies Mull, separated from Morven by its gloomy Sound. Southward, the view is closed by a range of unshapely hills, very green in color and unpicturesque in form, at the feet of which, but invisible, is Loch Feochan, another arm of the sea, and beyond the mouth of this loch stretches the seaboard, with numberless outlying islets, as far as the lighthouse of Easdale and the island of Scarba. Between the landmarks thus slightly indicated stretches the district of Lorne, some forty miles in length and fifteen in breadth; and, seen in clear, bright weather, free from the shadow of the rain-cloud, its innumerable green slopes and cultivated hollows betoken at a glance its peaceful character. There is, we repeat, greenness everywhere, save on the tops of the highest hills—greenness in the valleys and on the hillsides—greenness of emerald brightness on the edges of the sea—greenness on the misty marshes. The purple heather is plentiful, too, its deep tints glorifying the scene from its pastoral monotony, but seldom tyrannizing over the landscape. Abundant, also, are the signs of temporal prosperity—the wreaths of smoke arising everywhere from humble dwellings; the sheep and cattle crying on the hills; the fishing-boats and trading-vessels scattered on the firth; the flocks of cattle and horses being driven on set days to the grass-market at Oban.

This same town of Oban, prettily situated along the skirts of a pleasant bay, and boasting a resident population of some two thousand inhabitants, has been fitly enough designated the "key of the Highlands;" since, from its quaint quay, composed of the hulk of an old wreck, the splendid fleet of Highland steamers start for all parts of the western coast and adjacent islands. In summer-time a few visitors occupy the neat villas which ornament the western slopes above the town, and innumerable tourists, ever coming and going to the sharp ringing of the steamboat bell, lend quite a festive appearance to the little main street. As a tourist, the Wanderer first made the acquaintance of Oban and its people, and resided among them for some weeks, during which time there was a general conspiracy on the part of everybody to reduce him to bankruptcy; extortionate boatmen, grasping small tradesmen, greedy car-drivers, all regarding him as a lawful victim. He was lonely, and the gentle people took him in; he was helpless, and they did for him; until at last he fled, vowing never to visit the place again. Fate, stronger than human will, interposed, and he became the tenant of the White House on the Hill. He arrived in the fallow season, before the swift boats begin to bring their stock of festive travelers, and found Oban plunged in funereal gloom—the tradesmen melancholy, the boatmen sad and unsuspicious, the hotel-waiters depressed and servile, instead of brisk and patronizing. The grand waiter at the Great Western Hotel, one whom to see was to reverence, whose faintest smile was an honor, and who conferred a life-long obligation when he condescended to pour out your champagne, still lingered in the south, and the lesser waiters of the lesser hotels lingered afar with the great man. All was sad and weary, and, at first, all looks were cold. But speedily the Wanderer discovered that the people of Oban regarded him with grateful affection. He was the first man who, for no other reason than sheer love of silence and picturesqueness, had come to reside among them "out of the season." In a few weeks, he not only discovered that the extortioners of his former visit were no such harpies after all, but poor devils, anxious to get hay while the sun shone. He found that these same extortioners were the merest scum of the town, the veriest froth, underneath which there existed the sediment of the real population, which, for many mysterious reasons, no mere tourist is ever suffered to behold. He found around him most of the Highland virtues—gentleness, hospitality, spirituality. No hand was stretched out to rob him now. Wherever he went there was a kind word from the men, and a courtesy from the women. The poor pale faces brightened, and he saw the sweet spirit looking forth with that deep inner hunger which is ever marked on the Celtic physiognomy. Every day deepened his interest and increased his satisfaction. He knew now that he had come to a place where life ran fresh, and simple, and, to a great extent, unpolluted.

Not to make the picture tender, let him add that he soon discovered for himself—what every one else discovers, sooner or later—that the majority of the town population was hopelessly lazy. There was no surplus energy anywhere, but there were some individuals who, for sheer unhesitating, unblushing, wholesale indolence, were certainly unapproachable on this side of Jamaica. It so happened that the Wanderer wanted a new wing added to the White House, and it was arranged with a "contractor," one Angus Maclean, that it should be erected at a trifling expense within three weeks. A week passed, during which Angus Maclean occupied himself in abstruse meditation, coming two or three times to the spot, dreamily chewing stalks of grass, and measuring imaginary walls with a rule. Then, all of a sudden, one morning, a load of stones was deposited at the door, and the workmen arrived—men of all ages and all temperaments, from the clean, methodic mason to the wild, hirsute hodsman. In other parts of the world houses are built silently, not so in Lorne; the babble of Gaelic was incessant. The work crept on, surely if slowly, relieved by intervals of Gaelic melody and political debate, during which all labor ceased. Angus Maclean came and went, and, of course, it was sometimes necessary to advise with him as to details; and great was his delight whenever he could beguile the Wanderer into a discussion as to the shape of a window or the size of a door, for the conversation was sure to drift into general topics, such as the Irish Land question or the literature of the Highlands, and the laborers would suspend their toil and cluster round to listen while Angus explained his "views." In a little more than a month, the masonry was completed, and the carpenter's assistance necessary. A week passed, and no carpenter came. Summoned to council, Angus Maclean explained that the carpenter would be up "the first thing in the morning." Two days afterward, he did appear, and it was at once apparent that, compared with him, all the other inhabitants of Oban were models of human energy. With him came a lazy boy, with sleep-dust in his round blobs of eyes. The carpenter's name was Donald Mactavish—"a fine man," as the contractor explained, "tho' he takes a drap." The first day, Donald Mactavish smoked half a dozen pipes, and sawed a board. The next day, he didn't appear—"it was that showery, and I was afraid of catching the cold;" but the lazy boy came up, and went to sleep in the unfinished wing. The third day, Donald appeared at noon, looking very pale and shaky. Thus matters proceeded. Sometimes a fair day's work was secured, and Donald was so triumphant at his own energy that he disappeared the following morning altogether. Some times Donald was unwell; sometimes it was "o'er showery." Tears and entreaties made no impression on Mactavish, and he took his own time. Then the slater appeared, with a somewhat brisker style of workmanship. Finally, a moody plasterer strolled that way, and promised to whitewash the walls "when he came back frae Mull," whither he was going on business. To cut a long story short, the new wing to the White House was complete in three months, whereas the same number of hands might have finished it with perfect ease in a fortnight.

Thus far, we have given only the dark side of the picture. Turning to the bright side, we herewith record our vow that, whenever we build again, we will seek the aid of those same workmen from Lorne. Why, the Wanderer has all his life lived among wise men, or men who deemed themselves wise, among great book-makers, among brilliant minstrels, but for sheer unmitigated enjoyment, give him the talk of those Celts—flaming radicals every one of them, so radical, forsooth, as to have about equal belief in Mr. Gladstone and Mr. Disraeli. They had their own notions of freedom, political and social. "Sell my vote?" quoth Angus; "to be sure, I'd sell my vote!" And he would thereupon most fiercely expound his convictions, and give as good a reason for not voting at all as the best of those clever gentlemen who laugh at political representation. At heart, too, Angus was a Fenian, though not in the bad and bloodthirsty sense. Donald Mactavish, on the other hand, was of a gentle nature, inclined to acquiesce in all human arrangement, so long as he got his pipe and his glass, and was not hurried about his work. With playful humor, he would "draw out" the fiery Angus for the Wanderer's benefit. Then the two would come suddenly to war about the relative merits of certain obscure Gaelic poets, and would rain quotations at each other until they grew hoarse. They had both the profoundest contempt for English literature and the English language, as compared with their beloved Gaelic. They were both full of old legends and quaint Highland stories. The workmen, too, were in their own way as interesting—fine natural bits of humanity, full of intelligence and quiet affection. Noteworthy among them was old Duncan Campbell, who had in his younger days been piper in a Highland regiment, and who now, advanced in years, worked hard all day as a hodsman, and nightly—clean, washed, and shaven—played to himself on the beloved pipes, till overpowered with sleep. Duncan was simply delicious. More than once he brought up the pipes and played on the hillsides, while the workmen danced. These pipes were more to him than bread and meat. As he played them, his face became glorified. His skill was not great, and his tunes had a strange monotony about them, but they gave to his soul a joy passing the glory of battle or the love of women. He was never too weary for them in the evening, though the day's work had been ever so hard and long. Great was his pride and joy that day, when the house was finished, and, with pipes playing and ribbons flying, he headed the gleeful workmen as they marched away to the town.

From that day forward the White House on the

Hill remained silent in the solitude. Though the summer season came, and with it the stream of tourists and visitors, the Wanderer abode undisturbed. Far off he saw the white gleam of the little town across the long stretch of field and marsh, but he seldom bent his footstops thither, save when constrained by urgent business. Nevertheless, faces came and went, and bright scenic glimpses rose and passed, while day after day he found his love deepening for the Land of Lorne.

In a certain sense, the whole Hebrides are the Land of Lorne, Skye as much so as Kerrera, Coll and Tiree and Rum as much as Appin and Awe, Loch Scavaig, and Loch Eishart as much so as Lochs Feochan and Etive. The family house of Lorne began with a son of Somerled, Thane of Argyll and Lord of the Isles, who worried and bullied the Scottish king, Malcolm, until slain in battle at Renfrew. By a daughter of Olaus, King of Man, Somerled had two sons, Ronald and Dougall, the first of whom was the ancestor of the Lords of the Isles, or Macronalds, and the second of whom bequeathed his surname to the Lords of Lorne, or Macdougalls. Dougall got for his birthright certain mainland territories in Argyllshire, now known as the three districts of Lorne, but his name and fame stretched far further and embraced many of the isles. He resided in the stronghold of Dunstaffnage, with all the power and more than the glory of a petty prince. Thenceforward, the Macdougalls of Lorne increased and multiplied. At the time when Haco invaded the west (1263) they were great and prosperous, and fierce in forays against the Cailean Mòr, or

Knight of Loch Awe, from whom comes the ducal house of Argyll. For year after year the Macdougall of Lorne fought against the dominion of Bruce, who had slain the Red Comyn, Lorne's father-in-law, in the Dominican church at Dumfries; wherefore Bruce, when his power rose in Scotland, marched into Argyllshire to lay waste the country. John of Lorne, son of the chieftain, was posted with his clansmen in the Pass of Awe, a wild and narrow pathway, passing on below the verge of Ben Cruachan, and surrounded by precipices to all appearance inaccessible. The military skill of Bruce, however, enabled him to obtain possession of the heights above, whence his archers discharged a fatal volley of arrows on the discomfited men of Argyll, who were routed with great slaughter—John, their leader, just managing to escape by means of his boats on the lake. After this victory, Bruce "harried" Argyllshire, and besieging Dunstaffnage Castle, on the west shore of Lorne, reduced it by fire and sword, and placed in it a garrison and governor of his own. Alaster, the chieftain, at last submitted, but John, still rebellious, escaped to England. When the wars between the Bruce and Baliol factions again broke out in the reign of David II., the Macdougalls, with their hereditary enmity to the house of Bruce, were again upon the losing side. David II., and his successor, stripped them of the greater part of their territories, and in 1434 one Robert Stuart was appointed to administer their lands under the title of Seneschal of Lorne. In spite of all this terrible adversity, the Macdougalls still continued to exist, even to flourish in a private way. They retained the Castle of Dunollie, with the titles of chieftainship over the clan. But in the year 1715, the irrepressible blood burst forth again, and the Macdougall of the period, having joined the insurrection, found himself mulcted of his estate. Thirty years afterward, however, it was restored to the family, whom sad experience had rendered quiescent during the rebellion of that period. The present representative, a quiet major in the army, eats the Queen's bread, and preserves the family glory in a modest, unassuming way. He has a modern house and farm close to the ruins of Dunollie, the ancient stronghold of his race.

These same ruins of Dunollie stand on the very point of the promontory to the northwest of Oban, and form one of the finest foregrounds possible for all the scenery of the Frith. There is no old castle in Scotland quite so beautifully situated. On days of glassy calm, every feature of it is mirrored in the sea, with browns and grays that ravish the artistic eye. There is not too much of it left; just a wall or two, lichen-covered and finely broken. Seen from a distance, it is always a perfect piece of color, in fit keeping with the dim and doubtful sky; but in late autumn, when the woods of the promontory have all their glory—fir-trees of deep black green, intermixed with russet and golden birches—Dunollie is something to watch for hours and wonder at. The day is dark, but a strong silvern light is in the air, a light in which all the blue shadows deepen; while far off in the west, over green Kerrera, is one long streak of faint violet, above which gather strongly-defined

clouds in a brooding slate-colored mass. On such a
day—and such days are numberless in the Highland
autumn—the silvern light strikes strong on Dunollie,
bringing out every line and tint of the noble ruin,
while the sea beneath, with the merest shadow of the
cold, faint wind upon it, shifts its tints like a sword-
blade in the light, from soft steel-gray to deep, slumbrous blue. It only wants Morven in the background,
dimly purple with dark, plum-colored stains, and the
swathes of white mist folded round the high peaks, to
complete the perfect picture.

The visitor to the west coast of Scotland is, doubtless, often disappointed by the absence of bright colors
and brilliant contrasts, such as he has been accustomed to in Italy and in Switzerland, and he goes away
too often with a malediction on the mist and the
rain, and an under-murmur of contempt for Scottish
scenery, such as poor Montalembert sadly expressed
in his life of the Saint of Iona. But what many
chance visitors despise becomes to the living resident
a constant source of joy. Those infinitely varied
grays—those melting, melodious, dimmest of browns—
those silvery gleams through the fine neutral tint of
cloud ! One gets to like strong sunlight least; it
dwarfs the mountains so, and destroys the beautiful
distance. Dark, dreamy days, with the clouds clear and
high, and the wind hushed; or wild days, with the dark
heavens blowing past like the rush of a sea, and the
shadows driving like mad things over the long grass
and the marshy pool; or sad days of rain, with dim,
pathetic glimpses of the white and weeping orb ; or
nights of the round moon, when the air throbs with

strange electric light, and the hill is mirrored dark as ebony in the glittering sheet of the loch; or nights of the Aurora and the lunar rainbow—on days and nights like those is the Land of Lorne beheld in its glory. Even during those superb sunsets, for which its coasts are famed—sunsets of fire divine, with all the tints of the prism—only west and east kindle to great brightness; while the landscape between reflects the glorious light dimly and gently, interposing mists and vapors, with dreamy shadows of the hills. These bright moments are exceptional; yet is it quite fair to say so when, a dozen times during the rainy day, the heart of the grayness bursts open, and the rainbow issues forth in complete semi-circle, glittering in glorious evanescence, with its dim ghost fluttering faintly above it on the dark heavens?

"My heart leaps up when I behold
A rainbow in the sky!"

The Iris comes and goes, and is, indeed, like the sunlight, "a glorious birth" wherever it appears; but for rainbows of all degrees of beauty, from the superb arch of delicately-defined hues that spans a complete landscape for minutes together to the delicate, dying thing that flutters for a moment on the skirt of the stormcloud, and dies to the sudden sob of the rain, the Wanderer knows no corner of the earth to equal Lorne and the adjacent isles.

Two qualities are necessary to the enjoyment of these things. The first quality is quiescence, or brooding-power—the patient faculty of waiting while images are impressing themselves upon you, of relinquishing your energetic identity and becoming a sort of human tarn or mirror. If you want to be "shocked," galvanized, so to speak, you must go elsewhere, say to Chimborazo or the North Pole. The second quality necessary is (to be Hibernian) not altogether a quality, but the acquired conviction that rain is beautiful and mist poetical, and that to be wet through twice or thrice a day is not undesirable. In point of fact, for actual "downpours" of water, the Highlands are not much worse than the rest of Great Britain, but the changes are more sudden and incalculable. To abide indoors on account of wet or lowering weather may do very well in Surrey, but it will not do in Lorne; for if you want to see the finest natural effects—if you want to get the best sport on land and water—if you want to do in Lorne as Lorne does—you must think no more of rain there than you do of dust in the city. Abolish waterproofs, which were invented by the devil; away with umbrellas, which were devised for old women, and are only tolerable when Leech's pretty girls are smiling under them; don a suit of thick tweed, such as any cotter weaves, cut a stick from the nearest blackthorn bush, and sally forth in all weathers. Let your boots be just easy enough to let the water "out" when it has managed to get "in," and you will be quite comfortable. Those who tell you that a damp coat and a wet shoe mean danger to your health are only talking nonsense. Tight waterproof boots and macintoshes are more fatal things than cold and rain.

Let it not be gathered from what we have said that the climate of Lorne is bad, and the rain unceasing. On the contrary, there are, nearly every year, long intervals of drought, glaring summer days, when the landscape "winks through the heat," and the sea is like molten gold. What we mean to convey is, that some of the finest natural effects are vaporous, and occur only when rain is falling or impending, and that it is pitiful in a strong man to miss these from fear of a wet skin. As we write, in the late autumn season, there is little to complain of on the score of wet. We have not had a drop of rain for a fortnight. The days have been bright and short, and the nights starry and bright, with frequent flashes of the aurora. It is the gloaming of the year—

"—— To russet brown
The heather faded. On the treeless hill,
O'er-rusted with the red decaying bracken,
The sheep crawl slow."

This is the brooding hush that precedes the stormy, wintry season, and all is inexpressibly beautiful. The wind blows chill and keen from the north, breaking the steel-gray waters of the firth into crisp-white waves; and, though it is late afternoon, the western sky hangs dark and chill over the mountains of Mull, while the east is softly bright, with clouds tinted to a faint crimson. There is no brightness on any of the hills, save to the east, where, suffused with a roseate flush, stands Ben Cruachan, surrounded by those lesser heights, beautifully christened the "Shepherds of Loch Etive," a space of daffodil sky just above him and them, and then, a mile higher, like a dome, one magnificent rose-colored cloud. Thus much it is possible to describe, but not so the strange vividness of the green tints everywhere, and the overpowering sense of height and distance. Though every fissure and cranny of Cruachan seems distinct in the red light, the whole mountain seems great, dreamy, and glorified. Walking on one of the neighboring hills, the Wanderer seems lifted far up into the air, into a still world, where the heart beats wildly, and the eyes grow dizzy looking downward on the mother-planet.

In autumn, and even in winter, stillness like this, dead brooding calm, sometimes steals over Lorne for weeks together, and all the colors deepen and brighten; but at such times, as at all others, the finest effects are those of the rain-cloud and the vapor, and no overpowering sense of sunlight comes to trouble the vision.

Standing on the high hill behind his house, the Wanderer commands a wondrous view of the whole firth of Lorne, and not least noticeable in the prospect is the number of ancient ruins. There, to begin with, is Dunollie, a fine foreground to Morven. Farther north, close at the mouth of Loch Etive, Dunstaffnage stands on its promontory—a ruin on a larger scale, but, on the whole, less picturesque. Far across the firth, on the southern promontory of Mull, looking darkly on the waters of the gloomy sound,

> "Where thwarting tides, with mingled roar,
> Part the swart hills from Morven's shore,"

looms Duart, the ancient stronghold of the Macleans; and farther still, scarcely distinguishable in the dim distance,

> "Ardtornish, on her frowning steep
> 'Twixt earth and heaven hung,"

overlooks the same sound. Others there are, shut out from view by intervening hills and headlands; indeed, wherever a bold promontory juts out into the water, there has been a castle, and more or less of the ruins remain. What light and meaning they lend to the prospect! What a fine appeal they have to the human sentiment, quite apart from their æsthetic beauty, their delicious coloring. To call them castles is perhaps less correct than to describe them as private mansions of castellated form, with certain provisions against sudden assault. In each of them, of old, dwelt some petty chief with his family and retainers; and at intervals, for some great end, these chiefs could flock together, as they did on the occasion of the betrothal of the Maid of Lorne—

> "Brave Torquil from Dunvegan high,
> Lord of the misty hills of Skye
> Macneil, wild Barra's ancient thane,
> Duart, of bold Clan-Gillian's strain,
> Fergus, of Canna's castled bay,
> Macduffith, Lord of Colonsay,"

and any number of others—sea-eagles, building their nests on the ocean headland, and flitting from bay to bay by night to plunder and to avenge. They seem to have chosen the sites of their wild dwellings quite as much for convenience in embarking and for fishing purposes as for strategical reasons. Few of the old castles gain any strength from their situation. There are some, of course, not situated close to the water— such as Finlagin, in Isla, which was placed on an inland lake, and others on the islands of Loch Dochart and Loch Lomond. Stalker Castle stood on an island

not much bigger than itself; so did Chisamil. None
of these are protected against military attack, many
of them being commanded by rising ground, a few
volleys from which would have made short work of
the defenders. Most of them, like Duart yonder,
stand on rocks accessible only on one side, so that they
are well protected against personal assault. One
thing was never forgotten—the dungeon for the cap-
tive foe.

Dunollie shows to most advantage at a distance, as
a part of the landscape. The ruins consist only of a
portion of the keep, which is overgrown with ivy. But
the view from the promontory is very grand, and close
at hand there is the Dog-Stone (*Clach-a'-choin*), a
huge mass of conglomerate rock rising up from the
shore, and identified as the stake to which the great
Fenian king (*Righ na Feinne*) used to tie his dog
Bran. Bran! Fingal! At the very names, how the
whole prospect changes! The ruins on each headland grow poor and insignificant, and in the large
shadows of the older heroes the small chieftains disappear. The eyes turn to Morven and the "sound-
ing halls of Selma," and, for the moment, all other
associations are forgotten.*

From Dunollie to Dunstaffnage is only a few miles'
walk, and it is one to be undertaken by all visitors to
Oban. The road winds through low hills of thyme
and heather, past green slopes where sheep bleat and
cattle low, skirting pleasant belts of woodland, and
occasionally fields of waving corn, and passes on by

* For remarks on the **Ossianic poetry**, see Vol. II., the chapter
on Glen Sligachan.

the side of Loch Etive to the Pass of Awe; but leaving it some distance before it reaches the loch, you must strike along the seashore to the promontory, or isthmus, on which stands Dunstaffnage—a large square ruin, not very picturesque when so approached, though commanding a magnificent view. The custodian, who shows visitors over the castle, is a solemn young Celt, a gardener, who has quite a pretty little orchard adjoining his cottage. If you press him, he will give you the history of Dunstaffnage in a narrative fully as interesting, and nearly as reliable, as any tale of fairy-land, but distrust him, and turn to the guide-book, an extract from which we give below.*

* According to the Pictish chronicles, Kenneth MacAlpine transferred the seat of government from Dunstaffnage to Forteviot, in Perthshire, in 843. As the Norwegians began to make inroads upon the western coast of Scotland about this time, Dr. Jamieson thinks it highly probable that, on being deserted by its royal possessors, Dunstaffnage became a stronghold of the Norse invaders. For several centuries the place is lost sight of in the national annals, and only reappears during the eventful reign of Robert Bruce, who took possession of it after his victory over the Lord of Lorne in the Pass of Awe. At that time it belonged to Alexander of Argyll, father of John, Lord of Lorne. Old charters show that the castle and lands of Dunstaffnage were, in 1436, granted to Dugal, son of Colin, Knight of Loch Awe, the ancestor of the family in whose possession, as "Captains of Dunstaffnage," it has remained to the present day. The existing representative of the family is Sir Donald Campbell, Bart., of Dunstaffnage. As a stronghold of the clan Campbell, Dunstaffnage was maintained down to the rebellions in 1715 and 1745, when it was garrisoned by the royal forces. The old castle is said to have been dismantled by fire, in 1715. The nominal hereditary keeper of the castle is the Duke of Argyll.

The castle is built in a quadrangular form, 87 feet square with-

Perhaps, instead of engaging the faculties with doubtful tradition, it is wise to reserve the guide-book till you reach your home or inn, and to spend the whole time of your visit in looking at the surrounding prospect. Round the isles beneath the promontory, the tide boils ominously, setting in toward Connel Ferry, a mile distant, where Loch Etive suddenly narrows itself from the breadth of a mile to that of two hundred yards, causing the waters to rush in or out, at flood or ebb, with the velocity of a torrent shooting to the fall. If the wind is down, you can hear a deep sound, just as Sir Walter describes it:

―――"The raging
Of Connel with his rocks engaging;"

for the narrow passage is blocked by a ledge of rock, "awash" at half tide, causing a tremendous overfall, the roaring surge of which is audible for miles. Seen from here, Cruachan seems to have quite altered his position—surrounded by the great "Shepherds," he casts his gigantic shadow over the head of Loch Etive, and seems in close proximity to the Glencoe range. Turning westward, you look right across the great waters of Loch Linnhe, and see the long green island

in the walls, with round towers at three of the angles. The height of the walls is 66 feet, and their thickness 9 feet. The walls outside measure 270 feet; and the circumference of the rock on which the castle stands is 300 feet. The entrance seaward is by a staircase, but it is probable that in ancient times it was by a drawbridge. A brass gun is preserved on the battlements bearing the date of 1700, showing that it is not a wrecked trophy of a ship of the Spanish Armada (1588), as is usually reported.

of Lismore, or the Great Garden, stretching snake-like at the feet of the mountains of Morven; and, following the chain of these mountains northward, where they begin to grow dim in height and distance, tracing the mighty outlines of Kingairloch and Ardgower, you may catch a glimpse, dim to very dreaminess—a vague, momentary glimpse, which leaves you doubtful if you look on hill or cloud—of the monarch of Scottish mountains—Ben Nevis.

CHAPTER II.

PICTURES INLAND.

The Season — Cuckoos — Summer Days — Autumn - Winter — Moorland Lochs — The Fir Wood — The Moors and the Sea — Farm-houses and Crofters' Huts — Traces of former Cultivation on the Hills — The Ruined Sacters — Graveyard at Dunstaffnage — The Island of Inishail.

This is a marvelous land, a scene of beauty, ever changing, and giving fresh cause for joy and wonder. Every year deepens the charm. One never tires of Cruachan and the "Shepherds," or of Dunollie and Morven, or of the far-off glimpses of the sea. There are no two days alike. Last year, it seemed that every possible effect of sun and shadow had presented itself; and now not a week passes without producing some scenic loveliness which comes like a revelation. But the charm is moral as well as æsthetic. The landscape would be nothing without its human faces. Humanity does not obtrude itself in this solitude, but it is none the less present, consecrating the whole scene with its mysterious and spiritual associations.

As the year passes there is always something new to attract one who loves Nature. When the winds of March have blown themselves faint, and the April heaven has ceased weeping, there comes a rich sunny day, and all at once the cuckoo is heard telling his name to all the hills. Never was such a place for cuckoos in the world. The cry comes from every tuft of wood, from every hillside, from every projecting crag. The bird himself, so far from courting retirement, flutters across your path at every step, attended invariably by half a dozen excited small birds; alighting a few yards off, crouches down for a moment between his slate-colored wings; and finally, rising again, crosses your path with his sovereign cry—

"O blithe new-comer, I have heard,
I hear thee, and rejoice!"

Then, as if at a given signal, the trout leaps a foot into the air from the glassy loch, the buds of the water-lily float to the surface, the lambs bleat from the green and heathery slopes, the rooks caw from the distant rookery, the cock-grouse screams from the distant hill-top, and the blackthorn begins to blossom over the nut-brown pools of the burn. Pleasant days follow, days of high white clouds and fresh winds whose wings are full of warm dew. Wherever you wander over the hills, you see the lambs leaping, and again and again it is your lot to rescue a poor little one from the deep pool, or steep ditch, which he has vainly sought to leap in following his mother. If you are a sportsman you rejoice, for there is not a hawk to be seen anywhere, and the weasel and the foumart have not yet begun to promenade the mountains. About this time more rain falls, preliminary to a burst of fine summer weather, and innumerable glow-worms light their lamps in the marshes. At last, the golden days come, and all things are busy with their young. Frequently, in the midsummer, there is a drought for weeks together. Day after day the sky is cloudless and blue; the mountain lake sinks lower and lower, till it seems about to dry up entirely; the mountain brooks dwindle to mere silver threads for the water-ousel to fly by, and the young game often die for the lack of water; while afar off, with every red vein distinct in the burning light, without a drop of vapor to moisten his scorching crags, stands Ben Cruachan. By this time the hills are assuming their glory—the mysterious bracken has shot up all in a night, to cover them with a green carpet between the knolls of heather, the lichen is penciling the crags with most delicate silver, purple, and gold, and in all the valleys there are stretches of light yellow corn and deep green patches of foliage. The corn-crake has come, and his cry fills the valleys. Walking on the edge of the corn-field you put up the partridges—fourteen cheepers the size of a thrush, and the old pair to lead them. From the edge of the peat-bog the old cock-grouse rises, and if you are sharp you may see the young following the old hen through the deep heather close by. The snipe drums in the marsh. The hawk, having brought out his young among the crags of Kerrera, is hovering still as stone over the edge of the hill. Then, perchance, just at the end of July, there is a gale from the south, blowing for two days black as Erebus with cloud and rain; then going up into the northwest and blowing for one day with little or no rain; and dying away at last with a cold puff from the north. All at once, as it were, the sharp sound of firing is echoed from hill to hill; and on every mount tin you see the sportsman climbing with his dog ranging above and before him, the keeper following, and the gillie lagging far behind. It is the twelfth of August. Thenceforth, for two months at least, there are broiling days, interspersed with storms and showers, and the firing continues more or less from dawn to sunset.

Day after day, as the autumn advances, the tint of the hills is getting deeper and richer, and by October, when the beech-leaf yellows and the oak-leaf reddens, the dim purples and the deep greens of the heather are perfect. Of all seasons in Lorne the late autumn is, perhaps, the most beautiful. The sea has a deeper hue, the sky a mellower light. There are long days of northerly wind, when every crag looks perfect, wrought in gray and gold and silvered with moss, when the high clouds turn luminous at the edges, when a thin film of hoar-frost gleams over the grass and heather, when the light burns rosy and faint over all the hills, from Morven to Cruachan, for hours before the sun goes down. Out of the ditch at the roadside flaps the mallard, as you pass in the gloaming, and, standing by the side of the small mountain loch, you see the flock of teal rise, wheel thrice, and settle. The hills are desolate, for the sheep are being smeared. There is a feeling of frost in the air, and Ben Cruachan has a crown of snow.

When dead of winter comes, how wondrous look the hills in their white robes! The round red ball of the sun looks through the frosty steam. The far-off firth gleams strange and ghostly, with a sense of mysterious distance. The mountain loch is a sheet of blue, on which you may disport in perfect solitude from morn to night, with the hills white on all sides, save where the broken snow shows the red-rusted leaves of the withered bracken. A deathly stillness and a death-like beauty reign everywhere, and few living things are discernible, save the hare plunging heavily out of her form in the snow, or the rabbit scuttling off in a snowy spray, or the small birds piping disconsolate on the trees and dykes. Then Peter, the tame rook, brings three or four of his wild relations to the back door of the White House, and they stand aloof with their heads cocked on one side, while he explains their position, and suggests that they, being hard-working rooks who never stooped to beg when a living could be got in the fields, well deserve to be assisted. Then comes the thaw. As the sun rises, the sunny sides of the hills are seen marked with great black stains and winding veins, and there is a sound in the air as of many waters. The mountain brook leaps, swollen, over the still clinging ice, the loch rises a foot above its still frozen crust, and a damp steam rises into the air. The wind goes round into the west, great vapors blow over from the Atlantic, and there are violent storms.

Such is a mere glimpse of the seasons, as they pass in this pastoral land of Lorne; but what pen or pencil could do justice to their ever-changing wonders? Wherever one wanders, on hill or in valley, there is something to fascinate and delight. Those moorland lochs, for example! Those deep pure pools of dew distilled from the very heart of the mountains— changing as the season changes—lying blue as steel in the bright clear light, or turning to rich mellow brown in the times of flood. On all of them the water-lily blows, creeping up magically from the under-world, and covering the whole surface with white, green, and gold—its broad and well-oiled leaves floating dry in delicious softness in the summer sun, and its milk-white cups opening wider and wider, while the dragon-fly settles and sucks honey from their golden hearts. How exquisitely the hills are mirrored, the images only a shade darker than the heights above! Perhaps there is a faint breeze blowing, leaving here and there large flakes of glassy calm, which it refuses to touch for some mysterious reason, and the edges of which—just where wind and calm meet—gleam the color of golden fringe. Often in midsummer, however, the loch almost dries up in its bed; and innumerable flies—veritable gadflies with stings—make the brink of the water unpleasant, and chase one over the hills. In such weather there is nothing for it but to make off to the fir-woods, and there to dream away the summer's day, with the bell-shaped flowers around you in one gleaming sheet,

"Blue as a little patch of fallen sky,"

and the primroses fringing the tree-roots with pallid beauty that whitens in the shadow. The wood is delicious; not too dark and cold, but fresh and scented, with open spaces of green sward and level sunshine. The fir predominates, dark and enduring in its loveliness; but there are dwarf oaks, too, with twisted limbs and thick branches, and the mountain ash is there, with its innumerable beads of crimson coral, and the fluttering aspen, and the birch, whose stem is penciled with threads of frosty silver, and the thorns snowed over with delicate blossoms.

But, of course, the great glory of Lorne is the open moor, where the heather blows from one end of the year to the other. There is something sea-like in the moor, with its long free stretch for miles and miles, its great rolling hills, its lovely solitude, broken only by the cry of sheep and the scream of birds. Lakes and water-lilies are to be found far south. There are richer woods in Kent than any in the Highlands. But the moors of the western coast of Scotland stand alone, and the moors of Lorne are finest of all. Nowhere in the world, perhaps, does nature present a scene of greater beauty than that you may behold, with the smell of thyme about your feet, and the mountain bee humming in your ears, from any of the sea-commanding heights of Lorne. Turn which way you will, the glorious moors stretch before you; wave after wave of purple heather, broken only by the white farm with its golden fields, and the mountain loch high up among the hills; while the arms of the sea steal winding, now visible, now invisible, on every side, and the far-off firth, with its gleaming sail, stretches from the white lighthouse of Lismore far south to the Isla and its purple caves. Then the clouds! White and high, they drift overhead,

> "Slow traversing the blue ethereal field,"

and you can watch their shadows moving on the moor

for miles and miles, just as if it were the sea! Nor is the scene barren of such little touches as make English landscape sweet. There are bees humming everywhere, and skylarks singing, and the blackbird whistling wherever there is a bush, and the swift wren darting in and out of the stone dykes, like a swift-winged insect. There are flowers too—little unobtrusive things, flowers of the heath—primroses, tormentil, bog-asphodel, and many others. But nothing is purchased at the expense of freedom. All is fresh and free as the sea. After familiarity with the moor, you turn from the macadamized road with disgust, and will not even visit the woods till the fear of a sunstroke compels you. Did we compare the moor to the sea? Yes; but you yourself are like an inhabitant thereof; not a mere sailor on the surface, but a real haunter of the deep. What hours of indolence in the deep heather, so long as the golden weather lasts!

The white farm-house in the center of its yellow glebe does not altogether suit the great free landscape, but from a distance it serves as a foil to bring out the rocks and heather. Sweeter far is the crofter's little hut, so like the moor itself that you only recognize it by the blue wreath of peat-smoke issuing from its rude chimney. It is built of rough stones and clods, thatched with straw and heather, and paven with clay. Over its outer walls crawls a gorgeous trellis-work of moss and lichen, richer than all the carpets of Persia; and its roof is purple, green, and gold, such as no king ever saw in the tapestry of his chamber. This may seem a wild description of what tourists would regard as a wretched hut, fit only for a pig to live in; but find a painter with a soul for color, and ask *him*. Why, the very dirty children who stand at the door, shading their sunburnt faces to look at the passer-by, have tints in their naked skins and on their ragged kilts such as would fill a Titian's heart with joy. Here and there the hut is displaced to give place to a priggish cottage, with whitewashed walls and slate roofs; but the crofters, to do them justice, rather shun the kind innovation, and prefer their old tenements. Step into the hut for a light to your pipe, and look around you. The place is full of delicious peat-smoke, which at first blinds you, and then, as your eyes accustom themselves to it, clears away, to show you the old grandfather bending over the flame, the wife stirring the great black pot, and the cocks and hens perched all around on the beams and rafters. He who fears foul smells need not be afraid to enter here. Peat-smoke is the great purifier. It makes all smell sweet, and warms every cranny of the poor place with its genial breath.

The pieces of arable land are few, compared to the long stretches of moorland. The large farms have many acres of growing grain, and most of the little crofts have a tiny patch attached to them, from which they manage to grow a little corn and a few turnips and potatoes.

But wherever you wander over the moors, you will see piteous little glimpses of former cultivation—the furrow-marks which have existed for generations. Wherever there is a bit of likely ground on the hillside, be sure that it has been plowed, or rather dug with the spade. Standing on any one of the great heights, you see on every side of you the green slopes marked with the old ridges; and you remember that Lorne in former days was a thickly populated district. We have heard it stated, and even by so high an authority as the Duke of Argyll, that these marks do not necessarily indicate a higher degree of prosperity than exists in the same district at present. We are not so sure of that. Nor may the husbandry have been so rude; since the spade must have gone deep to leave its traces so long; and busy hands can do much, even to supply the want of irrigation. Attached to some of the existing crofts, which work entirely by hand-labor and till the most unlikely ground, we have seen some of the best bits of crop in the district. Be that as it may, the fact remains that once upon a time these hills of heather swarmed with crofts, and were covered with little fields of grain.

Remote, too, among the hills, in the most lonely situations, distant by long stretches of bog and moorland from any habitation, you will find here and there, if you wander so far, a ruin in the midst of green slopes and heathery bournes. This is the ruin of the old Shieling, which, in former days, so resounded with mirth and song.

"Oh, sad is the shieling,
Gone are its joys!"

as Robb Gunn sings in the Gaelic. Hither, ere sheep-farming was invented, came the household of the peasant in the summer-time, with sheep and cattle; and here, while the men returned to look after matters at home, the women and young people abode for weeks, tending the young lambs and kids, watching the milch-cow, and making butter and cheese that were rich with the succulent juices of the surrounding herbage. Then the milk-pan foamed, the distaff went, the children leaped for joy with the lambs, and in the evening the girls tried charms, and learned love-songs, and listened to the tales of their elders with dreamy eyes. Better still, there was real love-making to be had ; for some of the men remained, generally unmarried ones, and others came and went ; and, somehow, in those long summer nights, it was pleasant to sit out in a flood of moonlight, and whisper, and perhaps kiss, while the lambs bleated from the pens, and the silent hills slept shadowy in the mystic light. No wonder that Gaelic literature abounds in "Shieling songs," and that most of these are ditties of love ! The shieling was rudely built, as a mere temporary residence, but it was snug enough when the peat-bog was handy. In the wilds of the Long Island it is still used in the old manner, and the Wanderer has many a time crept into it for shelter when shooting wild fowl. The Norwegian saeter is precisely the same as the Scottish shieling, and still, as every traveler knows, flourishes in all its glory.

We are no melancholy mourner of the past ; rather a sanguine believer in progress and the future ; but alas ! whenever we look on the lonely ruins among the hills, we feel inclined to sing a dirge. The "Big Bed in the Wilderness," as the Gaelic bard named the saeter and pasture, is empty now—empty and silent—and the children that shouted in it are buried in all quarters of the earth ; aye, and many had reason to curse the cruelty of man ere they died, for they were driven forth across the waters from all that they loved. Some lived on, to see the change darker and darker, and then were carried on handy-spokes, in the old Scottish fashion, to the grave. Many a long summer day could we spend in meditation over the places where they sleep.

Highland churchyards are invariably beautiful and pathetic, but there are two in Lorne of perfect and supreme loveliness.

Adjoining the ancient stronghold of Dunstaffnage, which we have described in a former chapter, there is a fir-plantation fringing the promontory and overlooking the boiling tides at the mouth of Loch Etive; and in the heart of the plantation are the ruins of an old chapel, the four roofless walls of which still stand.* The ivy clings round the moldering walls, and the square space is filled with tombs and graves, long grass and weeds. Many dead lie there—dead that are now literally dust, and dead that only fell to sleep during the last generation. The old flat tombs, with their quaint-carved figures and worn-out inscriptions, were originally used to mark the graves of ancient chiefs and their families; but now they do duty as the gravestones of fishermen and herdsmen. Whole families of poor folk, who lived and died with the

---

* The original building, measuring only twenty-four yards by eight, is deformed by a modern addition at the east end, obscuring the altar window, which appears to have been very graceful, being in the early English style, with banded shafts and the dog-tooth ornament. Under the window a triple tablet extends round the chapel.

wash of the sea in their ears, rest together here with the sea-spray on their graves. At all seasons, even on the hottest summer day, there is a chill exhalation here, a feeling as of the touch of damp marble. The trees around snare the golden light, and twine it in and out of their dark branches till it is turned to faint silver threads. Flowers grow at the tree-roots, even in the grassy interstices between the graves; and fresh flowers are thrown regularly on the large marble tomb closed in at the eastern side of the ruin, the last meeting-place of the Campbells of Dunstaffnage.

Still more lovely is Inishail. It is a little island in the center of Loch Awe—the great fresh-water lake stretching for miles at the base of Ben Cruachan. At one extremity there is the ruins of a convent of Cistercian nuns; at the other, the old burial-place whither the dead are brought over water to this day. Low and silent, the isle floats upon the mighty loch, with its little load of dead. Once in a year, in the summer-time, the sky falls, and lies in one sheet of delicious blue-bells over the island, so that it looks a blest place indeed; one soft azure stain on the loch, in the long dreamy days, when the water is a glassy mirror; and the adjoining Black Isles cast their wooded reflections deep, deep down into the crystal gulf on which they swim. In the old days, the dead-boat would move slowly hither to the melancholy music of the bagpipes, echoing faint and far over the water; and still, at long intervals, it comes, but without the old weird music.

CHAPTER III.

THE HEART OF LORNE.

Loch Awe and its Ancient Legend—Summer Days on the Lake—The Legend of Fraoch Eilan—Kilchurn Castle—Effects of Moonlight and of Storm—View from Glenara—The Pools of Cladich—Duncan Ban of the Songs—His Coire Cheathaich—His Mairi Ban Og, and Last Adieu to the Hills—Songs of the Children of the Mist—The Pass of Awe—The Ascent of Ben Cruachan.

STANDING on the island of Inishail, you see outstretched before you one of the loveliest scenes in the world—the whole glorious expanse of Loch Awe, with its wooded and castled isles, the dark mouth of the Pass of Awe, and the towering heights of Ben Cruachan. This, indeed, may well be named the Heart of Lorne; for out of the mighty sheet of water innumerable brooks and rivulets stretch like veins to nourish all the land. The great mountain towers above, "varying momently his crest," and surveying the outstretched map of the Hebrides as far north as Canna, and as far south as the headland of Cantyre.

The ancient legend of Loch Awe is preserved in the beautiful tale of Bera. In the old dark days, far, far back in time, when there were great heroes on the earth, and great sages to guide their arms, Cruachan stood yonder, as he stands now—

" Struggling with the darkness all day long,
And visited all night by troops of stars ;"

and his scarce accessible heights were covered with great deer. All went well till there arose on Cruachan a fatal Well, fulfilling certain melancholy prophecy. Bera, the beautiful daughter of Grinan, the last of the sages of old, was charged to keep watch, and daily, as the last rays of the sun sank behind the mountain, to cover the mouth of the well with a mystic stone, marked with the strange runes of the sages. But Bera was a great huntress; and one day, after wandering far in pursuit of a mighty herd of deer, she returned to her seat so tired out that she fell to sleep beside the well. The sun sank, but Bera slept on, and the fatal well remained uncovered. At last, a thunderclap awoke her, and, springing up, she saw the raging of a fearful storm; and, behold! the fertile valley beneath her feet was flooded with a great water, stretching far out of sight in all directions, lashed to fury by the wild wind, and illumed by the lightning. The fatal deed once done, there was no remedy, and Loch Awe remains to this day, mystically fed and feeding, the veritable Heart of Lorne.

The coach from Inveraray to Oban dashes along the shores of the lake, waters at Dalmally, and so on through the Pass of Awe; and the drive is a glorious one; but he who would see Loch Awe indeed must live on its banks for weeks, watch it under all aspects of wind and cloud, and navigate its endless creeks and bays in an open boat. Few tourists do linger, save, of course, anglers, who come in spring after the ordinary loch-trout, and in autumn after the *salmo ferox;* but the great lake is full of interest for everybody, with its gorgeous and unapproachable effects for the painter, its wild old stories for the poet, its castles and graveyards for the antiquarian, and its general air of fascination for the idler and lover of beauty.

During the summer drought, Loch Awe is the hottest place in Lorne. The lake sinks in its bed day after day, till numberless hidden rocks begin to jut through the glistering water. No stream breaks the dead silence with its joyous voice, for every stream is dry; and Ben Cruachan is a sheet of red-fire, sharply defined at the edges against a sky insufferably blue. At such times a fresh breeze often blows on the seaboard a few miles away, but without creeping inland to the great lake, over and around which buzz innumerable flies of a venomous species, hovering in thousands round the cattle and driving the bare-legged herd-boy nearly mad. On the sides of Cruachan the adders swarm, though they are never found elsewhere in Lorne. But the scene is one of intoxicating beauty, calling up dreams of far-off Syria and its great lakes closed in by similar hills of stone, that scorch in the sunlight. For days together Loch Awe is a mirror without one speck or flaw, reflecting in its deep bosom the great clear mountains, the wooded islets, the gray castles moldering on their promontories; every shape and tint of the glorious scene, amid which you wander quietly, or rather, being wise, lie quiescent, just sheltered by the green bough of a tree, hovering

> "Between the dome above and the dome under,
> The hills above thee and their ghosts beneath thee!"

till life becomes so flooded with drowsy light that consciousness fades into a mere vacant dream, and all you behold appears beautifully unreal. Delicious it is in such weather to drift from place to place in a boat, slowly pulled by some swarthy Highlandman, on whose bare head the scorching beams fall harmless, and who, if he knows you well, may now and then break silence with some old tale or snatch of song. Just then the legend of Fraoch Eilan will be most acceptable, for you will have no difficulty in believing that Loch Awe is a veritable garden of the Hesperides; and the boatman will tell you, as he rows round the little island of Fraoch, how there was once on that island an enchanted garden, watched by a dragon; how the fair Mego longed for the fruit that grew there; how Fraoch, her lover, vainly endeavoring to gratify the longing of his beloved one, swam the lake and fought the dragon; and how, alas! when both Fraoch and the monster fell dead in fight, fair Mego died of unutterable grief. It is a story for the bright days, when the dog-star foams, and up above you the very hills seem to move in great glorified throbs. In your drowsy, semi-conscious state, you fully believe it, and see before you the golden apples dangling, and the golden dragon glaring—all a glitter of gold; and you dip your kerchief in the water, and bind it round your brows, and dangle your arm up to the shoulder in the cool water, as the boat glides on, suspended above a fathomless abyss of gold and blue.

But if Loch Awe can be hot and still, it can also be cold and wild. In windy weather its enormous expanse is as furious as a great arm of the sea, and the squalls plow the water into furrows of snow-white foam. On a dark day it is the blackest of all lochs—a very Acheron. But in any and every weather it preserves some kind of beauty, and has ever-varying attractions for the lover of nature—for every man, indeed, who is moved at all by the great forces of the world.

Perhaps the finest point of vantage in the whole loch is Kilchurn Castle; and Kilchurn, though beautiful exceedingly in dead-still summer weather, appears to most advantage when the wind is high and the waters wild. The ruin stands at the upper end of the lake, on a rock which was originally an island, but is now a sort of peninsula, connected by a flat alluvial meadow with the higher shore; and though its stones have been outrageously plundered to supply materials for a church and an inn at Dalmally, though every scrap of wood it ever contained has been pilfered and burnt, enough of the old place still remains to spiritualize the whole landscape; a few crumbling walls being enough for the purpose in all such cases. Built originally at the time of the Crusades, in 1440, and occupied by a British garrison as late as 1745, Kilchurn still abides, and will abide for many a year to come, if not altogether demolished by the hand of man. Time has dealt gently with it, merely penciling the walls with soft lichens and golden moss; and so far as time is concerned, it may be a ghost in the moonlight for a thousand years to come.

Of course, Kilchurn is beautiful in moonlight—all old castles are, especially when they stand close upon the water; but the effects of moonlight, although doubtless far more defined than is generally supposed by people who do not study Nature for themselves, belong more to the imagination than the eye, if, indeed, we are not continually moved by moonlight for peculiar physiological reasons, just as lunatics are moved, though in less measure. Fault has been found by Mr. Philip Hamerton with poets in general, and Sir Walter Scott in particular, because they seem to think that the moon "does not respect local color, but translates everything into black and white;"* and the same writer describes very amusingly how he, after reading Scott's lines about Melrose, and getting into the ruins furtively, his head full of melodious rhyme, discovered that the "ruins gray" were red; and was afterward informed "that the Minstrel was so little in earnest on the subject as never to have taken the trouble to drive over from Abbotsford and see Melrose for himself, as he had so warmly recommended everybody else to see it." Still, Scott was right, and Hamerton is wrong, in spite of the false epithet "gray;" for what Scott meant to imply was simply that moonlight supplied a certain imaginative mystery; a weird, silvern glamor,

* See some remarks on this subject in Mr. Hamerton's "Painter's Camp," an admirable book, in which the attempts to describe natural effects, from a painter's point of view, are almost painfully honest and faithful; painfully so, because betraying the dissatisfaction of an æsthetic mind almost convulsed by the tremendous truths of Nature, driven again and again to the despairing fear that absolute faithfulness to Nature is impossible, and trying, amidst its despair, to be rational at all hazards, rather than sentimental over the inadequacy of human effort. The result is a style curiously blending profound artistic feeling with enormous self-consciousness, and betraying an alarming leaven of technicality, even in the sphere of ideas.

in which all old ruins become most impressive. For the same reason,

> "He who would see Kilchurn aright
> Must visit it by pale moonlight,"

not on account of the effects of color, though many of these, as Mr. Hamerton has finely shown, are most delicately defined and beautiful, but simply because moonlight is *in esse* a more emotional light than sunlight.

But on some dark day, when Cruachan is black with shadow, and the rain-cloud driving past, when the loch is broken into great waves with crestlike head and hollows as black as ink, and when the wild lines of the rain shoot down in light over the old ruin, Kilchurn becomes a spirit; indeed, the almost human center of the scene. Look which way you will, it is the cynosure. Wild mists cloud the gorges of the Pass of Awe, the wind moans in the blackness of Cruachan, and Kilchurn, with the waves lashing at its feet, stares through the air like a human face, strangely relieved against the dazzling greenness of the meadow which links it to the land. What, indeed, are all the effects of moonlight to that desolate look of loneliness and woe, mingled with secret strength to resist the elemental strife?

> "But a mere footstool to you sovereign lord,
> Huge Cruachan (a thing that meaner hills
> Might crush, nor know that it had suffered harm):
> Yet he, not loth, in favor of thy claim
> To reverence, suspends his own; submitting
> All that the God of Nature hath conferred,
> All that he holds in common with the stars,

"To the memorial majesty of Time,
Impersonated in thy calm decay!"

Truly does the old ruin remain paramount, while mountains, torrents, lakes, and woods unite to pay it homage. It is the most perfect foreground possible for a mountain picture, forming not only a poetic center of human interest, but a fine scale wherewith to measure the mighty proportions of the hills and the wild expanse of troubled waters.

The distance from Inveraray to the banks of Loch Awe is about sixteen miles, the first fourteen of which are chiefly pleasant because every one of them removes you a little farther from Inveraray, that most depressing of fish-smelling Highland towns; but about two miles from that lake there is a wretched hut, the owner of which sells—or used to sell until very recently—a very good "dram" to the pedestrian, inspired with which fine spirit he is ready to look with treble rapture on the magnificent view from the top of the hill above Cladich. Ben Cruachan towers to the heavens in all his gigantic beauty, with dark heather-clad flanks and red-tinted crags, and at his feet the great lake stretches broad and deep, studded with grassy and woody islets, which are green as emerald in summer time, and in the winter season dark-red with the withered bracken and fern. In the time of snow this scene becomes strange and impressing in the extreme. The spectator from the hill has a feeling of being suspended up in the air, and the sense of height and distance conveyed by the great white mountain is almost painful. From the far-off cone of Cruachan a white smoke of drift-snow rises with the wind and blows away against the pale green of the cloudless sky. The dark-wooded flanks of the mountain contrast with the white snows and dim azure shadows of the bare crags and precipices. If the lake is a dead calm, as is usually the case at such times, the effect is still more mysterious, as every feature of the spectral scene is repeated in a fathomless gulf of crystal clearness.

At the foot of the hill is the little inn of Cladich, a cozy nest for anglers and all such peace-loving men; and close to the inn there is a burn, shaded with trees and ferns, and fringed in spring-time with primroses and blue-bells. Oh! the pools of Cladich! the nut-brown pools, clear as amber, fed by little falls foaming as white as snow, and full of tiny trout that dart hither and thither, with dark shadows on the bottom of polished rock! Many a bath have we taken there of yore, lying for hours like a very freshwater Triton, clad as Adam, pipe in mouth; and the friend of our boyhood in the next "bath," limbed like a young fawn, and little thinking of the terrible City by whose breath he died! To us, as we write, Cladich seemed the sweetest spot in the world, and we could linger on, describing its loveliness, page after page, calling up memories of long summer days on the lake, dreamy musings on the wooded Black Isles, and walks by moonlight among the woods and falls behind the little inn—an inn with linen milky white, and the scent of heather in every room, and sometimes a plate of pansies in fresh water on the table. But to brood over these happy times would be to weary the reader. Away from Cladich! Away by the road that winds northward along the shores of the lake, and, after affording a magnificent view of Kilchurn, reaches the village of Dalmally, a pleasant little place, with a good inn, a church, a picturesque bridge, and, best of all, a solid stone monument to Duncan Bàn.

What Burns is to the Lowlands of Scotland, Duncan Bàn is to the Highlands; and more: for Duncan never made a poem, long or short, which was not set to a tune, and he first sang them himself as he wandered like a veritable bard of old. Duncan MacIntyre, better known as Donacha Bàn, or Fair-haired Duncan, was born here in Glenorchay in 1724, and he died at Edinburgh in 1812, in the golden days of the "Edinburgh Review." His had been a long life, if not an eventful one. For about forty-five years he dwelt among these hills, haunting "Coire Cheathaich" at all hours, and composing his mountain music; and sometimes traveling about the country to collect subscriptions to his poems, dressed in the Highland garb, with a checked bonnet, over which hung a large bushy tail of a wild animal; a badger's skin, fastened by a belt, in front; a hanger by his side, and a soldier's wallet strapped to his shoulders. During these expeditions he was recognized wherever he went by his peculiar appearance. On one occasion, a forward young man asked him, "If it was he that made Ben Dourain?" "No," replied the old man, "Ben Dourain was made before you or I were born; but I made a poem in praise of Ben Dourain." "He spoke slowly," writes the recorder of the circumstance, "and seemed to have no high opinion of his own poems, and said little of Gaelic poetry; but said that officers in the army told him about the Greek poets, and Pindar was chiefly admired by him."*

When Duncan Bàn was forty-four years of age, he dictated his poems to a clergyman, who wrote them down for publication. For years they had been floating in the poet's mind to music of their own, and many had been carried from mouth to mouth across the Hebrides. They are simple in form as the hills, as sweet and gentle in sound as the mountain brooks, and many are most lengthy and elaborate, just like Highland tales, not because the subject is great in itself, but because the singer is so in love with it that he could sing about it forever. "Coire Cheathaich, or the Misty Corri," is the masterpiece, being the description of the great corri in Glenorchay, where Duncan loved to roam. Here it is in English. Not a word is lost, but any Highlandman will tell you that no English could convey the unutterable tenderness and rich music of the original:

COIRE CHEATHAICH; OR, THE GLEN OF THE MIST.

    My beauteous corri! where cattle wander—
      My misty corri! my darling dell!
    Mighty, verdant, and covered over
      With wild flowers tender of the sweetest smell;
    Dark is the green of thy grassy clothing,
      Soft swell thy hillocks most green and deep,
    The cannach blowing, the darnel growing,
      While the deer troop past to the misty steep.

* Mackenzie's "Beauties of Gaelic Poetry."

Fine for wear is thy beauteous mantle,
   Strongly woven, and ever-new,
With rough grass o'er it, and, brightly gleaming,
   The grass all spangled with diamond dew;
It's round my corri, my lovely corri,
   Where rushes thicken and long reeds blow;
Fine were the harvest to any reaper
   Who through the marsh and the bog could go.

Ah, that's fine clothing!—a great robe stretching,
   A grassy carpet most smooth and green,
Painted and fed by the rain from heaven
   In hues the bravest that man has seen—
'Twixt here and Paris, I do not fancy
   A finer raiment can ever be—
May it grow forever!—and, late and early,
   May I be here on the knolls to see!

Around Ruadh Awridh what ringlets cluster!
   Fair, long, and crested, and closely twined,
This way and that they are lightly waving,
   At every breath of the mountain wind.
The twisted hemlock, the slanted rye-grass,
   The juicy moor-grass, can all be found,
And the close-set groundsel is greenly growing
   By the wood where heroes are sleeping sound.

In yonder ruin once dwelt MacBhaidi,
   'Tis now a desert where winds are shrill;
Yet the well-shaped brown ox is feeding by it
   Among the stones that bestrew the hill.
How fine to see, both in light and gloaming,
   The smooth Clach Fionn so still and deep,
And the houseless cattle and calves most peaceful'
   Grouped on the brow of the lonely steep.

In every nook of the mountain pathway
   The garlic-flower may be thickly found—
And out on the sunny slopes around it
   Hang berries juicy and red and round—

THE HEART OF LORNE.

The penny-royal and dandelion,
    The downy cannach together lie—
Thickly they grow from the base of the mountain
    To the topmost crag of his crest so high.

And not a crag but is clad most richly,
    For rich and silvern the soft moss clings;
Fine is the moss, most clean and stainless,
    Hiding the look of unlovely things;
Down in the hollows beneath the summit
    Where the verdure is growing most rich and deep,
The little daisies are looking upward,
    And the yellow primroses often peep.

Round every well and every fountain
    An eyebrow dark of the cress doth cling;
And the sorrel sour gathers in clusters
    Around the stones whence the waters spring;
With a splash and a plunge and a mountain murmur
    The gurgling waters from earth upleap,
And pause and hasten, and whirl in circles,
    And rush and loiter, and whirl and creep!

Out of the ocean comes the salmon,
    Steering with crooked nose he hies,
Hither he darts where the waves are boiling—
    Out he springs at the glistening flies!
How he leaps in the whirling eddies!
    With back blue-black, and fins that shine,
Spangled with silver, and speckled over,
    With white tail tipping his frame so fine!

Gladsome and grand is the misty corri,
    And there the hunter hath noble cheer;
The powder blazes, the black lead rattles
    Into the heart of the dun-brown deer;
And there the hunter's hound so bloody
    Around the hunter doth leap and play,
And madly rushing, most fierce and fearless,
    Springs at the throat of the stricken prey.

Oh, 'twas gladsome to go a-hunting
  Out in the dew of the sunny morn !
For the great red stag was never wanting,
  Nor the fawn, nor the doe with never a horn.
And when rain fell and the night was coming,
  From the open heath we could swiftly fly,
And, finding the shelter of some deep grotto,
  Couch at ease till the night went by.

And sweet it was when the white sun glimmered,
  Listening under the crag to stand—
And hear the moorhen so hoarsely croaking,
  And the red cock murmuring close at hand ;
While the little wren blew his tiny trumpet,
  And threw his steam off blithe and strong,
While the speckled thrush and the redbreast gaily
  Lilted together a pleasant song !

Not a singer but joined the chorus,
  Not a bird in the leaves was still.
First the laverock, that famous singer,
  Led the music with throat so shrill ;
From tall tree-branches the blackbird whistled,
  And the gray bird joined with his sweet " coo-coo ;"
Everywhere was the blithesome chorus,
  Till the glen was murmuring through and through.

Then out of the shelter of every corri
  Came forth the creature whose home is there ;
First, proudly stepping, with branching antlers,
  The snorting red-deer forsook his lair ;
Through the sparkling fen he rushed rejoicing,
  Or gently played by his heart's delight—
The hind of the mountain, the sweet brown princess,
  So fine, so dainty, so staid, so slight !

Under the light green branches creeping
  The brown doe cropt the leaves unseen,
While the proud buck gravely stared around him
  And stamped his feet on his couch of green ;

Smooth and speckled, with soft pink nostrils,
　With beauteous head, lay the tiny kid;
All apart in the dewy rushes,
　Sleeping unseen in its nest, 'twas hid.

My beauteous corri! my misty corri!
　What light feet trod thee in joy and pride,
What strong hands gathered thy precious treasures,
　What great hearts leapt on thy craggy side!
Soft and round was the nest they plundered,
　Where the brindled bee his honey hath—
The speckled bee that flies, softly humming,
　From flower to flower of the lonely strath.

There thin-skinned, smooth in clustering bunches,
　With sweetest kernels as white as cream,
From branches green the sweet juice drawing,
　The nuts were growing beside the stream—
And the stream went dancing merrily onward,
　And the ripe red rowan was on its brim,
And gently there in the wind of morning
　The new-leaved sapling waved soft and slim.

And all around the lovely corri
　The wild birds sat on their nests so neat,
In deep warm nooks and tufts of heather,
　Sheltered by knolls from the wind and sleet;
And there from their beds, in the dew of the morning,
　Uprose the doe and the stag of ten,
And the tall cliffs gleamed, and the morning reddened
　The Coire Cheathaich—the Misty Glen!

One such poem conveys, even in a translation, a better idea of the writer's mind than whole chapters of expository criticism. How the Highlandman broods over every feature of the darling scene, from the weird "mountain ruin, where a family once dwelt," down to the little wren "flinging off his steam" (a queer and very favorite Gaelic expression) in the sunshine! Was a brook ever described better, as it

"Pauses and hastens, whirls in circles,
Rushes and loiters, and whirls and creeps?"

To Duncan the corri is a perpetual feast. With a painter's eye he hungers over the tints of the moss on the crags, the blue-black back and silver spangles of the salmon, the thin-skinned, smooth-clustered nuts on the green branches, the dark-green eyebrow of cresses round the mountain well; and to him also all the sounds have maddening sweetness: the moorhen croaking, the thrushes and redbreasts warbling, the whole glen "breathing a choral strain;" till at last, in one supreme poetic flash, he sees the dun doe and great stag springing up in the dew of a May morning, and the "red light" flaming on every crag of the corri. His was no mere song for beauty's sake; there was love at the heart of it. To him the corri meant life and freedom, and the fresh air of the world—it meant youth and its memories, passion and its dreams, deep-seated religion and its mystery. The love he put into "Coire Cheathaich" took another form in Mairi Bàn Og, which is esteemed the finest love-song in the Gaelic language, and is addressed, not to his sweetheart—not to a passing mistress, such as Burns immortalized—but to his wife; is, in a word, the epithalamium of Duncan, the Highland forester, on his marriage with Mary "of the ale-house." Every word is warm as sunshine, but holy and pure. He broods over his bride's beauty as he broods over nature, missing no detail, blessing the "clerk-given right" which makes the beauty all his own. He describes the "soft and round maiden with curly hair;" her "breath sweet as apples growing;" her "smooth lidded" blue eye; her body "as pure and white as cannach;" her warm hand, like a lady's; her little foot in its tight-fitting shoe; he tells us how "Mairi" milks the cattle by the river, with the calves leaping round her; how she wanders light-footed to the lone mountain shieling; how she sits "sewing bands and plain seams," or "working embroidery," in the candle-light of the cottage, at night; and he adds, with true Highland pride, how she bears in her veins the "blood of the King and MacCailean," and of the Macdonald "who was chief in Sleat." No love is too deep for her, no gift too great; and he will kill for her "swans, seals, wild geese, and all birds"—nay, she has but to give the word, and she shall have the antlers of the best deer in the forest. Nothing is more remarkable in this love-song than the sacredness of its passion; in it Duncan Bàn has correctly represented not only his own feelings, but the popular Highland sentiment about marriage. In Lorne and the Western Hebrides, the purity of the popular mind on this subject is most remarkable. The Highlander may sometimes err through excess of animal passion, but he is never consciously indecent, and he is utterly innocent of the "gaudriole."

Happy years had Duncan Bàn in Glenorchay, drinking into his soul every tint of the glorious landscape, and loving the more the longer he looked. For six years he was sergeant in the Breadalbane Fencibles, and when that regiment was disbanded, in 1799, he procured, by the influence of the Earl of Breadalbane, a place in the City Guard of Edinburgh, those poor old veterans so savagely described by Ferguson in "Leith Races":

> "Their stumps, erst used to filabegs,
>   Are dight in spatterdashes,
> Whase bailant hides scarce fend their legs
>   Fra weet and weary splashes
>   O' dirt that day!"

He was then seventy-five years of age. About this time he composed a quaint, long rhyme, in praise of Dunedin, or Edinburgh; and the poem, although not one of his inspired productions, is deeply interesting from its quaint touches of wondering realism. The old man, with his sharp hunter's eye, missed nothing, as he wandered in the strange streets. He describes the castle, the battery, the abbey, the houses, " wealthy and great;" the building of the parliament, where "reasonable gentlemen" administered justice, with free power to "hang the offender up high;" the swells in the street, with powder in their curled hair, and a "bunch like silk on the top;" the pretty ladies, with stays to keep them straight and thin, beauty-spots on their faces, strong, tight, and pointed shoes, with (adds the poet) "heels much too high;" the coaches, and the hard-hoofed horses frisking and prancing, so much finer than any reared on Highland pastures. All this was pleasing for a time, while it had the charm of novelty; but, doubtless, the heart of the old bard wearied for the hills. Some years after, on the 19th of September, 1802, he visited his home, and wandered a long day among the scenes he loved so well, and then and there composed the most beautiful of all his poems—"The Last Farewell to the Hills." He was then seventy-eight years old.

THE LAST ADIEU TO THE HILLS.

Yestreen I stood on Ben Dorain, and paced its dark-gray path ;
Was there a hill I did not know—a glen, or grassy strath ?
Oh ! gladly in the times of old I trod that glorious ground,
And the white dawn melted in the sun, and the red-deer cried around.

How finely swept the noble deer across the morning hill,
While fearless played the fawn and doe beside the running rill ;
I heard the black and red cock crow, and the bellowing of the deer—
I think those are the sweetest sounds that man at dawn may hear.

Oh ! wildly, as the bright day gleamed, I climbed the mountain's breast,
And when I to my home returned, the sun was in the west ;
'Twas health and strength, 'twas life and joy to wander freely there,
To drink at the fresh mountain stream, to breathe the mountain air.

And oft I'd shelter for a time within some shieling low,
And gladly sport in woman's smile, and woman's kindness know.
Ah ! 'twas not likely one could feel for long a joy so gay !
The hour of parting came full soon—I sighed, and went away.

And now the cankered withering wind has struck my limbs at last ;
My teeth are rotten and decayed, my sight is failing fast ;
If hither now the chase should come, 'tis little I could do ;
Though I were hungering for food, I could not now pursue.

But though my locks are hoar and thin, my beard and whiskers white,
How often have I chased the stag with dogs full swift of flight !
And yet, although I could not join the chase if here it came,
The thought of it is charming still and sets my heart on flame.

Ah! much as I have done of old, how ill could I wend now,
By glen, and strath, and rocky path, up to the mountain's brow!
How ill could I the merry cup quaff deep in social cheer!
How ill now could I sing a song in the gloaming of the year!

Those were the merry days of spring, the thoughtless times of youth;
'Tis Fortune watches over us, and helps our need, forsooth;
Believing that, though poor enough, contentedly I live,
For George's daughter, every day, my meat and drink doth give.*

Yestreen I wandered in the glen; what thoughts were in my head!
There had I walked with friends of yore—where are those dear ones fled?
I looked and looked; where'er I looked was naught but sheep! sheep! sheep!
A woeful change was in the hill! World, thy deceit was deep!

From side to side I turned mine eyes—alas! my soul was sore—
The mountain bloom, the forest's pride, the old men were no more.
Nay, not one antlered stag was there, nor doe so soft and slight,
No bird to fill the hunter's bag—all, all were fled from sight!

Farewell, ye forests of the heath! hills where the bright day gleams!
Farewell, ye grassy dells! farewell, ye springs and leaping streams!
Farewell, ye mighty solitudes, where once I loved to dwell—
Scenes of my spring-time and its joys—forever fare you well!

After that, Duncan Bàn returned to Edinburgh, and remained in the City Guard till about 1806, when, having saved a few pounds from his wages and the

---

* "George's daughter" was the musket carried by him as a member of the City Guard, and servant of King George. The value of his "meat and drink" was fivepence or sixpence a day.

profits of his published poems, he was enabled to retire and spend his remaining years without toil of any kind. He was eighty-eight years old when he died. On the 19th of May, 1812, he was buried in the Greyfriars' Burying Ground, Edinburgh; and a few years ago the monument was raised to his memory in Glenorchay. His fame endures wherever the Gaelic language is spoken, and his songs are sung all over the civilized world. Without the bitterness and intellectual power of Burns, he possessed much of his sentiment, and all of his personal tenderness; and as a literary prodigy, who could not even write, he is still more remarkable than Burns. Moreover, the old, simple-hearted forester, with his fresh love of nature, his shrewd insight, and his impassioned speech, seems a far completer human figure than the Ayrshire plowman, who was doubtless a glorious creature, but most obtrusive in his independence. Poor old Duncan was never bitter. The world was wonderful, and he was content to fill his humble place in it. He had "an independent mind," but was quite friendly to rank and power wherever he saw them; for, after all, what were they to Coire Cheathaich, with its natural splendors? What was the finest robe in Dunedin to the gay clothing on the side of Ben Dorain? Burns never saw Nature as Duncan Bàn saw her; was never merged into her, so to speak, never became a part of flying cloud and brooding shadows; rather petted and fondled her like a mistress, with most unutterable tenderness, but no awe. Burns was the intellectual being, man, lord of the earth and all its creatures, their lover till the end, but always their lord; bitter with the world, bitter with his own sins; too proud to gauge ale-barrels, but not too proud to get dead drunk or to debauch women; hurled down like a torrent by his own sheer force and strength, a divine singer, a shameless satirist, the lover of " Mary in heaven," and the undoubted author of some of the filthiest " suppressed poems " in the " Merry Muses."* Duncan Bàn " of the Songs " was a silent man, not specially intellectual, content to hawk his poems about the country, and sing them at the fireside, with scarce a touch of satire in his whole nature, with a heart quite pure and fresh to the end, when, as an old man, he bade the hills " farewell forever." In the life of Burns we see the light striking through the storm-cloud, lurid, terrific, yet always light from heaven. In the life of Duncan Bàn there is nothing but a gray light of peace and purity, such as broods over the mountains when the winds are laid. Burns was the mightier poet, the grander human soul; but many who love him best, and cherish his memory most tenderly, can find a place in their hearts for Duncan Bàn as well.

As we quit the Highland poet's grave, and follow the highway to the Pass of Awe, there is other music in our ears besides that of " Coire Cheathaich " and the " Last Farewell;" for did not the " Children of the Mist," haunting like mountain deer the secret gorges of Cruachan, utter many a lyrical plaint full of music

---

* The woefullest picture in the world is the last portrait of Burns, which we regret to see inserted in Dr. P. H. Waddell's otherwise invaluable edition of the poet's works. This portrait, once seen, haunts the beholder for ever.

and heart's agony ? Readers of the "Legend of Montrose" and the "Lady of the Lake" know now by heart the wrongs of the Macgregors, the "clan that was nameless by day;" and Gaelic literature abounds with songs recording the sufferings and threats of the bloody outlawed clans—songs most weird and terrible, with frequent glimpses of wild tenderness. One of the best of these is the "Hills of the Mist," the tradition concerning which states that the singer, after having hidden her hunted kinsmen in a bed within the mountain shieling, sat down on the floor and crooned to herself a song bewailing their non-appearance:

"Oh, where are my kinsmen? Oh, where do they wander?
I watch for them lonely; I wait and I ponder."

And the pursuers, listening outside and noting the terrible agony of her voice (no counterfeit that, for might not the butchers enter at any moment and detect her ruse?) passed on in the darkness without searching the shieling.

The Pass of Awe is very beautiful, the road winding high up among the crags and woods and overlooking the wild waters of the river. Close to the bridge which spans the stream took place the famous fight between Bruce's followers and those of John of Lorne, when the bodies of the latter, miserably overthrown, choked and rendered bloody the impetuous flood. Along this path walked Mrs. Bethune Baliol, escorted by the exuberant Donald Macleish, on that memorable occasion when she saw the tree, the waterfall, and the solitary human figure—"a female form seated by the stem of the oak, with her head drooping, her hands clasped, and a dark-colored mantle drawn over her head, exactly as Judith is represented in the Syrian medals as seated under her palm-tree."* The form of the miserable woman, still as a corpse or a marble statue, haunts the eye of the traveler at every step; rock, tree, and falling water assume her likeness; and the ear is filled with her memorable words of grief—

"My beautiful! my brave!"

There is no shape of fiction so closely wedded to an actual scene. The Pass of Awe and the Highland Widow are inseparable. The one solitary human soul, in its unutterable dolor, surrounded by somber crags and corries, and water plunging from pool to pool with sullen roar, is more truly regent of the place than all the traditional figures of clansmen and Children of the Mist.

Following the road along the Pass of Awe, you reach Tyanuilt, whence the ascent of Ben Cruachan is tolerably easy. Mountain climbing is always glorious, be the view obtained at the highest point ever so unsatisfactory; for do not pictures arise at every step, beautiful exceedingly, even if no more complex than a silver-lichened boulder half buried in purple heather and resting against the light-blue mountain air; or a mountain pool fringed with golden mosses and green cresses, with blue sky in it and a small white cloud like a lamb; or a rowan tree with berries red as coral, sheltering the mossy bank where the robin sits in his nest? He who climbs Cruachan will see not only these small things, but he will behold a series of crag

* Scott's "Highland Widow."

pictures of unapproachable magnificence—corries red and rugged, in the dark fissures of which snow lingers even as late as June, pyramids and minarets of granite glistering in the sunshine through the moisture of their own dew, stained by rain and light into darkly beautiful hues, and speckled by innumerable shadows from the passing clouds. There is a certain danger in roaming among the precipices near the summit, as the hill is subject to sudden mists, sometimes so dense that the pedestrian can scarcely see a foot before him; but in summer-time, when the heights are clear as amber for days together, the peril is not worth calculating. On a fine, clear day, the view from the summit—which is a veritable red ridge or cone, not a flat table-land like that of some mountains—is very peculiar. It can scarcely be called picturesque, for there is no power in the eye to fix on any one picture; and, on the other hand, to liken it to a map of many colors would be conveying a false impression. The effect is more that of a map than of a picture, and more like the sea than either. The spectator loses the delicate æsthetic sense, and feels his whole vision swallowed up in immensity. The mighty waters of Awe brood sheer below him, under the dark abysses of the hill, with the islands like dark spots upon the surface. Away to the eastward rise peaks innumerable, mountain beyond mountain, from the moor of Rannoch to Ben Lomond, some dark as night with shadow, others dim as dawn from sheer distance, all floating limitless against a pink horizon and brooded over by a heaven of most delicate blue, fading away into miraculous tints, and filling the spirit with intensest awe; while in the west is visible the great ocean, stretching arms of shining sheen into the wildly broken coast, brightening around the isles that sleep upon its breast—Tiree, Coll, Rum, Canna, Skye—and fading into a long vaporous line where the setting sun sinks into the underworld. Turn where it may, the eye is satisfied, overcharged. Such another panorama of lake, mountain, and ocean is not to be found in the Highlands. As for Lorne, you may now behold it indeed, gleaming with estuaries and lakes—Loch Linnhe, the Bay of Oban, and the mighty Firth as far south as Jura, and, northward over the moors, a divine glimpse of the head of Loch Etive, blue and dreamy as a maiden's eyes. The head swims, the eyes dazzle. Are you a god, that you should survey these wonders in such supremacy? Look which way you will, you behold immensity—measureless ranges of mountains, measureless tracts of inland water, the measureless ocean, lighted here and there by humanity in the shape of some passing sail smaller to view than a sea-bird's wing. For some little time at least the spectator feels that spiritual exhaltation which excludes perfect human perception; he yields to a wave of awful emotion, and bows before it as before God. He can be æsthetic again when he once more descends to the valleys.

CHAPTER IV.

SPORT ON THE MOORS AND LOCHS.

Grouse and Black-game Shooting—A September Day on the Moors—The Grouse-shooter—Peat Bogs—Arrival of Snipe and Woodcock—Mountain Lochs and other Haunts of Wild-fowl—False and True Sportsmen.

SPORT on the moors of Lorne is what sport should be—a great deal more like wild-shooting than is generally the case on the great moors of the north. The game is not numerous, but strong, wary, full of health and strength. There is no overcrowding, as on the Perthshire and Aberdeenshire moors. In addition to Argyllshire grouse, bright, rufus-breasted, full-chested, altogether the finest bird to be found in this country, and beyond all measure superior to the smaller-sized and darker-plumaged bird of the eastern moors, there are black-game in abundance, a few partridges, brown and blue hares, a sprinkling of snipe, and a large number of wild-fowl. Roe-deers are plentiful in some districts, but the red-deer is seldom found. The *salmo ferox* abounds in Loch Awe, and all the rivers afford more or less salmon angling, while many of the small mountain lochs are as full of excellent trout as a pond in Surrey is full of sticklebacks. We have heard greedy sportsmen, used to wholesale butchery of bird and beast, complain of the barrenness of Lorne, and certainly Lorne is barren as compared with the great moors farther north; though it has this one great advantage, that it affords excellent sport long after the birds have packed elsewhere, and not a shot is to be had except by driving. In Lorne, moreover, the game in no way injures the population—is not numerous enough to ruin the farmer and poor crofter; is not valuable enough to be preserved at the cost of human lives. Any true sportsman will find his appetite fully gratified, though not by enormous "bags." All his skill will come into requisition—all his faculties will be duly tested.

Yearly, when the 12th of August dawns, the sound of shooting echoes from hill to hill, over the purple sea of moorland that surrounds the White House on the Hill; and the dogs leap eagerly in the kennel whenever their master passes; and overhead, on the top of the knoll, a cock-grouse crows cheerily in the sunshine. But the Wanderer is not to be tempted. The 20th of August is time enough to touch grouse in most seasons; and the black-game should invariably be left in peace till the 1st of September. Of course, where the object is merely to secure a large number of birds, the earlier in the season one commences the better; but it is scarcely conceivable how any rational being can find pleasure in butchering a poor bird when it is no bigger than a chicken and a great deal stupider, and when it is as easily hit as a target at thirty yards. Grouse-shooting is poor sport till the birds run well, instead of lying like stones at the mere sound of a distant footstep, and till they rise on the wing, swift and strong as an old cock, directly after the dog has fairly caused them to draw together and crouch. Black-game shooting on the moors is unmanly sport. The birds won't get up, and are again and again collared by the over-eager dog, and when they do rise, early in the season, why, a boy might hit them with a pea-shooter as they dash clumsily away. But black-game shooting at evening flight, when the birds are wild beyond measure, and come down in hundreds to feed on the corn sheaves, is quite another sort of sport, worthy of any man with a clear eye and steady nerves. By this time the young cock is getting something like his adult plumage, and is a fair prize, both as an edible and for the sake of his feathers. He is wonderfully wary and keen-sighted when feeding on the ground, but will seldom break his flight. Often on the moors, while lunching in the shade of some woody knoll, we have been disturbed by a flock of black-game whizzing past, one after another, a few yards distant, and not altering their course by an inch, even when they perceived their danger and saw some of the advance-guard dropping stone-dead to the flash and report of the gun.

On some morning in the month of September, the moor is in all its glory, stretching its mighty billows in all directions in one streak of luxurious purple and glittering green, broken up here and there by great rocks and lichened crags, and all flooded with the light of the sun. The sportsman sweats and pants, the dogs hang out their tongues and work heavily, unguided by a breath of wind; the gillie lies on his stomach and dips his heated face in every burn; and by midday you have killed perhaps a couple of brace of birds. Then comes the long delicious siesta by the brink of some crystal pool of the stream, and (after the lightest possible lunch) the pipe or cigar, in the enjoyment of which you lie on your side in the dry old heather, and watch the small shadows, cast by clouds as white as wool, moving noiselessly and sleepily over the free expanse of the heath— brooding at times as still as stones—at times hastening together like a flock of sheep, with the golden gleam on every side of them. If you are fortunate, about this time there comes a shower; just a sprinkling for a few minutes, soft as dew on the grass at dawn, scented as a maiden's breath. The moor sparkles, the air feels fresh and free, and when you loosen the dogs, they no longer toil wearily with lolling tongues, but work in narrowing runs up the faintest possible breath of wind, draw swift and steady to the deep patch whither the pack have run, and become all in a moment rigid, with fixed eyes and dilating nostrils. Now and again, in such weather, the best dog in the world will miss his game, or, running unawares into the thick of them, scatter them like chaff. Of course, as is well known, each member of the broken pack will, at the beginning of the season, lie like a stone, wherever you mark it down, and sometimes almost suffer you to seize it with your hand. As the day advances, and the heat lessens, the bag increases; and about sunset, when the birds have left the springy bogs and betaken themselves to the dry knolls of young heather to feed, you will have sport in perfection.

The signs of a good grouse-shooter are few and unmistakable. He must be a steady walker, not so swift as to weary the dogs, not slow enough to spoil them, and not given to puffing like a porpoise when climbing the hillside. He must be a good snap shot, ready at any moment to take a chance when it comes, with or without a point; he must account for two birds out of every pack that rises; and he should kill his birds, dead. He must be silent, for talking, above all things, spoils sport; sober, for dram-drinking endangers both himself and his companions; good-humored, or the keepers and gillies will hate him and spoil his chance whenever they can; and, above all, humane, never shooting at a bird with the faintest chance of merely wounding it and letting it get away to die. In addition to all this, he must be a man to whom the moor is familiar at all seasons, who knows the haunts of birds in all sorts of weathers, who understands the whole theory of heather-burning, who is as well acquainted with every natural sign as the mountain-shepherd himself. Most men, of course, leave all things to their keepers, come to their moor on the 12th, and are taken about in due course at the beck and nod of "Donald." Some of those men shoot well; few of them are worthy of the name of sportsmen. Merely to be able to present a gun and knock down a mark is a feat that any "hedge-popper" can attain. Practical knowledge, loving observation of nature, power of silence, take time to grow; but they are essential. In addition to them may be mentioned a certain capacity of enduring physical discomfort, without which the grouse-shooter is no better than any pigeon-killer in the suburbs of London.

There are no very bad bogs in Lorne, though occasionally, while grouse-shooting, we have seen a brother sportsman disappear almost up to the arm-pits, and dragged him with some difficulty out of the oozy earth and green, slimy subterranean pools. In hot weather, the grouse frequent the parts where the peat is cut and piled, and drink at the black pools in the hollows. At this time, the black-game come there also for the same purpose. In a "peat-bog" not fifty yards square, we have put up from twenty to thirty black-game singly, each crouching unseen till fairly run upon by the dog, and consisting of several old hens and their packs of young. They will lie, too, in the queerest holes imaginable, on the sides of ditches. We have seen our setter rigid and moveless over a hole where only a water-rat might be expected to dwell, and where a gray hen was huddled up for the sake of the coolness and shade. The old cock is never to be found in such places. He broods alone and sulky, in some spot where he can have a free flight out of the way of danger. The most favorite of all places for young black-game in the heat of the day are the deep patches of bracken and fern on the moor, where they can run about with a very forest of greenness above their heads; but they soon learn to prefer the corn-fields, from the fact that the latter combine both food and shelter. Many sportsmen greatly annoy the farmer by covertly sending their dogs into the standing corn, and shooting the startled birds from the edges. This practice is most reprehensible, and should be discountenanced by all true sportsmen. Anything that interferes, however slightly, with the rights of others, should be abandoned; and the farmer's crop is of infinitely more importance to the world than the shooter's gamebag.

But we are being betrayed into a treatise on grouse-shooting, whereas it is merely our intention to sketch in a general way the possibilities of sport in Lorne.

As the season advances, the birds grow scarcer and scarcer—less and less approachable. A white frost sometimes tames the red grouse, never the black; and both sooner or later form into great packs, which pass away like a cloud, long ere the sportsman gets within gun-range. A little may be done by driving, but not much. Instead of harassing the grouse late in the season, it is better to turn one's attention to other game. Hares and rabbits abound in many districts, especially the blue hare, which goes to earth like a cony. About November the local snipe, reinforced by legions from the north, swarm in all the bogs and marshes, unless it is very wet, when they scatter in every direction over the damp hillsides. One fine night the little "jacks" arrive, sprinkling themselves all over the country, and offering chance after chance, in their peculiar fashion, to blundering sportsmen. Last of all come the woodcocks, two or three at a time—first taking to the deep clumps on the hillside, and afterward selecting winter quarters by the side of the runlets that water the hazel-woods. Many of them, however, only rest a few days in

Lorne, and then disappear, in all probability winging farther south. Those which linger through the whole winter often remain to breed in the spring.

The lochs among the hills abound in wild-fowl, many of which breed there. There is one small mere, not a mile distant from the White House on the Hill, which we have seen as thickly covered with teal and widgeon as a duckpond in the Zoological Gardens. At such times, however, it is exceedingly difficult to get a shot; so numerous are the eyes watching, and so easily do the birds take the alarm, that "sitting-shots" are out of the question. The best plan is for the sportsman to place himself in ambush, at one end of the water, send his man to disturb the birds at the other, and trust to chance for a shot flying. If the affair is properly managed, he may fire five or six times, as fast as he can load; and perhaps the teal, less wary than the larger duck, may alight on the water, within a few yards of his ambush. Directly frost comes, the small lochs are abandoned, and the wild-fowl betake themselves to the arms of the sea. In a severe season, when all the fresh-water meres are frozen over, the salt-water lochs afford excellent sport; the better, in our opinion, because the birds are wild beyond measure, and will test all the shooter's powers of skill and patience.

We will not detain the reader by any further enumeration of the sports of Lorne, particularly as our notion of sport is peculiar, and has nothing in common with the ideas of men who delight in slaughter. To us, sport is only desirable in so far as it develops all that is best and strongest in a man's physical nature, tries his powers of self-patience and endurance, quickens his senses, and increases his knowledge of and reverence for created things. In so far as it renders him callous to suffering and selfish in his enjoyments, sport is detestable. There are yearly let loose upon the moors of Scotland a set of men who are infinitely less noble than the beasts and birds they murder; who are brutal without courage, and conceited without dignity; who degrade all manly sports by their abominable indifference to the rights alike of fellow-men and dumb creatures. Fortunately, all sportsmen in Scotland are not men of this sort; a few fine-souled gentlemen are sprinkled here and there; but there is far too much brutal murder on all hands, by beings who take a savage pleasure in the mere slaughter of things as tame as hens and sheep. The true test of a day's sport is not the number of head secured, but the amount of skill and pluck requisite to secure it! Depend upon it, also, the man who recklessly and wantonly takes away the lives of dumb things merely for the sake of killing, would, if his wretched neck was as secure in one case as in the other, assist with equal pleasure at the massacre of his fellow-men. Many of the men who joined in the infernal carnival of murder in India some years ago, and, in so doing, left on this nation a taint which God will sooner or later avenge on our boasted civilization, had first developed the taste for blood in the pheasant coverts of England and the swarming moors of the north.

Wild-fowl shooting on the sea-fjörds, otter-hunting on Kerrera, salmon-angling in Loch Awe, sea-fishing on the firth—any of these might supply matter for a separate chapter, if we were to chronicle one tithe of our experience; but we are compelled to pass on to more moving matter, only remarking, in conclusion, that, although the lover of battues and wholesale slaughter may find himself better served elsewhere, the true sportsman will never regret a season spent with rod and gun, afloat and ashore, on the lochs and moors of Lorne.

CHAPTER V.

THE FIRTH OF LORNE.

The *Ocean Queen*, or *Coffin*—Shon Macnab's Race with the Barber—Lachlan Finlay—From Crinan to the Dorus Mhor—Hebridean Tides—Scarba—The Gulf of Corryvreckan—Its Horrors and Perils—Luing and the Small Isles—The Open Firth—Easdale and its Quarriers—Tombs at the Door—Miseries of Calm—Gylen Castle and the Island of Kerrera—King Haco's Invasion of the Hebrides—A Puff from the Southeast—The Island of Mull—Johnson and Boswell in the Hebrides—A Run to Tobermory—Loch Sunart—A Rainy Day—Ardtornish Castle—Anchored between Wind and Tide—Night on the Firth—Troubles of Darkness—Farewell to the *Ocean Queen*—Arrival of the *Tern*.

THE Firth of Lorne stretches from Loch Crinan (a spot familiar to every Highland tourist) as far as the entrance to the Sound of Mull; after passing which, it changes its name to Loch Linnhe, and creeps northward, ever narrowing till it reaches Bannavie, and forms the narrow estuary of Loch Eil.

Strictly speaking, only the mainland coast as far as Loch Crinan appertains to Lorne, but in old times Mull was included, as well as many of the far-off islands. Be that as it may, the Firth of Lorne is a glorious sheet of salt water, fed by the mighty tides of the Atlantic, and forming, both on the islands and on the mainland, a line of sea-coast not easily matched for loneliness and beauty. Numerous islands, large and small, stud the waters, forming narrow passages, through which the tide boils with terrific fury. Great heights, grassy and rocky, rise everywhere out of the sea, casting dark shadows. Everywhere the black teeth of the reef threaten the seaman. Innumerable bays and land-locked lakes lie close in the shelter of the coast; but the anchorages are nearly all bad and dangerous, on account of the submerged rocks and the foul bottom.

To see this firth aright, to enjoy its wondrous scenery in a way quite impossible to the ordinary tourist, the Wanderer secured the *Ocean Queen*, a small yacht of nine tons, thirty-four feet long, seven and a half feet beam, and drawing precisely six feet of water aft. She was the crankiest vessel ever built by the hand of man, and was speedily known by the nickname of the *Coffin*. Her mainsail was an enormous sheet of canvas, though luckily somewhat old and tearable; and she carried also a gaff-topsail. Her speed, running before the wind, was very great; and, beating to windward, she managed finely as long as she could carry canvas. She was quite unfit for a dangerous coast like that of Lorne, where the storms are sudden and the squalls terrific; but she had a neat little cabin and snug forecastle, so that she made a tolerable floating-home. Many a fright did the Wanderer get in her. Latterly, he managed to render her pretty snug by running in the bowsprit, and sailing her with the foresail only and single-reefed mainsail; but, from first to last, she was as fickle as an unbroken filly; her vilest quality of all being her awkwardness in "coming about," even under the most experienced management.

Having secured this noble vessel, the Wanderer had to look about for a suitable person to assist him in managing her—no difficult task, it may be imagined, on a fishing-coast and close to a fishing-town; but, in good truth, he was doomed to a bitter experience. After trying several impostors, who betrayed themselves in a day, he secured the services of Shon Macnab, a gigantic Gael, six feet three in his shoes, and about twenty years of age. A fine specimen of the sailor was Shon, with his great red face, flaming whiskers, and huge hands; and he knew how to move about the boat as well as an east-country fisherman, and was altogether smart at his work, from taking in a reef to climbing up the rigging to set the gaff-topsail. But Shon had two most inevitable faults—he was inordinately vain and utterly untruthful. No man knew how to handle a boat but Shon Macnab; all his townsmen were poor pretenders. No one could pilot a boat on the west coast but Shon; he knew every rock and shallow, and every sideway, from the Mull of Cantyre to Cape Wrath. Unfortunately, however, Shon had never been farther from Oban than Ardnamurchan, and his knowledge of the coast consisted of a sort of second-sight—very gratifying to the possessor, but liable to get the confiding owner of a boat into serious trouble. All went well with Shon for a time; but at last, mad with success, he secretly wagered " the Barber" to race the latter's vessel, an open fore-and-aft boat, very superior in seaworthiness, from Oban round the Lady's Rock and back round Kerrera, a distance of about forty miles. So one day the Wanderer came down to the shore just in time to see the *Ocean Queen* rounding the Maiden Island on her way to the Lady's Rock, and side by side with her the Barber's boat. It was blowing half a gale of wind, and the Barber soon turned back to the bay; but Shon, with a picked crew of Gaels, all wild with whisky, doubtless, still held on his wild career; while the Wanderer, climbing the heights above the town, watched his vessel, and expected every minute to see it submerged. A big sea was rolling in the firth, and the little boat, too sorely pressed under canvas, was sadly knocked about. She reached Oban in the afternoon, with only a tear in the mainsail; but her planks were slightly strained, and she was never as tight after that day. Although Shon begged wildly for pardon, the Wanderer was inexorable, and sent him about his business.

For some little time it seemed as if no fit person would appear to take Shon's place. Several candidates appeared, but were rejected on various scores —greediness, dirtiness, stupidity, or old age. At last the Wanderer discerned a small tradesman in the village, who had been a herring-fisher, and whose only present occupation was to sit on a sack and whittle wood with a knife, while his wife managed the shop. Lachlan Finlay was from the "high-hill country," on the skirts of Morven, and was a true Celt of the quieter kind—very cold and distant on first acquaintance, but affectionate in the extreme. Every day that the Wanderer sailed with Lachlan he liked him better. He was tolerably good at his work—he was thoroughly truthful, and as simple-hearted as a child. He had the "boating mind" of a boy, and was never happy without his pocket-knife to work with. His "pouches" were full of nails, bits of string and other odds and ends. He was as clean as an infant, mind and body, while having a keen perception of the value of money.

As Lachlan knew nothing of the coast, the Wanderer had to work his way about by the government charts, picking his steps, so to speak, from place to place, with extreme caution, and ever dreading the hidden dangers of the firth. Many a narrow escape had the *Ocean Queen* in those days—at one time swinging to her doom on the fierce tide of Dunstaffnage, and only being saved by superhuman endeavors to tow her out of the tideway with the punt; at another, bumping and scratching on the submerged rocks to the north of the Maiden Island; sometimes caught in the open, and having to run for life; at others drifting in the darkness on some unknown and dangerous portion of the coast. One adventure of this sort is as good as another, and as in the course of a certain cruise we had an opportunity of seeing the whole scenery of the firth, let us here chronicle our experience.

We had run up to Crinan to meet a friend from the south. Having taken him on board, we slipped out of the basin at daybreak, with all canvas set, save the gaff-topsail, and ran with the light breeze on our quarter across to the Dorus Mhor, or Big Gate, a narrow passage formed by the peninsula and islands of Loch Craignish. At spring-tides, the tide in the Dorus runs five miles an hour, and, when there is a breeze, the cross seas are terrific. Running with wind and tide, the *Ocean Queen* actually flew; but while she was shooting through the Dorus the waves broke fiercely over her counter, and as the boiling tide dragged at her this way and that, it was a task of no ordinary skill to keep her steady with the helm. The steamship plows her way through the passage, though sometimes with difficulty, and those who stand on her deck look down on the boiling gulf in safety; but it is different with those who sit in a tiny craft, with the water lapping around and over them, and the bubbling roar painfully audible. These tide-ways are ugly indeed to the seaman's eye. How the water hisses and swirls, now like green glass with its own motion, now broken into foam, now rushing to the overfall and plunging down! How the cross-currents tug at the little craft, as if seeking to drag her to her doom! Sometimes a huge coil of seaweed marks the hidden rock, a floating tangle gives a false alarm, whirling on the surface of the waters ahead. The tides of the Dorus Mhor and the adjoining Sound of Scarba are only equaled by the tides of the Kyles of Skye.

On the present occasion there was no danger, and as the dawn blossomed into full bright day, we left the Dorus Mhor behind, and, keeping close along the mainland, which stretched far along to the right, we followed the inner channel of the Firth of Lorne. We were soon abreast of Scarba, a single conical mountain, rising abruptly out of the sea, and fashioning itself into an island about three miles long, very precipitous and rocky, but having on the eastern side a series of thinly-wooded declivities, which, in the gentle light of the summer morning, were touched with tints of quite ethereal beauty. Between Scarba and Jura, which stretches far to the southward, is a narrow sound, opening on the great dim ocean, and, looking through the passage, we ever and anon caught a white gleam, as of great waves breaking in the distance. Yonder lay the far-famed Gulf of Corryvreckan, and it was to escape the force of the tide, which sets for miles toward the dreaded passage, that we were keeping so close to the mainland shore. Corryvreckan is the Hebridean Maelstrom, ever regarded with fearful eyes by the most daring sailors of the inland deep. Poets may be allowed to sing, like Campbell, of "the distant isles that hear the loud Corbrechtan roar;" or, like Scott, of

> "Scarba's isle, whose tortured shore
> Still rings to Corryvreckan's roar;"

but it is no mere poetical dread that fills our Lachlan's heart as he leans against the mast and searches the distance. From infancy upward, the name of yonder gulf has been to him a word of awe and terror. He has heard of great ships being swallowed up whole, torn into pieces by the teeth of hidden reefs, and vomited out in fragments miles away on the Islay shore. He has seen old men turn pale by the very fireside at the mention of Corryvreckan. He believes that the ebb tide in Corryvreckan, "when the wind is from the west, would drown a man-of-war as easily as the shell of a nut." He has, nevertheless, heard stories of vessels that have passed safely through the terrific place; but these, to him, were no less than miracles, brought about by a special Providence.

. The Wanderer used to smile at the yarns of sailors and fishermen, with their dark accumulation of mystic terrors; but the more he navigated the waters in his unprofessional way, the less skeptical he grew. In good truth, familiarity with the sea, instead of breeding contempt, only strengthens the sense of awe. Its dangers are not forever on the surface; they present themselves slowly and upon occasion. When the Wanderer first began to sail small craft, he saw little or no peril; now, every day afloat increases his caution and respect for the elements; and if he goes on in the same ratio for a few years longer, he will be afraid to venture on the water at all. In seafaring matters, distrust the man who seems stupidly indifferent to danger, and over-confident. Choose the man who has his eye cast forever to windward, with that hungry watchfulness so peculiar to the skilled fisher. Never forgive him if, in sailing in an open boat, you catch him fastening the sheet, though only with a half hitch; for, be certain, the man who does that is irreclaimable, and will drown you some day.

Of course, the accounts of Corryvreckan are exaggerated—the danger consisting not in the whirlpools, but in the terrific sea raised by the wind when contending with the tidal wave and the long Atlantic swell in the narrow passage of the sound. In times of storm the place is indeed perilous, and verily capable of drowning a large vessel. Caught in the numberless currents, a ship becomes at once unmanageable, and must drive whither Fate directs—either to strike on some corner of the coast, or to spring her planks and sink to the bottom; or, perhaps—as happened on one traditional occasion—to be swept in safety out of the tide along the Jura shore. In the most dangerous part of the gulf, where it is a hundred fathoms deep, there is a submerged pyramidal rock, rising precipitously to within fifteen fathoms of the surface, and the result is a subaqueous overfall, causing in its turn infinite gyrations, eddies, and counter-currents. There is most danger at the flood-tide, which sets from the eastward, through the gulf, at the rate of ten or twelve miles an hour, and encounters the whole swell of the Western Atlantic rolling into the narrow sound. At turn of tide there is a brief lull, during which, in calm weather, boats have passed through; but the attempt is at all times to be avoided, as the slightest miscalculation as to the tides, or the sudden rising of the wind, would render escape impossible. At all times Corryvreckan "roars," the sound being audible even close to the mainland shore. The poet Campbell heard it at a distance of many leagues, at Downie House, close to Loch Crinan. He compares its effect in calm weather, when all the surrounding seas are still, to the sound of innumerable chariot-wheels.

Quitting the Peninsula of Craignish, we had reached the shores of the Island of Luing, which, with Seil, Shuna, and small isles innumerable, lies so close to the mainland as almost to form a portion of the coast of the Nether Lorne. Seil is separated from the mainland by a channel of only a few yards, forming a rapid, river-like sound, two miles in length. Low and undulating, these isles present few points of beauty, but up behind them lies Loch Melfort, a salt-water lake of rare loveliness, surrounded by magnificent cliffs of ivy-clad gneiss. Out beyond them, to the west, and lying close to and due north of Scarba, are Lunga and the Black Isles. Closed in on each side, we were running before the wind up the broad passage known as the Sound of Scarba, and were soon struggling in the tideway opposite the Black Isles, on the largest of which a lighthouse is situated. A few minutes later, however, we were clear of all the isles, and saw before us the glories of the great firth stretched out in the golden light of a summer day.

Due west of our little vessel stretched the open Atlantic, growing dimmer and dimmer in distance, with a ghostly ship afar, beating southward under full sail; but down to the northwest, fifteen miles away, rose the gigantic mountains of Mull, their deep purple hues mingling with mist upon the peaks; while farther north yet, the white lighthouse of Lismore gleamed with the gleam of breaking waves at its base—and above and beyond mountains innumerable darkened the distance. Straight before the yacht's bow the firth sparkled, its waters visible for many a mile, and a whole fleet of fishing-boats, large and small, white-sailed and red-sailed, were drifting in the slack tide, over a broad patch of dead calm, off the great cliffs of the island of Kerrera, which mingled with the mainland on the starboard bow. The breeze that had brought us thus far was dying fast, and scarcely had we run three miles ahead, and got abreast of the little island of Easdale, when it died away altogether, suddenly as breath from a mirror, and left us rolling about most uncomfortably on the smooth sea. It is ever thus in summer; no wind can be relied on for many hours together; and hence the great danger of navigating the inland channels, with their fierce tides.

The boat which conveys the ordinary tourist to Oban calls at Easdale, but few strangers pay any attention to the unpicturesque little island. Easdale is, nevertheless, worth a visit, for the sake of its slate quarries, which are perhaps the finest in Scotland; still more for the sake of its population, all dependent on the quarries, all born in the locality, and living quite isolated there, summer and winter. Many old superstitions that have died their lingering death elsewhere still flourish here, together with many primitive manners and customs. The men of Easdale are true Celts—daring boatmen and intense dreamers—speaking the fine tongue that many southerners deem nearly extinct, but which still remains the common and cherished speech of Lorne and the Hebrides. He who walks among their houses will note, here and there, large slabs of stone set up on end. These have been purchased and preserved—does the reader guess for what purpose? For gravestones; reserved by the owners to mark their own places of rest. Here and elsewhere in the Hebrides, one not only finds the islander preparing his own shroud, but buying his own tombstone. There they stand, daily monitors of the Inevitable, with the great ocean murmuring forever close to them—a daily preacher of the Eternal.

It is always weary work, waiting for the wind; to look this way and that, in dim hope and expectation, despairingly whistling according to the sailors' superstition; to see the water darken miles off, and the shadow creeping nearer and nearer, and then, just as you expect your sails to fill, miserably dying; or worse still, as on the present occasion, to watch with fierce chagrin the breeze at your back, which for hours together blows pleasantly a hundred yards behind you, and there, for some mysterious reason, pauses, and won't come a single inch nearer; or, worst of all, to drift on the swift current, in spite of all your efforts, toward some dreaded danger, from which only a smart "puff" could bear you away in safety. He who uses a sailing-boat* must recommend to his spirit many hard virtues, foremost among which is patience. The wind is ever perverse, and will serve no man's will. It is most perverse of all on an island coast like that of the Hebrides. Breezes of all sorts are bred among the clouds of the hill-tops, and they are ever rushing down when least expected. An experienced eye can see them coming, but that is all. Even in summer, it is impossible to predict the weather with much certainty.

For hours we drifted on a glassy sea, beguiling part of the time by popping unsuccessfully at a shoal of porpoises, which tumbled for some minutes about a hundred yards from the vessel, in pursuit of the herring, doubtless, for numberless gulls and terns screamed in the air or floated like ourselves on the

* A good story is told of the old Clyde bargeman who, sailing slowly on the firth, and finding himself passed by the first steamboat, watched the latter till almost out of earshot, and then, unable to keep silence any longer, bawled out: "Ayo! get awa' wi' your *Deil's reek*" (Devil's smoke); "I'm just sailing as it pleases the *breath o' God!*" And there is something in this idea of the "breath of God," after all, apart from the comic connection in the anecdote.

water. The tide still took us in the right direction, and we grew nearer and neare to the fleet of fishing boats becalmed off Kerrera; until at last, to our disgust, a nice puff of wind struck them ahead, and, beating slowly northward, they drew one by one toward the opposite shores of Mull.

It was now afternoon, a dimly-bright spring afternoon, and we were floating off Gylen Castle, the shadow of which was clearly visible in the smooth sea. Gylen, like Dunollie, was an old stronghold of the Lords of Lorne. Its gray tower stands on a precipice overlooking the ocean, in the center of a desolate bay, which has been washed and torn into the wildest forms of crag and scaur by the roll of the Western Sea. It commands a full view of the boundless Atlantic. The heights of Kerrera above it are dark and verdureless, and deepen its look of loneliness and desolation. Even on this summer day it appears pitiful and lonely; but in darker days, when it looms through the sad mist like a ghost, it seems to have a look of almost human sorrow. Many a wild scene of life and revel has it beheld. Now its only inhabitants are the owl and the wild-rock pigeon, the latter of which builds in great numbers among the rocky cliffs of the island.

This said island of Kerrera, although not strikingly picturesque in form, possesses such peculiar fascinations as grow upon the imagination. It is separated from the mainland by a narrow strait or sound, half a mile wide, at the northern extremity of which lies the beautiful bay of Oban; is four miles long and two miles broad; and presents an irregular surface of hill and dale, on which can be had a harder day's walking than anywhere else in Lorne. It is a great haunt of the otter, and its crags shelter birds of prey of all descriptions, from the hooded crow to the peregrine falcon. But its chief attractions are on the coast, and the way to behold them is to spend the long day in rowing right round its shores. The cliffs and outlying islets form themselves into pictures of rare beauty, shifting with the lights and shadows of heaven and ocean. The waters on both sides are dangerous for sailing vessels, being sown everywhere with reefs and shallows; studded on the outer coast with many small black islands, in the neighborhood of which are all sorts of submerged dangers; and most unpleasant of all is the narrow inner sound, which is full of rocks not all marked in the charts. Beating to windward up the Sound of Kerrera is disagreeable work; the short tacks are so wearisome, besides being full of danger to one not well acquainted with the coast. The squalls off the coast of the mainland, when the southeast wind blows, are sharp and sudden, often striking you straight from the heights without ruffling an inch of the sound to windward. Woe betide the helmsman who fails to "luff" skillfully at such times. On certain days, no skill is of much avail. The puffs come and go, with intervals of calm; and just as the vessel has lost all way in the latter, and is lying dead still, the squall leaps upon her like a tiger, and she staggers on, half drowned, happy to escape with her mast above water.

One never stands on Kerrera without thinking of King Haco's memorable invasion of Lorne and the

Isles, which is recorded in our second volume. Here, in Kerrera, King Alexander II. had that weird dream, when St. Olaf, St Magnus, and St. Columba appeared to him and warned him to return home to Scotland; and here the king, having disregarded the warning, died of a mysterious distemper.* Hither, to the same anchorage, doubtless, (Horse-shoe Bay?) came the Norwegian monarch, and found King Dugal and other Hebrideans waiting to receive him. From the Kyles of Skye to Loch Ranza and Loch Long, there is scarcely a portion of the coast that the great invasion does not render memorable. Nothing has changed since then. Tobermory, and Kerrera, and Loch Ranza, and the other places where the Norwegian vessels lay, are our anchorages to this hour. Standing on the high cliffs of Kerrera, and gazing across the Firth of Lorne to the opening of the Sound of Mull, we have often pictured the quaint Norwegian vessels issuing one by one out of the distance, with "Haco the aged" in the largest—" built wholly of oak, containing twenty-seven banks of oars, and adorned with heads and necks of dragons overwrought with gold." There is no finer figure in history than that of Haco the King, with his stately generosity, his deep piety.

' The actions of the just
Smell sweet, and blossom in the dust!'

He was a prince indeed, sowing thought and order wherever he stepped, and when the end was near,

* ' Konongr sagdi draumin; ok fysto flestir at hann skylldi afto snúa. Enn hann villdi Pat egi; litlu sidarr tók hann sótt ok andadiz.' (See Vol. II. the " Saga of Haco the King.")

bearing his lingering illness with holy calm. "He desired Norwegian books might be read to him day and night; first, the 'Lives of Saints,' and when they were ended, the 'Chronicles of our Kings from Haldan the Black,' and so of all Norway's kings, one after another." Nor did he forget his followers, great or small, but bequeathed them loving gifts; and with his dying breath he left orders for the guidance of Magnus his son, in dealing with the people and the army. Finally, surrounded by the Wise Men of his kingdom, he passed "from this home's life," leaving a name and fame that smell sweet to the present day.

The summer calm did not last long, and it was broken with ominous suddenness. All at once, a low faint moan was heard, the water darkened in Kerrera Sound, and the great boom swung over with a violent tug at the mast as the sail filled. "Take in a reef, Lachlan, for we're going to have as much as we can carry!" Lachlan laughed and hesitated, but the Wanderer, whose experience told him what was coming, brought the boat up to the wind, handed the helm to his southern friend, and sprang at the reef points—Lachlan assisting vigorously, though with a very skeptical air. The wind *did* come, blowing on our quarter with considerable force, and it soon became necessary to take off the foresail and lower the peak of the mainsail. Thus eased, the *Ocean Queen* bowled round the southern point of Kerrera and out into the dancing waters of the open firth. As she ran between Kerrera and the islands at its extremity, we saw the great cormorants sitting bolt upright in a long row on one of the isles with their dirty white patch at the throat like a street-preacher's neck-cloth. We passed just out of gunshot, and fired a salute into the air above their heads. A few plunged into the sea, dived, and emerged a hundred yards away; the greater number took wing and went flapping across the firth slowly, close to the sea; but a few great fellows, swollen with fish, merely rolled their long heads from side to side, and sat still on their thrones.

The wind was now so strong that it would have been impossible to carry canvas beating to windward; flying with the wind on our quarter and occasionally lowering the peak to the puffs, we got along capitally, at the rate of seven or eight miles an hour. How the bright waves danced and sparkled!

> "Merrily, merrily bounds the bark,
>   On a breeze from the southward free,
> So shoots through the morning sky the lark,
>   Or the swan through the summer sea."

The sky brightened, partaking of the wind's gladness. The fleet of fishing-boats were now running swiftly toward the Sound of Mull, at the mouth of which the lighthouse of Lismore, with the wild ebb-tide foaming at its base, stood in bright relief against the great Morven mountains. Every boat there, big or small, was bound for the Long Island or Outer Hebrides, along the wild shores of which the herring were flashing, and one and all, after a month's fishing, would follow the mysterious flight of the fish southward. Noticeable among them was an Isle of Man "jigger," running neck and neck with a double lug-sailed boat from Newhaven, while west-country smacks innumerable lagged behind. There was more pluck and spirit, more calm resolution to fight with the great forces of the world, more gentleness of heart and strength combined, on board that little fleet, than could readily be found in any camp of war. There they flew, going " as it pleased the breath of God!" They passed the dark shores of Mull, they shot one by one round the base of the dark castle of Duart, and they faded, with a last ghostly gleam, in the dark shadows that slept then, and sleep almost always, on the Sound of Mull.

It had been our original intention to make Oban that night, but to do so we should have had to beat considerably to windward, and the breeze was too strong. We were compelled, in despite of our inclination, to run right after the fishing-boats into the Sound of Mull. The wind had already raised a considerable sea, and we surged forward with the waves dashing in white foam behind us, sometimes almost breaking into the cockpit where we sat. We were soon close under the shadow of Mull, with Kerrera far away on our weather quarter, and Duart castle drawing every moment nearer and nearer on the port bow. There was no prospect of any first-rate anchorage, short of Tobermory, which was thirty miles away up the Sound. True, there were three lochs, with tolerable shelter and holding-ground, along the coast of Mull, which we were skirting, but the entrances were all more or less dangerous—Loch Buy being not only perilous, but quite unknown to us; Loch Spelve partly known, but always perilous on account of submerged rocks in a passage only a few yards wide; and Loch Don, exposed to the full force of the sea when the wind blew as it was then blowing. In the Sound of Mull itself, it was not much better. Duart Bay and Craignure were far too open, Loch Aline could not be well entered against the ebb-tide, and Scallastle had one great disadvantage, owing to our ignorance of the rock-sown waters which surround it. However, if the wind continued to blow at that rate, we should be snug in Tobermory in less than three hours.

As we flew through the water toward Duart, we had a fine view of Mull and its mountains, on the peaks of which the sun was now pouring soft purple light. The coasts of the great island, particularly to the southward, where they are washed by the Atlantic, are wild and precipitous, and assume forms only less beautiful than the basaltic crags on the northeast coast of Skye. Inland, all is dreary and unpicturesque as compared with other surrounding islands. Of course, where there are great hills, with occasional moorland lochs and frequent glimpses of the sea-arm winding far into the land, there must be beauty, abiding and ever-varying; where there is heather, there must be glorious color; but, taken comparatively, Mull is uninviting and wearisome, save only to the sportsman, who will find its moors tolerably abundant in wild-fowl of all kinds and its high corries frequented by the red-deer.

To our mind, by far the pleasantest picture connected with Mull is that of good old Doctor Johnson traversing its weary wilds on horseback in company with Boswell. "Mr. Boswell thought no part of the Highlands equally terrific;" but the Doctor was lionhearted. If any final proof were wanted that Johnson had in him the soul of a hero, it is to be found in the chronicle of his northern tour. In the autumn of 1773 (after trying in the summer " to learn *Dutch*," and being " interrupted by inflammation of the eyes "), he set out, an old man of sixty-four, for the Hebrides, then deemed almost inaccessible. For week after week he faced hardships and dangers unexampled in his honest experience; trudged footsore on endless moors, lay half-drowned in the bottom of leaky Highland boats, faced the fury of real Highland storms, got drunk with mad Highland lairds, and showed at every step the patience of a martyr and the pluck of a soldier. His journal is delicious reading, with its solemn indifference to barbaric "scenery," its quaint pedantic love for antiquities, its calm tone of intellectuality, its deep and fervent piety. Boswell's journal is still more delightful, full of life and unconscious humor, abounding in delicious touches. The glimpses of the oracular conduct and conversation are superb. How Johnson stood out in the dusky moor at Glenelg, and abused his faithful follower in such terms that " Bozzy " could sleep little the night after—" Dr. Johnson's anger had affected me much." How Johnson drank whisky-toddy in Skye and gave his ideas about a seraglio;* and how, when a pretty little lady

---

* " Thursday, Sept. 16—After the ladies were gone from table, we talked of the Highlanders not having sheets : and this led us to consider the advantage of wearing linen."

" *Johnson*—All animal substances are less cleanly than vegetable. Wool, of which flannel is made, is an animal substance; flannel, therefore, is not so cleanly as linen. I remember I used

sat on his knee and kissed him, the old boy "kept her on his knee and kissed *her*, while he and she drank tea," all the company being much "entertained to see him so grave and pleasant." How he had honor everywhere, and won love to crown it. How nightly he turned his dear, purblind, gentle face to God, and communed with his own soul, as it was his wont to do, especially on his birthday.* There are no sweeter

to think tar dirty; but when I knew it to be only a preparation of the juice of the pine, I thought so no longer. It is not disagreeable to have the gum that oozes from a plum-tree upon your fingers, because it is vegetable; but if you have any candlegrease, any tallow upon your fingers, you are uneasy till you rub it off. I have often thought that if I kept a seraglio the ladies should all wear linen gowns, or cotton—I mean stuffs made of vegetable substances. I would have no silk; you cannot tell when it is clean; it will be very nasty before it is perceived to be so. Linen detects its own dirtiness."

"To hear the grave Dr. Samuel Johnson, 'that majestic teacher of moral and religious wisdom,' while sitting solemn in an arm-chair in the Isle of Skye, talk *ex cathedra* of his keeping a seraglio, and acknowledge that the supposition had *often* been in his thoughts, struck me so forcibly with ludicrous contrast that I could not but laugh immoderately. He was too proud to submit, even for a moment, to be the object of ridicule, and instantly retaliated with such keen sarcastic wit, and such a variety of degrading images, of every one of which I was the object, that though I can bear such attacks as well as most men, I yet found myself so much the sport of all the company, that I would gladly expunge from my mind every trace of this severe retort."
—*Boswell's Tour to the Hebrides.*

* The following is among Dr. Johnson's "Prayers and Meditations":

"TALISKER, in Skye, Sept. 24, 1773.

"On last Saturday was my sixty-fourth birthday. I might, perhaps, have forgotten it, had not Boswell told me of it; and,

bits of literature in the world than these few notes of a "Tour to the Hebrides," made in the wild autumn season by Boswell and Johnson.

It was at Loch Buy, the mouth of which we had just passed in the *Ocean Queen*, that Johnson met "a true Highland laird, rough and haughty, and tenacious of his dignity, who, hearing my name, inquired whether I was of the Johnstons of Glencoe or the Johnstons of Ardnamurchan." Johnson and Boswell both record the fact, but the former is silent about a still more amusing subject. On the morning

<hr>

what pleased me less, told the family at Dunvegan. The last year is added to those of which little use has been made; I tried in the summer to learn Dutch, and was interrupted by an inflammation in my eye. I set out in August on this journey to Skye. I find my memory uncertain, but hope it is only by a life unmethodical and scattered. Of my body I do not perceive that exercise or change of air has yet either increased the strength or activity. My nights are still disturbed by flatulences. My hope is—for resolution I dare no longer call it—to divide my time regularly, and to keep such a journal of my time as may give me comfort on reviewing it. But when I consider my age and the broken state of my body, I have great reason to fear lest death should lay hold upon me while I am only yet designing to live. But I have yet hope.

"Almighty God, most merciful Father, look down upon me with pity! Thou hast protected me in childhood and youth; support me, Lord, in my declining years. Preserve me from the dangers of sinful presumption. Give me, if it be best for me, stability of purposes and tranquillity of mind. Let the year which I have now begun be spent to thy glory, and to the furtherance of my salvation. Take not from me thy Holy Spirit, but as death approaches prepare me to appear joyfully in thy presence, for the sake of Jesus Christ our Lord. Amen."

after their arrival, Lady Lochbuy proposed that he (the Doctor) should have some cold "sheep's head" for breakfast. Sir Allan "seemed surprised at his sister's vulgarity; but," says Boswell, "from a mischievous love of sport, I took her part, and very gravely said, 'I think it is but fair to give him an offer of it, and if he does not choose it, he may let it alone.' So, when Johnson entered the room, Lady Lochbuy said to him, 'Do you take any cold sheep's head, sir?' 'No, MADAM!' he thundered, in a tone of surprise and anger." The sequel is perfect, in Boswell's own words: "'It is here, sir,' said she, supposing he had refused it to save the trouble of bringing it in. Thus they went on at cross purposes, till he confirmed his refusal in a manner not to be misunderstood; while I sat quietly by, and enjoyed my success." Why the good Doctor should have refused a capital dish, in such a way, is quite beyond the question.

We were soon rounding Duart Point, with the Lady's Isle and Lismore Lighthouse on our quarter. The ordinary Highland tourist has an opportunity of seeing this part of the firth upon the deck of his steamer, and it is at all times a sight worth seeing— the tides between the Lady's Rock and the Lighthouse causing innumerable whirls, eddies, and countercurrents, very similar to those of the Dorus Mhor, and of course in rough weather raising a very heavy sea. As we passed, all around rock and lighthouse was white with foam, save where the eddies whirled the surface smooth. Leaving the boiling sheet behind us, we ran into the Sound of Mull; past Duart Castle and Duart Bay; past the little village of Craignure and the wood-fringed hills of Scallastle; past the great Highlands of Morven, which rose to the right, with bluff, red-tinted crags descending sheer into the sea; past Ardtornish Castle on its promontory, and the tiny entrance to "green Loch Aline's land-locked bay"—and ere long we were abreast of the outlying rocks and isles of Salen, with Aros Castle looming distinct against the sunset, and saw Ben More and Bentalloch, the monarchs of Mull, rise up suddenly behind us, darkening as the sunlight faded. Still the wind blew on our quarter, and, now in smooth water, we rushed along, leaving on our right the parish of Morven, with its fine stretches of green land and bushy wood, and on our left the land of Mull, seeming wilder and more precipitous the nearer we drew to Tobermory. It was a glorious race. Ere dark we had passed several of the fishing fleet, and were fast gaining on some of the others; and still the breeze kept just steady and strong enough for us to carry canvas. Old castles and fantastic headlands faded and darkened as we sailed. Picture after picture grew and changed. The moon rose as we passed Calve Island and swept round to Tobermory Bay; and here, as it was necessary to come close up to the wind, the little vessel half-drowned herself in lying over under her great sail. Five minutes after, however, the anchor was down in the bay, and all parties on board the little yacht turned in, thoroughly exhausted with the pleasure and excitement of the day.

It is not our purpose to describe Tobermory. To our mind, putting aside the excellence of its bay as an anchorage, it is simply the ugliest and dreariest place

in the islands. The climate is detestable, the rainfall
unceasing, the inns vile, all things abominable. Yet
this is an ungenerous description, since Tobermory
commands a fine view of the mouth of that most
delightful of Highland lakes, Loch Sunart, and of the
adjoining mountains of Ardnamurchan. On the
present occasion we were anxious to get back to
Lorne as soon as possible. When day broke it was
raining hard, but to our joy the little wind there was
came from the west. As we ran out of the bay, the
dim lights of dawn were dappling the base of the
hills of Ardnamurchan, and the waters of Sunart
loomed dark below, with a still gleam of silvery calm
stretching across the mouth in the neighborhood of
the black Stirks—two small rocky isles. Mighty
veils of gray vapor covered the distant mountains,
save in one distant place to the north, where the darkness was rent by a moist gleam of light and showed
the livid peak of some great hill. Behind us, as we
ran east, the great Ocean loomed, with the slant
shadows of the rain drawn in long streaks between
water and cloud, and the sea glittering below like
dark-blue steel misted with breath. All the heavens
was clouded, but, in Lachlan's parlance, "she was
going to be a good day."

It was a good day, and a long one. The wind
came and went, shifting between west and west-by-
south, often failing altogether; and the rain fell,
more or less, constantly. We made slow work of it,
though we carried our gaff-topsail, and though now
and then we got a squall which shook and buried the
boat. By three in the afternoon we were only off the

mouth of Loch Aline, fifteen miles from our starting-place, floating on the slack tide, and hardly making an inch of way. But, nevertheless, it was a day to be remembered. Never did the Wanderer feast his vision on finer effects of vapor and cloud; never did he see the hills possessed with such mystic power and meaning. The "grays" were everywhere, of all depths, from the dark, slumberous gray of the unbroken cloud-mass on the hill-top to the silvery gray of the innumerable spears of the rain; and there were bits of brown, too, when the light broke out, which would have gladdened the inmost soul of a painter. One little picture, all in a sort of neutral tint, abides in his memory as he writes. It was formed by the dark silhouette of Ardtornish Castle and promontory, with the winter sky rent above it; and a flood of white light behind it just reaching the stretch of sea at the extremity of the point, and turning it to the color of glistening white-lead. That was all; and the words convey little or nothing of what the Wanderer saw. But the effect was ethereal in the extreme, finer by far than that of any moonlight.

After we had been becalmed for an hour off the Sheep Islands, which lie between Loch Aline and Scallasdale, we saw the water blacken far behind us, and Lachlan began to whistle up the wind; but it was eight miles off and traveling very slowly, though there seemed plenty of it. It was quite another hour before it reached us, and then it seemed very undecided whether to blow on or die; gaining in vigor, however, it took us by fits and starts to within a mile of the lighthouse of Lismore; grew still stronger, and took us another half mile nearer ; and finally, for no reason that we could discover, refused to go with us an inch farther. We were now in the midst of the fierce ebb-tide setting from the Lady's Rock, with the waves leaping round us and the eddies whirling, and a roar like thunder in our ears. Then occurred a succession of Tantalus-tricks of the most aggravating sort. Where the tide boiled there was not a breath of wind, and we were whirled backward, this way and that, till we again reached the black shadow where the wind was blowing. Then the wind, which was really strong, drove us again into the tide—which in its turn again drove us backward. This occurred again and again, in spite of all our skill. The breeze came on only by inches, though our superstitious Lachlan whistled madly. By and by we began drifting rapidly up the broad arm of the firth, which runs northward between Morven and the long green island of Lismore, and only by frantic pulling with the long oars did we get out of the way of an ugly rock lying half a mile out from the island. By this time we were miserably wet and cold—and hungry, too, for we had fared scantily. At last, to our joy, a breeze came off the Morven shore to reinforce the lazy breeze from the sound, and we ran on bravely till we got into the full strength of the tide-way just abreast of the lighthouse. Here, though the breeze continued, we stuck, fairly anchored between wind and tide, and, in spite of all the efforts of the helmsman, whirling about at the mercy of the elements, with the waves leaping round us and the foam leaping over us, and the savage water roaring as if to swallow the little boat. " Up with the topsail, Lachlan !" It was done, and the yacht dived forward a few yards, with her bowsprit submerged, and the green waves rolling off her bows. But the wind was yet no match for the tide. Now we got forward a short distance; then we swept back in an eddy. An hour passed thus. More than once we were swept so uncomfortably near to the lighthouse that we had to beat up to windward with the tide—and then we should have foundered indeed, if Lachlan had not been smart in hauling down the gaff-topsail. Not for another half hour, when the tide began to slacken, did we get through the narrow passage, and by that time all on board were dripping from head to foot; and the little yacht, hull and sail, was bathed in salt water. Do you wonder that our first act, on reaching the smooth water of the firth, was to get out the whisky-bottle and serve round the glorious spirit with no niggard hand?

Out in the open firth the breeze was slack and fitful, but we crept slowly over toward Oban, the white smoke of which was visible seven miles away between the north end of Kerrera and the woody promontory of Dunollie. Northward, we saw the long dark arm of Loch Linnhe—here and there dotted with isles and rocks—closed in suddenly where the house of Airds gleamed like a wreath of snow in the midst of its woody bay, and surrounded on all sides by mountains slowly darkening in twilight. Dim and melancholy loomed Dunstaffnage to the east, with Ben Cruachan and the Shepherds of Loch Etive blackening behind her. Far southward, off Kerrera, there was already a ghostly gleam on the ocean, cast by the invisible moon.

But if we looked for moonlight we were doomed to disappointment. When we had reached the center of the firth it was quite dark; and, to add to our troubles, the wind had died entirely away, as is its wont on many summer nights, when dead calm lasts from evening to dawn. There was nothing for it but to put out the long oars, and pull the little yacht toward the anchorage, five miles distant. Lachlan worked one oar manfully, singing a monotonous Gaelic chant peculiar to him, while the Wanderer labored at the other. As the mist and darkness deepened, it became impossible to tell what progress was being made. Gradually, moreover, the whole land changed its form, and it became uncertain where lay the narrow entrance to Oban Bay. He who has never been afloat on such a night, off such a coast as that of Lorne, can scarcely conceive how mysteriously it seems to change, eluding the knowledge of the most experienced pilots. Clouds seem mountains; shadows, islands; islands, shadows; all is ghostly and confused. For a long time we were steering by what seemed the Maiden Island, which lies at the mouth of the entrance to Oban, but we found presently that we had been looking at a solid bank of mist sleeping in the silent sea. At last, we found ourselves in the shadow of Kerrera, but Kerrera is six miles long, and we knew not what part of the island we were approaching; so that at any moment we might strike one of those rocks and reefs with which its shores are sown. It therefore became expedient to let the yacht lie off, while the Wanderer rowed in the punt toward the land and tried to make out the bearings of the coast. A few strokes of the paddles, and he was alone in the solid black shadow—literally "darkness visible"—of the island. He rowed on for some minutes, and then leant on his oars to reconnoiter. The darkness was awful, the stillness was deathlike, broken only by the wash of the fathomless water, and the dreary moan of the sea-birds roosting on the isles. Once or twice the curlew uttered, far off in the night, his weird, melancholy whistle, as he flew from one ghostly bay to another; but neither by sight nor sound could the Wanderer discover his precise whereabouts. The more he rowed, the more the land changed shape and receded. All was mysterious darkness. In sheer despair, he turned back toward the yacht, which was lost in the gloom. He shouted. The cliffs moaned an answer; and a sea-gull screamed. He shouted again and again. At last, faint and far away, he heard another voice crying; and so guided, he at last got on board the yacht.

Not for hours after, when the atmosphere became somewhat clearer, did we succeed in making out the shape of the land, and when we did so, we found we had drifted far down Kerrera, and were not a hundred yards from one of the worst outlying reefs. It was weary work pulling along the dark coast of the island. By the time we got to our anchorage dawn was breaking; and just as we hauled down our sails, a fresh morning breeze sprang up and whistled merrily in the rigging.

During the little voyage that has just been recorded, the *Ocean Queen* had behaved tolerably, for the simple reason that she had no chance of showing her worst qualities, namely, crankness under canvas and awkwardness in "coming round." On other occasions she fully justified her soubriquet of the *Coffin*. Whenever the wind blew hard, she could not carry a rag of canvas "beating;" and when squalls came, it was a miracle she floated at all, so wildly did she heel over and ship the green water. She was certainly a prize for any used-up person in search of a new sensation. Then, again, her clumsiness occasioned other perils. Twice, in the tideway off the mouth of Loch Etive, she was nearly swept to destruction because she would not answer the helm. Once, she was driven like a straw past the great rock at the mouth of Loch Aline, actually scraping the weeds thereon, and only escaping by an inch.* In short, she supplied the owner's system with a series of gratuitous galvanic shocks, which a very daring person might have deemed pleasant excitement, but which to the Wanderer's mind was anything but delightful. Even a soldier in war-time is not always under fire, or he would soon sicken and grow weary; but in the *Ocean Queen* we were ever

* The worst of these sharp boats is this: if they *do* take the ground, whether running on a sandbank or striking on a reef, they heel over and fill at once, in spite of all your efforts to save them; and, in nine cases out of ten, "legs" (or wooden props for the sides) are quite useless. Now, a broad-bottomed fishing-boat sits on a rock or mudbank as snugly as a bird, provided she does not fill, and can wait for the next tide to float her off into deep water.

more or less in peril, all the ferocious elements being leagued against a cockshell.

Not without great reluctance, however, did the Wanderer part with the *Ocean Queen*. Crank and fitful as she was, frequently as she had put his life in danger, he had learned to regard her with affection. How many a glorious scene he had beheld from that little cockpit! how many a golden day he had wasted, stretched full length on that narrow deck! With all her faults, the little yacht was beautiful to look upon, and very snug for her tonnage.

But when the little *Tern* came in her place, the fickleness of man's heart was proven, for the old love was gone in a moment, and the new love took its place. The *Tern* was two tons smaller, and belonged to the same family—being a racer which had won several prizes; but she had far better "bearings," being much shorter in proportion to her beam. She, too, was of course a toy; a mere little wind-straw of a boat, though destined to weather many a storm that tried bigger vessels. In her tiny cabin, where it was impossible to sit upright, we were to sleep for many months, while exploring the strange shores of the Hebrides, from Lorne to the Long Island. Lachlan Finlay went back to his shop, there to resume his old occupation of sitting on a sack and whittling sticks; and in his place, when the little *Tern* was ready for sailing, her tiny cabin well stocked with all the necessaries for a long cruise, Hamish Shaw, the pilot, came from his fishing in the Firth of Clyde and swung up his hammock in the forecastle, just as the cuckoos were swarming over every hill in Lorne.

CHAPTER VI.

THE "TERN'S" FIRST FLIGHT.

The *Tern* Afloat—Off Ardnamurchan—First Glimpses of the Isles—The Cuchullin Hills—General Reflections—Flashing Forward—The Party on Board—The Scaur of Eig—Rum—Birds of the Ocean—Muck—Sunset on the Waters—Loch Scresort, Rum—The Gaelic Skipper—The Widow—A Climb among the Peaks—View of the Western Ocean from Rum—The *Tern* weighing Anchor—Kilmory Bay—First View of Canna—At Anchor.

WHEN the little cutter *Tern*, agile and beautiful as the sea-swallow from which she takes her name, weighed anchor in Tobermory Harbor, and began to work westward through the Sound of Mull toward Ardnamurchan, the long swell coming in from the Atlantic was beginning to whiten under a stiff breeze from the northwest; and it became a question whether or not she should fold down her wings and run back to her nest in the bay.

We looked wistfully to windward, and began to doubt our wisdom in venturing so far on board so tiny a craft—seven tons register, open "aft," and rigged with a heavy boom and racing mainsail sure to bring her on her broadside in stormy weather. The gloomy prognostics of both fair-weather yachtsmen and hard-weather seamen were sharply remembered, as the big rollers began to break wildly over our weather-bow, and the strong wind to lay the decks under to the very edge of the cockpit "combing." But the Viking in the blood prevailed. A third reef was taken in the mainsail, and the little craft was urged on; and scarcely had she beaten two miles and a half to windward, when the breeze died suddenly away, and the waters, washing troublously, grew weaker and weaker, till the tops of the long heaving rollers were almost calm. A light air and a strong tide soon carried the *Tern* outside of Ardnamurchan, where, dripping and quivering like a thing of life, she has paused nearly becalmed, with the lonely islands whither she is bound opening one by one on the dim and shadowy sea.

To the south lies Mull in mist, piling her dull, vast hills out above the line of breaking foam; while away to the southwest, cairn after cairn, looming through the waters, show where barren Coll is weltering in the gloomy waste. To the far west, only cloud resting on cloud, above the dim, unbroken water-line of the Atlantic. But northward all brightens, for the storm has passed thence with the wind, and the sunlight has crept out cold and clear on craggy Rum, whose heights stretch gray and ghostly against a cloudless sky. Hard by, in shadow, looms the gigantic Scaur of Eig, looking down on the low and grassy line of Muck,

"Set as an emerald in the casing sea."

Beyond all these, peeping between Rum and Eig, penciled in faint and ghostly peaks, hued like the heron's breast, are the wondrous Cuchullin Hills of Skye—born of the volcano on some strange morning in the age of mighty births. The eye seeks to go on farther. It rests on those still heights, and in a moment the perfect sense of solitude glides into the soul; thought seems stationary, brooding over life subdued.

For a sight such as that words are the merest pencil-scratches, and for the feeling awakened by such sights there is no kind of symbol at all. In trying accurately to describe nature, one glides at once into the mood of the cicerone; for the moment of enjoyment has past, and the pain of explanation has begun. The *still* power of waters is not quite to be felt until the very body and blood have known their stormy might; and how better know their might than by slipping out upon the waste in as tiny a vessel as can live thereon? The smaller the craft, the fewer the fellow-beings at hand, the intenser the enjoyment both of storm and calm. It is a proud pleasure to dash like a sea-fowl under the very mouth of the tempest, conscious of the life in one's veins, drunken as it were with the excitement and uncertainty of the hour— awake to every quiver of the little yielding creature under the wings of which you fly, feeling its panting breath come and go with your own, till, perchance, its wings are folded down close, and it swims with you for very life before the elements which follow screaming in its track. After a flight so fine, the soul is ready for strange, calm waters and melancholy peaks, fit to feel the pathos and sweetness of things at rest, ending with that dim, pathetic tremble, amid which we seem to feel God's shadow in our souls. In this life, and perhaps in lives beyond, there seems need of some such preparation for great spiritual peace; and it is therefore a poor soul which has not felt some very rough weather.

The British lover of beauty wanders far, but we question if he finds anywhere a picture more exquisite than opens out, vista after vista, among these wondrous Isles of the North. Here, year after year, they lie almost neglected, seen only by the hard-eyed trader and the drifting seaman; for that mosaic being, the typical tourist, seldom quits the inner chain of mainland lakes, save, perhaps, when a solitary "Saturday Reviewer" oozes dull and bored out of the mist at Broadford or Portree, takes a rapid glare at the chilly Cuchullins, and, shivering with enthusiasm, hurries back to the south. The heights of Rum, the kelp-caverns of Islay, the fantastic cliffs of Eig, scarcely ever draw the sight-seer; Canna lies unvisited in the solitary sea; and as for the Outer Hebrides—from Stornoway to Barra Head—they dwell ever lonely in a mist, warning off all fair-weather wanderers. A little, a very little, has been said about these isles; but to all ordinary people they are less familiar than Cairo, and farther off than Calcutta.

Forbidding in their stern beauty, isolated and sea-surrounded, they possess no superficial fascinations; their power is one that grows; their spell is that of the glamour, holding only the slowly-selected soul. Not merely because these isles are so strangely, darkly lovely, but because we owe to them so much that is noblest and best in the heart of our modern life, did it seem fitting to attempt some faint pictures of their scenery and their people; and to wander from island to island, mixing freely with poor folk, seeing and noting what may afterward pass into noble nourishment for the heart, is the errand of those on board the little *Tern*.

" For many a tale
Traditionary round the mountains hung,
And many a legend, peopling the dark woods."

As the eye became more and more accustomed to hill and sea, as the first mood of awe and pleasure at the weird vistas wore away, human figures, group after group, before invisible, loomed slowly into view: the kelp-burner moving blackly through the smoke of his fire on the savage shore; the herrin-fishers tossing at their nets, while the midnight sea gleams phosphorescent below and the clouds blacken in the lift above; the wild, wandering women, foul with the fish they are gutting, shrieking like the cloud of gulls that hovers over their heads; the quaint country-folk streaming down the little ports on holidays and fair-days; the shepherd on his hill; the lobster-fisher in the quiet bay; the matron grinding her corn and weaving her petticoat with instruments hundreds of years "behind the age"—and all these moving against so mighty a background, and speaking a speech stranger to common ear than any modern tongue of Europe—a speech old as the hills and full of their mysterious music and power. Here surely was something for the eye and heart to rest upon, a life subtly coloring ours through many generations, yet preserved quite fresh and unchanged by the spirit of the waters— a life far more surely part of us and ours than that of Florence, or Paris, or Wiesbaden.

To lie becalmed in the little *Tern* off the terrible Rhu, the Ardnamurchan, most dreaded by those best acquainted with its mighty tides and fierce waters, is by no means an unmixed pleasure. Yonder stretches the ocean, dead-still now, but likely to be roused in an instant into frenzy; and, even more to be dreaded, half a mile on the starboard bow, the gloomy cliffs of the point seem coming nearer, as the fitful eddies of the tide swing the vessel this way and that. Out go the long oars, and slowly, very slowly, the *Tern* draws from the shore. Two long hours of hard pulling, with scarcely any perceptible progress, is not altogether desirable, even in the presence of a scene so fair; and one whistles for the wind more and more impatiently. At last the waters ripple black to the northward, the hugh mainsail-boom swings over with a heavy jerk, and in a minute the *Tern* flashes ahead, full of new life, and the sky brightens over a fresh and sparkling sea, and, with hearts leaping, all canvas set, and the little kittiwakes screaming in our track, we leave the mighty Rhu behind.

We are four—the skipper, the pilot, the Wanderer, and the cook—only the seaman being a sailor by profession. The skipper, to describe him briefly, is a wild, hirsute being, generally inclined (as Walt Whitman puts it) to "loafe and invite his soul." The pilot is of another turn, a Gaelic fisher, deep in knowledge of small craft, and full of the dreamy reasonings of his race. As for the Wanderer—

"A subtle-souled psychologist,
All things he seemed to understand,
Of old or new, or sea or land,
But his own mind—which was a mist;"

in other words, he is a nondescript, a mooner on the

skirts of philosophy, whose business it is to take notes by flood and fell, and cater for the kitchen with rod and gun. What he provides is prepared to perfection by the cook, in a den about the size of an ordinary cupboard, and served up in a cabin where Tom Thumb might have stood upright, and a shortish man have just lain at full length. Over the sleeping accommodation let us draw a veil.

As the *Tern* flies nearer to the mighty Scaur of Eig, a beetling precipice, towering 1300 and odd feet above the sea, the sun is sloping far down westward behind the lofty peaks of Rum; and in deep, purple shadow, over the starboard bow, the rugged lines of the mainland, from Loch Moidart to the Sound of Sleat, open up, gloam strangely, and fade, ridge after ridge, away. The distant Cuchullins grow yet more ghostly against the delicate harebell of the sky, catching on their peaks the roseate tints of sunset; and the mountains of Rum deepen more and more in under-shadow, as the light flames keener on their rounded heights. The wind falls again, faint airs come and go, and the low sound of the sea becomes full of a strange hush. At such an hour, one remembers with a chill shiver the terrible story of the Cave of Eig. In the old bloody days, the inhabitants had given dire offense to the Macleods, and the chief came over, with all his clan at his heels, to butcher the offenders. But not a soul was visible—only the white snow; for it was winter-time. Every inhabitant— man, woman, and child—had taken refuge in the great cave. The Macleods were about to return to their boats when they discovered footprints in the snow. Tracing these, they came to the mouth of the great cave. Then, with a devilish ingenuity, the cruel chief ordered a great fire of turf and fern to be lit at the mouth of the cavern. There was no escape; all the poor shrieking folk were suffocated. This is no mere legend, but horrible truth. Until very recently, the cave was full of human bones, and some remain still, though the busy hands of visitors have carried off the most perfect remains. "Something ails it now—the place is curst!" One sees and hears it all—the flame shining lurid in the white snow, the black, smoky cloud at the mouth of the cave, the grimly-grinning caterans piling up the fire with wild yells, and the wild shrieks of the murdered floating out upon the winter wind!

> "On Scooreigg next a warning light
> Summoned her warriors to the fight;
> A numerous race, ere stern Macleod
> O'er their bleak shores in vengeance strode!
> When all in vain the ocean-cave
> Its refuge to its victims gave.
> The chief, relentless in his wrath,
> With blazing heath blockades the path:
> In dense and stifling volumes rolled,
> The vapor filled the caverned hold!
> The warrior-threat, the infant's plain,
> The mother's scream, were heard in vain;
> The vengeful chief maintains his fires,
> Till in the vault a tribe expires!
> The bones which strow that cavern's gloom,
> Too well attest their dismal doom."

As we draw close under the lee of Rum, the still sea is darkened on every side with patches as of drifting sea-weed, and there is a still flutter as of innumerable little wings. Hither and thither, skimming the water in flocks of eight or ten, dart the beautiful shearwaters (*puffini Anglorum* of the ornithologists), seizing their prey from the sea with their tender feet as they fly; while under them, wherever the eye rests, innumerable marrots and guillemots float, dive, and rise. All these have their nests among the purple-shaded cliffs close at hand. The black and green cormorants are there too, wary and solitary; and the gulls, from the lesser black-backed to the little kittiwake, gather thickly over one dark patch of floating birds astern, where, doubtless, the tiny herring are darting in myriads. Save for the fitful cry of the kittiwakes, or the dull, croaking scream of a solitary tern beating up and down over the vessel, all is quite still, and the presence of these countless little fishers only deepens the solitude. Quite fearless and unsuspicious, they float within oar's length of the vessel, diving swiftly at the last moment, and coolly emerging again a few yards distant. Only the cormorant keeps aloof, safe out of gun range. Rank and unsavory as this glutton is, his flesh is esteemed by fishermen, and he is so often hunted that he is ever on the watch for danger.

Low, undulating, grassy, yonder is Muck—the Gaelic Eilan-na-Muchel, or Isle of Swine—Buchanan's *Insula Porcorum*. It is green and fertile, an oasis in the waste. Muck, Eig, Rum, and Canna form collectively the Parish of Small Isles, with the pastor of which Hugh Miller took his well-known geologic cruise. It must be no lamb-hearted man who carries the gospel over these waters during winter weather.

Lower, deeper sinks the sun, till he is totally hidden behind the hills. Haskeval and Haleval, the two highest peaks of Rum, throw their shadows over the drifting *Tern*, while from some solitary bay inland the oyster-catchers and sealarks whistle in the stillness. A night mist coming from the west deepens the gloaming, and we look rather anxiously after a harbor. Somewhere, not far away, below the two peaks, lies a little loch, with safe anchorage; but no eyes, except those of a native, could pick it out in the darkness. We drift slowly upward on the flood-tide, eagerly eyeing every nook and cranny in the shadowy mass at our side. Just as the day dawns, we spy the mouth of the loch, and launching the long oars, make wearily toward it; but the anchor is soon down, all cares are over for the time being, and, after pipes and grog, all hands turn in for a nap.

Our slumbers are sweet, though short, and ere long we are up on deck, looking around on Loch Scresort. Viewed in the soft, sparkling light of a windless summer morning, it is as sweet a little nook as ever Ulysses mooned away a day in, during his memorable voyage homeward. Though merely a small bay, about a mile in breadth, and curving inland for a mile and a half, it is quite sheltered from all winds, save the east, being flanked to the south and west by Haskeval and Hondeval, and guarded on the northern side by a low range of heathery slopes. In this sunny time the sheep are bleating from the shores, the yacht lies double—yacht and shadow—and the still bay is painted richly with the clear reflection of the mountains:

"Not a feature of the hills
Is in the mirror slighted."

On the northern point of the loch, where the old red sandstone is piled in torn, fantastic heaps high over the sea, gulls innumerable sit and bask. "Croak! croak!" cries the monstrous-hooded crow at their backs, perched like an evil spirit on the very head of the cliffs, and squinting fiercely at the far-off sheep. A bee drones drowsily past the yacht, completing the sense of stillness and pastoral life.

Scattered along the southern side of the bay are a few poor cottages, rudely built of stone and roofed with peat turfs, and at the head of the loch is a comfortable, whitewashed house, the abode of Captain Macleod of Dunvegan, the tenant of the island. There is, moreover, a rude stone pier, where a small vessel might lie secure in any weather, and off which a battered old brigantine is even now unloading oatmeal and flour. Casting loose the punt, we row over to the vessel, and begin to chat with the shrewd-looking ancient skipper, who is superintending the passage of the sacks into a skiff alongside. In that extraordinary dialect called Gaelic-English, which may be described as a wild mingling of Gaelic, bad Irish, and Lowland Scotch, he gives us to understand that he is at once the owner and master of his craft, and that he cruises from island to island during the summer, bartering his cargo of food for whatever marketable commodities the poor folk of the place may have prepared. His great trade is with the fishers, who pay him in dried fish, chiefly ling and cod; but all is fish that comes to his net, and can be anyhow cashed in the south. Doubtless, the odds of the bargains are quite on his side. In answer to our queries as to the general condition of the islanders, he shakes his gray head dismally, and gives us to understand that but for him, and for such as he, many a poor household would perish of starvation.

Starvation, however, does not seem the order of the day in Loch Scresort. On landing, and making for the first hut at hand, we find the cow, with her calf by her side, tethered a few yards from the dwelling, two pigs wallowing in the peat-mire close by, and at least a dozen cocks, hens, and chickens, running to and fro across the threshold, where a fresh, well-fed matron, with a smile for the stranger, salutes us in the Gaelic speech. With that fine old grace of hospitality which has fled forever from busier scenes, she leads us into her cottage—a "but" and a "ben." The apartment into which we are shown, despite the damp earthen floor and mildewy wall, is quite a palace for the Highlands; for it has a wooden press bed, wooden chairs and table, and a rude cupboard, shapen like a wardrobe; and the walls are adorned, moreover, by a penny almanac and a picture cut out of the "Illustrated London News." Drink fit for the gods is speedily handed round, in the shape of foaming bowls of new milk fresh from the udder—a cup of welcome invariably offered to the traveler in any Highland dwelling that can afford it. A few friendly words warm up the good woman's heart, and she begins to prattle and to question. She is a childless widow, and her "man" was drowned. She dwells here all alone; for all her relatives have emigrated to Canada, where she hopes some day to join them. On hearing that we have passed through Glasgow, she asks eagerly if we know a woman called Maggie, who sells eggs; the woman's surname she does not remember, but we must have noticed her, as she is splay-footed and has red hair. She has never been farther south than Eig, and hence her notion of big cities. She longs very much to see Tobermory and its great shops—also to look up a distant kinsman, who has flourished there in trade. She tells us much of the laird and his family—the "folk in the big house;" they are decent, pious people, and kind to the poor. Will she sell us some eggs? Well, she has not heard the price of eggs this season, but will let us have some at fivepence a dozen. She loads the pilot with a basketful of monsters, and we go on our way rejoicing.

Casting our eyes up the hill as we leave the cottage, we meet a pair of steadfast eyes regarding us over a knoll a few yards distant; and lo! the head and antlers of a noble stag, a veritable red deer from the peaks. He has wandered down to prey upon the little patch of corn, from which the widow with difficulty drives him and his mates many times in the day. A royal fellow! Conscious of his immunity, he stares coolly at us with his soft yet powerful eyes. We approach nearer—he does not move—a pistol-shot would stretch him low; but suddenly espying our retriever, who has lingered behind, lapping up some spilt milk, he tosses his head disdainfully, and turns to go. As Schneider, the dog, runs toward him, he breaks into a trot, then bounds suddenly over a boulder, and is off at full speed. The dog pursues him eagerly, but the fleet-footed one speeds silently away, floating lightly upward to the heights, and leaving his panting pursuer far behind.

But the eye, following him upward, rests on the peaks, and is sublimed by a sudden sense of the silences broken only by the red deer's splash in some dark tarn. Fading gradually upward from deep green to ashen gray, mingling softly into the white little cloud that poises itself on the highest peak of all, the mountains lie in the crystalline air of a hazeless summer day. Every rock comes out clear, every stream shows its intense white seam against the hillside, and the knolls of crimson heather in the foreground seem visible to the tiniest leaf.

The temptation is too great, and we are soon vigorously facing the lesser range of heights. On all the knolls around us the white canna-grass waves in the wind, and the yellow iris peeps among the green twigs of under-grass, and in the hollows here, where the peat is cut and piled for drying, we stop and pluck bog-asphodel. Higher we speed, knee-deep now in the purple heather—from which the dog scares moor fowl under our very feet. The air rarefies, full, as it were, of holier, deeper breath. The deep red of the heather dies away into brown and green, and yet a few paces farther, only green herbage carpets the way—boulders thicken, the hill-side grows still more steep, till at last, quite breathless with exercise and the sharp fine air, we get among the graystone cliffs and the hugely-piled boulders of the peaks.

The great, glorious world lies around and beneath us—mountains, crags, and their shadows in a violet sea. Close at hand, to the northward, see Canna, with her grim shark's teeth of outlying rock jutting up here and there, far out in the westward ocean; and behind her tower the Cuchullin Hills of Skye, sharpening into peak on peak, blue mists brooding on their base, but all above snowed over with livid layers of hypersthene, and seamed with the black-forked bed of torrents that in wild weather twist down like lightning to the hidden lakes below.

Far down westward on the ocean there is a long low line, as of cloud, on the horizon. That is the Outer Hebrides, our Ultima Thule. The low levels are veiled by distance, but the hills and promontories—now a dull headland, beyond a stretch of highland—loom here and there through the mist—

"The dreamy grief of the gray sea."

With a feeling distantly akin to that of the old wanderers of the waters, gazing from their frail barks at the cloud of unexplored demesne, we eye our distant quarry. A far flight for the tiny *Tern*, on seas so great and strange! Weary with a long-reaching gaze, our eye drops downward on the western side of the isle whereon we stand. The low, grassy swell of the Minch breaks in one thin, creamy line against that awful coast—a long range washed into cliffs and precipices, and unbroken by a single haven or peaceful creek. When the mists and vapors gather here, and the southwester comes pouring in upon these shores, and the sea rises and roars as it can roar only on rocky coasts, many a brave ship goes to pieces yonder. There is then no hope on this side of time. Not a soul is there to look on from the land, and he who drifts living as far as the shore is dashed to pieces on its jagged wall. There is no pause, no suspense. A crash, a shriek, and nothing remains but spindrift and splintering planks.

After a long ramble, we regain our punt, and are soon busy hoisting sail on board the yacht, for a fresh breeze has sprung up, which should waft us swiftly on to Canna. Up goes the *Tern's* white wings, and we fly buoyantly away, the faint scent of *honeysuckle* floating from the rocks as we round the jagged point of the bay. It is the last farewell of Loch Scresort— the last, sweet breath of a sweet place. The sun shines, the spray sparkles, and with happy hearts and backward-looking eyes we speed along on the joyful, gentle sea.

The breeze stiffens, blowing on our quarter, and the little *Tern*, though she carries a double reef in the mainsail, has soon about as much as she can bear; but cheerily she foams through it, veritably "like a thing of life," fearless, eager, quivering through every fibre with the salt fierce play—now dipping with a stealthy motion into the green hollow of the waves, then rising, shivering on their crest, and glancing this way and that like a startled bird; drifting sidelong for a moment as if wounded and faint, with the tip of her white wing trailing in the water, and again, at the wind's whistle, springing up and onward, and tilting the foam from her breast in showers of silver spray.

Though the breeze is so keen, there is neither mist nor rain. Far away yonder to the west, a slight gray streak hovers over the clear sea-line—and from thence, as from the out-pursed lip of a god, the invisible wind is blown. All is fresh and clear—the peaks of Rum, the far-off mainland—all save the white Cuchullins, which have suddenly clothed themselves with their own smokes and vapors, through which they loom at intervals, Titan-like and forlorn. From the blank, stony stare of hills so ghostly in their beauty, yet so human in their desolation, one turns to look at Kilmory Bay, which opens before us as we round the northern shores of Rum. It is a little space of shingly sand, yellow and white and glistening, slipped in between grim crags and under the shadow of the mountains. The thin cream line of foam stirs not on its edge, as the deep soft billows roll inward and lessen over shallows. Above, on the slope of the hill, there are stretches of grassy mead as green as any in Kent, and cattle grazing thereon; and still higher, the heights of heather die away into hues of gray moss and lichen, till the stony peaks are penciled grimly on the quiet azure of the sky.

Canna is now in full view. The "castled steep," as Scott calls its high cliff, towers in deep brown shadow, surrounded by green heights of pasture, while below is one long line of torn crags and caves, in the lee of which, on a stretch of nearly calm sea, the gulls and guillemots gather, and the solan goose drops like a stone to its prey. The breeze now strikes nearly dead ahead, and the *Tern* has a sore struggle of it beating onward. Not until she is close in upon the jagged cliffs does the narrow entry into the harbor open, and it is a difficult job, indeed, to pick our way through the rocks, in the teeth of wind so keen ; but directly we round the corner of the cliffs, the little landlocked bay opens safe and calm, and, gliding into five-fathom water, we cast anchor just opposite the laird's house.

CHAPTER VII.

CANNA AND ITS PEOPLE.

The Laird of Canna—His Kingly Power—Prosperity of the State—The Island—The Old Tower—Canna in Storm and in Calm—The Milking—Twilight—A Poem by Davy Gray—Haunts of the Ocean Birds—Whispers from the Sea—The Canna People—The Quiet Life—The Graveyard on the Hillside.

THE Laird of Canna might fitly be styled its king; for over that lonely domain he exercises quite regal authority, and he is luckier in one respect than most monarchs—he keeps all the cash. His subjects number four-score—men, women, and children. Some till his land, some herd his sheep. For him the longline fishers row along the stormy coasts of Rum, for him the wild boors batter out the brains of seals on the neighboring rocks of Haskeir; the flocks on the crags are his, and the two smacks in the bay; every roof and tenement for man or beast pays him rent of some sort. The solid modern building, surrounded by the civilized brick wall, is his palace—a recent erection, strangely out of keeping with the rude cabins and heather houses in the vicinity. Yet the Laird of Canna is not proud. He toiled hard with his hands long before the stroke of good fortune which made him the heritor of the isle, and even now he communes freely with the lowest subject, and is not above boarding a trading-vessel in the bay in his shirt-sleeves. A shrewd, active, broad-shouldered man is the laird, still young, and as active as a goat. Though he sits late at night among his books, he is up with the grayest dawn to look after his fields. You meet him everywhere over the island, mounted royally on his sturdy little sheltie, and gazing around him with a face which says plainly,

> "I am monarch of all I survey;
> My right there is none to dispute."

But at times he sails far away southward, in his own boats, speculating with the shrewdest, and surely keeping his own. In the midst of his happy sway he has a fine smile and a kindly heart for the stranger, as we can testify. The great can afford to be generous, though, of course, if greatness were to be measured by mere amount of income, the laird, though a "warm" man, would have to be ranked among the lowly. He has in abundance what all the Stuarts tried in vain to feel—the perfect sense of solitary sway.

Think of it—dreamer, power-hunter, piner after the Napoleonic! A fertile island, a simple people, ships and flocks all your own, and all set solitary and inviolate in the great sea; for how much less have throats been cut, hearths desolated, even nations ruined! There is no show, no bunkum, no flash-jewelry of power, but veritable power itself. In old days, there would have been the gleaming of tartans, the flashing of swords, the sound of wassail, the intoning of the skald, but now, instead, we have the genuine modern article—a monarch of a speculative turn, transacting business in his shirt-sleeves. The realm flourishes, too. Each cotter or shepherd pays his rent in labor, and is permitted a plot of ground to grow potatoes and graze a cow. The fishermen are supported in the same way. Both sexes toil out of doors at the crops, and take part in the shearing, but the women have plenty of time to watch the cow and weave homespun on their rude looms. All on the isle, excepting only the laird himself, belong to the old Romish faith, even the laird's own wife and children being Catholics. There is no bickering, civil or religious. The supreme head of the state is universally popular, and praised for his thoughtfulness and generosity—a single example of which is as good as a hundred. It is said to be the custom of many Highland proprietors, notably those of Islay, to levy a rent on those who burn the seaweeds and tangles on their shore, charging the poor makers about a pound on every ton of kelp so produced. Not so the Laird of Canna. "He charges nothing," said our informant, a wild old Irish wanderer, whom we found kelp-burning close to our anchorage; "the laird is too decent a man to take *rint for the rocks!*"

One might wander far, like those princes of Eastern fable who went that weary quest in search of kingdoms, and fare far worse than here. Though environed on every side by rocks and crags, and ringed by the watery waste, Canna is fat and fertile, full of excellent sheep-pastures and patches of fine, arable ground. Its lower slopes, in times remote, were enriched by the salt sea-loam, and its highest peaks have been manured for ages by innumerable sea-fowl. Huge sheep of the Cheviot breed cover all the slopes, finding their way to the most inaccessible crags; long trains of milch-cows wind from the hills to the outside of the laird's dairy, morning and gloaming; and in the low, rich under-stretches of valley are little patches of excellent corn, where the loud "creek-creek" of the corn-crake sounds harshly sweet. So much for the material blessings of the island. Now, let us note those other blessings which touch the eye and soul.

It is a fish-shaped island, about five miles long and a mile and a half broad, throwing out, by a small isthmus on the western side, a low peninsula of grassy green. The main island forms a ridge, the cliffs of which rise on the northern side to about one thousand feet above the level of the sea, and descend on the southern side to the shore, by a succession of terraces of dazzling greenness, supported on magnificent columns of basalt. In the space between the peninsula (which, being separated from the mainland at high water, is sometimes called Sandy Island) and the southeastern point of the mainland, lies the harbor, and across the isthmus to the west lies another greater bay, so sown with grim little islands and sunken rocks as to be totally useless to navigators in any weather. The peninsula is somewhat low, but the crags of the main island tower to an immense height above the level of the sea.

In a tiny bay opening to the east, towers the lofty rock whereon was situated the old tower, a few fragments of which are to be seen by any one making the difficult ascent. Here it was that a Lord of the Isles confined one of his mistresses — a story still current in the island, and familiar to strangers from Scott's lines:

> " Signal of Ronald's high command.
> A beacon gleamed o'er sea and land,
> From Canna's tower, that, steep and gray,
> Like falcon-nest o'erhangs the bay.
> Seek not the giddy crag to climb,
> To view the turret scathed by time ;
> It is a task of doubt and fear
> To aught but goat or mountain deer.
> But rest thee on the silver beach,
> And let the aged herdsman teach
>   His tale of former day ;
> His cur's wild clamor he shall chide,
> And for thy seat by ocean's side
>   His varied plaid display ;
> Then tell, how with their chieftain came,
> In ancient times, a foreign dame
>   To yonder turret gray.
> Stern was her lord's suspicious mind,
> Who in so rude a jail confined
>   So soft and fair a thrall !
> And oft, when moon on ocean slept,
> That lovely lady sate and wept
>   Upon the castle-wall,
> And turned her eye to southern climes,
> And thought, perchance, of happier times,
> And touched her lute by fits, and sung
> Wild ditties in her native tongue.
> And still, when on the cliff and bay
> Placid and pale the moonbeams play,
>   And every breeze is mute,
> On the lone Hebridean's ear
> Steals a strange pleasure, mixed with fear,
> While from that cliff he seems to hear
>   The murmur of a lute,
> And sounds, as of a captive lone

> That mourns her woes in tongue unknown.
> Strange is the tale—but all too long
> Already hath it staid the song—
>   Yet who may pass them by,
>   That crag and tower in ruins gray,
>   Nor to their hapless tenant pay
>   The tribute of a sigh?"

There is scarcely an old ruin in the north but is haunted by some spirit such as this—and there is a ruin on every headland.

Canna is the child of the great waters, and such children, lonely and terrible as is their portion, seldom lack loveliness—often their only dower. From the edge of the lapping water to the peak of the highest crag, it is clothed with ocean gifts and signs of power. Its strange under-caves and rocks are colored with rainbow hues, drawn from glorious-featured weeds; overhead, its cliffs of basalt rise shadowy, ledge after ledge darkened by innumerable little wings; and high over all grow soft greenswards, knolls of thyme and heather, where sheep bleat and whence the herd-boy crawls over to look into the raven's nest. On a still summer day, when the long Atlantic swell is crystal smooth, Canna looks supremely gentle on her image in the tide, and out of her hollow under-caves comes the low, weird whisper of a voice; the sunlight glimmers on peaks and sea, the beautiful shadow quivers below, broken here and there by drifting weeds, and the bleating sheep on the high swards soften the stillness. But when the winds come in over the deep, the beauty changes—it darkens, it flashes from softness into power. The huge waters boil at the foot of the crags, and the peaks are caught in mist; and the air, full of a great roar, gathers around Canna's troubled face. Climb the crags, and the horrid rocks to westward, jutting out here and there like sharks' teeth, spit the lurid white foam back in the glistening eyes of the sea. Slip down to the water's edge, and amid the deafening roar the spray rises fa above you in a hissing shower. The whole island seems quivering through and through. The waters gather on all sides, with only one long, glassy gleam to leeward. No place in the world could seem fuller of supernatural voices, more powerful, or more utterly alone.

It is our fortune to see the island in all its moods; for we are in no haste to depart. Days of deep calm alternate with days of the wildest storm. There is constant change.

Everywhere in the interior of the island there are sweet pastoral glimpses. On a summer afternoon, while we are wandering in the road near the shore, we see the cattle beginning to flock from the pastures, headed by two gentle bulls, and gathering round the dairy house, where, in "short-gowns," white as snow, the two head dairymaids sit on their stools. The kine low softly, as the milk is drawn from the swelling udder, and now and then a calf, desperate with thirst, makes a plunge at his mother and drinks eagerly with closed eyes till he is driven away. Men and children gather around, looking on idly. As we pass by, the dairymaid offers us a royal drink of fresh, warm milk, and with that taste in our lips we loiter away. Now we are among fields, and we might be in England— so sweet is the scent of hay. Yonder the calm sea glimmers, and one by one the stars are opening like forget-me-nots, with dewdrops of light for reflections in the water below. Can this be Canna? Can this be the solitary child of the ocean? Hark! That is the corn-crake, crying in the corn—the sound we have heard so often in the southern fields! As we listen, our eyes are dim indeed, for we are murmuring the tender rhyme of the poet of Merkland—lines never yet published till now, but treasured up by us as something passionately sweet. It seems his very voice we hear, murmuring them in the twilight.

THE CORN-CRAKE.

I've listened now a full half-hour,
Nor knew that voice possessed the power
Of Lethe's fabled wave to bless
My spirit with forgetfulness.

The night is calm as my desire.
I see the stars, yet scarcely see,
So sweetly melteth all their fire
Into the blue serenity.
The mountains mingle with the haze,
And the three glorious sycamores
That stand before three cottage doors,
And throw warm shadows on the floors
On beautiful sunshiny days,
Come out in firmer, blacker lines,
Where softly bright a crescent shines.
A famous crescent is it still
Which seems to love this Merkland Hill
As well as ever Helicon,
And shines with as intent a will
On Luggie, as it ever shone
On Castaly in days of yore,
When poesy was deepest lore
And love the customary glee;
A land—a land of Arcady.

But whether in that land of dreams,
When sun had set and many streams
Were mingling in one murmurous moan,
Through alder coverts flowing on,
Thy voice, dear Corn-crake! sounded through
The calmness, when the dear cuckoo
Had fallen asleep in shady glen,
Far from the paths of mortal men,
I cannot tell; yet I uphold
That never a more vernal cry,
From lawn or air, or hedge or wood,
Filled all the eager, hungry sky,
Or charmed a sylvan solitude.

O Corn-crake! will you never weary?
You cry as if it were thy duty,
And thy voice were all thy beauty.
Do you cry that I may hear thee?
Not a bird awake but thee,
Except, across the dim, dim sea,
The voluptuous nightingale,
Singing in an orange dale.

By a word, by a tone, we are carried into a dream; the nightingale sings, and the Scottish poem dies away among all the perfumes of the south!

When there is little or no sea, it is delightful to pull in the punt round the precipitous shores, and come upon the lonely haunts of the ocean-birds. There is one great cliff, with a huge rock rising out of the waters before it, which is the favorite breeding haunt of the puffins, and while swarms of these little creatures, with their bright, parrot-like bills and plump, white breasts, flit thick as locusts in the air, legions darken the waters underneath, and rows on rows sit brooding over their young on the dizziest edges of the cliff itself. The noise of wings is ceaseless, there is constant coming and going, and so tame are the birds that one might almost seize them, either on the water or in the air, with the outstretched hand. Discharge a gun into the air, and, as the hollow echoes roar upward and inward to the very hearts of the caves, it will suddenly seem as if the tremendous crags were loosening to fall; but the dull, dangerous sound you hear is only the rush of wings. A rock farther northward is possessed entirely by gulls, chiefly the smaller species; thousands sit still and fearless, whitening the summit like snow, but many hover with discordant scream over the passing boat, and seem trying with the wild beat of their wings to scare the intruders away. Close in shore, at the mouth of a deep, dark cave, cormorants are to be found, great black "scarts," their mates, and the young, preening their glistening plumage leisurely, or stretching out their snake-like necks to peer with fishy eyes this way and that. They are not very tame here, and should you present a gun, will soon flounder into the sea and disappear; but at times, when they have gorged themselves with fish, so awkward are they with their wings, and so muddled are their wits, that one might run right abreast of them and knock them over with an oar.

Everywhere below, above, on all sides, there is nothing but life—birds innumerable, brooding over their eggs, or fishing for the young. Here and there a little fluff of down, just launched out into the great world, paddles about, bewildered, and dives away from the boat's bow with a faint, troubled cry. On the outer rocks gulls and guillemots, puffins on the crags, and cormorants on the ledges of the caves. The poor reflective human being, brought into the sound of such a life, gets quite scared and dazed. The air, the rocks, the waters, are all astir. The face turns for relief upward, where the blue sky meets the summit of the crags. Even yonder, on the very ledge, a black speck sits and croaks; and still further upward, dwarfed by distance to the size of a sparrowhawk, hovers a black eagle, fronting the sun.

There is something awe-inspiring, on a dead calm day, in the low, hushed wash of the great swell that forever sets in from the ocean; slow, slow it comes, with the 'regular beat of a pulse, rising its height, without breaking, against the cliff it mirrors in its polished breast, and then dying down beneath with a murmuring moan. What power is there! what dreadful, fatal ebbing and flowing! No finger can stop that under-swell, no breath can come between that and its course; it has rolled since Time began—the same, neither more nor less, whether the weather be still or wild—and it will keep on when we are all dead. Bah! that is hypochondria. But look! what is that floating yonder, on the glassy water?

> "Oh! is it fish, or weed, or floating hair,
> O' drownèd maiden fair?"

No; but it tells as clear a tale. Those planks formed lately the sides of a ship, and on that old mattress, with the straw washing out of the rents, some weary sailor pillowed his head not many hours ago. Where is the ship now? Where is the sailor? Oh! if a magician's wand could strike these waters, and open

them up to our view, what a sight should we see—
the slimy hulls of ships long submerged; the just
sunken fish-boat, with ghastly faces twisted among
the nets; the skeleton suspended in the huge under-
grass and monstrous weeds; the black shapes, the
fleshless faces, looming green in the dripping foam
and watery dew! Yet how gently the swell comes
rolling, and how pleasant look the depths this summer day—as if Death were not, as if there could be
neither storm nor wreck at sea!

More hypochondria, perhaps. Why the calm sea
should invariably make us melancholy we cannot tell,
but it does so, in spite of all our efforts to be gay.
Walt Whitman used to sport in the great waters as
happily as a porpoise or a seal, without any dread,
with vigorous animal delight; and we, too, can enjoy
a glorious swim in the sun, if there is just a little
wind, and the sea sparkles and freshens full of life.
But to swim in a dead calm is dreadful to a sensitive
man. Something mesmeric grips and weakens him.
If the water be deep, he feels dizzy, as if he were suspended far up in the air.

We are harping on delicate mental chords, and forgetting Canna; yet we have been musing in such a
mood as Canna must inevitably awaken in all who
feel the world. She is so lonely, so beautiful; and
the seas around her are so full of sounds and sights
that seize the soul. There is nothing mean, or squalid,
or miserable about Canna; but she is melancholy
and subdued—she seems like a Scandinavian Havfru,
to sit with her hand to her ear, earnestly listening to
the sea.

That, too, is what first strikes one in the Canna people—their melancholy look; not grief-worn, not sorrowful, not passionate, but simply melancholy and subdued. We cannot believe they are unhappy beyond the lot of other people who live by labor, and it is quite certain that, in worldly circumstances, they are much more comfortable than the Highland poor are generally. Nature, however, with her wondrous secret influences, has subdued their lives, toned their thoughts, to the spirit of the island where they dwell. This is more particularly the case with the women. Poor human souls, with that dark, searching look in the eyes, those feeble flutterings of the lips! They speak sad and low, as if somebody were sleeping close by. When they step forward and ask you to walk into the dwelling, you think (being new to their ways) that some one has just died. All at once, and inevitably, you hear the leaden wash of the sea, and you seem to be walking on a grave.

"A ghostly people!" exclaims the reader; "keep me from Canna!" That is an error. The people do seem ghostly at first, their looks do sadden and depress; but the feeling soon wears away, when you find how much quiet happiness, how much warmth of heart, may underlie the melancholy air. When they know you a little, ever so little, they brighten, not into anything demonstrative, not into sunniness, but into a silvern kind of beauty, which we can only compare to moonlight. A veil is quietly lifted, and you see the soul's face; and then you know that these folk are melancholy, not for sorrow's sake, but just as moonlight is melancholy, just as the wash of water is melancholy, because *that* is the natural expression of their lives. They are capable of a still, heart-suffering tenderness, very touching to behold. We visit many of their houses, and hold many of their hands. Kindly, gentle, open-handed as melting charity, we find them all; the poorest of them as hospitable as the proudest chieftain of their race. There is a gift everywhere for the stranger, and a blessing to follow—for they know that after all he is bound for the same bourne.

Theirs is a quiet life, a still passage from birth to the grave; still, untroubled, save for the never-silent voices of the waves. The women work very hard, both indoors and afield. Some of the men go away herring-fishing in the season, but the majority find employment either on the island or the circumjacent waters. We cannot credit the men with great energy of character; they do not seem industrious. An active man could not lounge as they lounge, with that total abandonment of every nerve and muscle. They will lie in little groups for hours, looking at the sea, and biting stalks of grass—not seeming to talk, save when one makes a kind of grunting observation, and stretches out his limbs a little farther. Some one comes and says: "There are plenty of herring over in Loch Scavaig—a Skye boat got a great haul last night." Perhaps the loungers go off to try their luck, but very likely they say: "Wait till to-morrow —it may be all untrue;" and in all probability, before they get over to the fishing-ground, the herrings have disappeared.

Yet they can work, too, and with a will, when they

are fairly set on to work. They can't speculate, they can't search for profit; the shrewd man outwits them at every turn. They keep poor—but, keeping poor, they keep good. Their worst fault is their dreaminess; but surely as there is light in heaven, if there be blame here, God is to blame here, who gave them dreamy souls! For our part, keep us from the man who could be born in Canna, live on and on with that ocean-murmur around him, and elude dreaminess and a melancholy like theirs!

"Bah!" cries a good soul from a city; "they are lazy—like the Irish, like Jamaca niggers; they are behind the age; let them die!" You are quite right, my good soul; and if it will be any comfort to you to hear it, they, and such as they, are dying fast. They can't keep up with you; you are too clever, too great. You, we have no doubt, could live at Canna, and establish a manufactory there for getting the sea turned into salt for export. You wouldn't dream—not you! Ere long these poor Highlanders will die out, and with them may die out gentleness, hospitality, charity, and a few other lazy habits of the race.

In a pensive mood, with a prayer on our lips for the future of a noble race destined to perish locally, we wander across the island till we come to the little graveyard where the people of Canna go to sleep. It is a desolate spot, commanding a distant view of the Western Ocean. A rude stone wall, with a clumsy gate, surrounds a small square, so wild, so like the stone-covered hill-side all round, that we should not guess its use without being guided by the fine stone mausoleum in the midst. That is the last home of the Lairds of Canna and their kin; it is quite modern and respectable. Around, covered knee-deep with grass, are the graves of the islanders, with no other memorial-stones than simple pieces of rock, large and small, brought from the seashore and placed as foot-stones and head-stones. Rugged as water tossing in the wind is the old kirkyard, and the graves of the dead therein are as the waves of the sea.

In a place apart lies the wooden bier, with hand-spokes, on which they carry the cold men and women hither; and by its side—a sight, indeed, to dim the eyes—is another smaller bier, smaller and lighter, used for little children. Well, there is not such a long way between parents and offspring; the old here are children too, silly in worldly matters, loving, sensitive, credulous of strange tales. They are coming hither, faster and faster; bier after bier, shadow after shadow. It is the tradesman's day now, the day of progress, the day of civilization, the day of shops; but high as may be your respect for the commercial glory of the nation, stand for a moment in imagination among these graves, listen to one tale out of many that might be told of those who sleep below, and join me in a prayer for the poor islanders whom they are carrying, here and in a thousand other kirkyards, to the rest that is without knowledge and the sleep that is without dream.

CHAPTER VIII.

EIRADH OF CANNA.

"She was a woman of a steadfast mind,
Tender and deep in her excess of love;
Not speaking much, pleased rather with the joy
Of her own thoughts."
WORDSWORTH'S "EXCURSION."

THERE was a man named Ian Macraonail, who lived at Canna in the sea. In the days of his prosperity God sent him issue—five lads and a lass. Now Ian had great joy in his five sons, for they grew up to be fine young men, straight-limbed, clean-skinned, clever with their hands; and in the girl he had not joy, but pain, for she was a sickly child and walked lame, through a trouble in the spine. Her name was Eiradh, and she was born to many thoughts.

When she was born she cried; nor did she cease crying after long days; and folk seeing that she was so sickly a child, thought that she would die soon. Yet Eiradh did not die, but cried on, so that the house was never quiet, and the neighbors, when they heard the sound in the night, said, "That is Ian Macraonail's bairn; the Lord has not yet taken her away." When she was three years old she lay in the cradle still, and could not run upon her feet; and then foul sores came out upon her head. After they burst, she had sound sleeps, and her trouble passed away.

The mother's heart was glad to see the little one grow stiller and brighter every day, and try to prattle like other children at the hearth; and she nursed her little care, slowly teaching her to move upon her feet. Afterward they taught her how to use a little crutch of wood, which Ian himself cut in the long winter nights when he was at home.

Ian Macraonail was a just man, and his house was a well-doing house; but Eiradh saw little of her father's face. In the summer season, he was far away, chasing the herring on the great sea, and even on the stormy winter days he was fishing cod and ling with a mate on the shores of Skye and Mull. When he came home he was wet and sleepy, and all the children had to keep very still. Then Eiradh would sit in a corner of the hearth, and see his dark face in the peat-smoke. If he took her upon his knee, she felt afraid and cried; so that the father said, "The child is stupid; take her away." But when he took her young brother upon his knee, the boy laughed and played with his beard.

For all that, the mother held Eiradh dear above all her other children, because she was sickly and had given her so much care.

Ian had built the house with his own hands, and it looked right out upon the sea. All the day and night the water cried at the door. Sometimes it was low and still and glistening; and it was pleasant then to sit out on the sand and throw stones into the smooth and glassy tide. But oftenest it was wild and loud, shrieking out as if it were living, dashing in the seaweed and planks of ships, and seeming to say, "Come out here, come out here, that I may eat you up alive!" All the night long he cried on, while the wind tore at the roof of the house, and would have carried it far away, if the straw ropes and heavy stones had not been there to hold it down.

Then Eiradh would hide her head under the blankets and think of her father upon the sea.

The water cried at the door. When Eiradh's eldest brother grew up into a strong youth, he went away with his father upon the sea. He stayed away so long that his face grew strange. When he came home he was sleepy and tired, like his father, and said little to his sister and brothers. But one day he brought Eiradh home a little round-eyed owl, like a little old woman in a tufted wig. Eiradh was proud that day. When the calliach opened its mouth and roared for food, she laughed and clapped her hands; and she made the bird a nest in an old basket, and fed it with her own hands. She loved her great brother very much after that, and was happy when he came home.

The water cried at the door. One day Eiradh's second brother joined his father and brother upon the sea, and ever after that was sleepy and tired like the others when he came home.

The mother said to Eiradh, "That is always the way—boys must work for their bread." But Eiradh thought to herself, "It is the sea calling them away. I shall soon not have a brother left in the house."

The water cried at the door, till all Eiradh's five brothers went away. Then it was very lonely in the dwelling, and the days and nights were long and dull. When the fishers came home, their faces were all strange to her, and they seemed great, rough men, while she was only a little sickly child. But they were kind. They told her wild stories about the sea and the people they had seen, and laughed out loud and merry at the wonder in her great, staring eyes. They told her of the great whales and the sea-snakes that have manes like a horse and teeth like a saw; and how the old witch of Barra smoked her pipe over her pot and sold the fishermen winds.

One night, when Eiradh was twelve years of age, she sat with her mother over the fire, waiting for her father and brothers to come home in the skiff from Mull. It was a rainy night, late in the year. Now, the mother had been ailing for many days with a heaviness and pain about the heart, and she said to Eiradh: "I feel sick, and I will lie down upon the bed to rest a little." Eiradh kept very still, that her mother might sleep, and the pot, with the supper in it, bubbled; the rain went splash-splash at the door, till Eiradh fell to sleep herself. She woke up with a loud cry, and, looking round her, saw her father and brothers in the room. The steam was coming thick like smoke from their clothes, their faces were white, and they were talking to one another. She called to them not to make a noise, because mother was sleeping; but her father said in a sharp voice, "Take the girl away; she is better out of the house!" Then a neighbor woman stepped forward, out of the shadow of the door, and said, "She shall go with me." When the woman took her by the hand and led her to the other house through the rain, she was so frightened she could not say a word. The woman led her in,

and bade her seat herself beside the fire, where a man
sat smoking his pipe and mending his nets. Then
Eiradh heard her whisper in his ear, as she passed
him, "This is lame Eiradh with the red hair; her
mother has just died."

It seemed to Eiradh that the ground was suddenly
drawn from under her feet, and she was walking high
up in the air, and all around her were voices crying,
"Eiradh! Eiradh with the red hair! your mother has
just died." When that passed away, a sharp thread
was drawn through her heart, and she could scarcely
cry for pain; but when the tears came, they did her
good, washing the pang away. But it was like a
dream.

It was like a dream, too, the day the woman took
her by the hand and led her back to the house. The
sea was loud that day—loud and dark—and it seemed
to be saying, "Eiradh! Eiradh! your mother has just
died." The home was clean and still; father was sitting
on a bench beside the fire in his best clothes,
looking very white. When she went in he drew her
to him and kissed her on the forehead, and she sobbed
sore. The woman said, "Come, Eiradh," and led her
aside. Something was lying on the bed all white, and
there was a smell like fresh-bleached linen in the air;
then the woman lifted up a kerchief, and Eiradh saw
her mother's face dressed in a clean cap, and the gray
hair brushed down smooth and neat. Eiradh's tears
stopped, and she was afraid—it looked so cold. The
woman said, "Would you like to kiss her, Eiradh,
before they take her away?" But Eiradh drew her
breath tight, and cried to be taken out of the house.

That night she slept in the neighbor's house, and the next day her mother was taken to the graveyard on the hill. Eiradh did not see them take her away; but in the afternoon she went home and found the house empty. It was clean and bright. The peat-fire was blazing on the floor, and there were bottles and glasses on the press in the corner. By and by her father and brothers came in, all dressed in their best clothes, and with red eyes; and many fishermen —neighbors—stood at the door to take the parting glass, and went away quite merry to their homes. But the priest came and sat down by the fire with her father and brothers, and patted Eiradh on the head, telling her not to cry any more, because her mother was happy with God. She went and sat on the ground in a corner, looking at them through her tears. Her father was lighting his pipe, and she heard him say, "She was a good wife to me;" and the priest answered, "She was a good wife and a good mother; she has gone to a better place." Eiradh wondered very much to see them so quiet and hard.

With that, the days of Eiradh's loneliness began. She had no mother to talk to her in the long nights when her father and brothers were away upon the sea; but she used to go to the neighbor-woman's house and sleep among the children. Oftener than ever before, she loved to sit by the water and listen, playing alone, so that her playmates used to say, "Eiradh is a stupid girl, and likes to sit by herself." One day she went to the graveyard on the hill and searched about for the place where her mother was laid. The grass was long and green, and there were great woods everywhere; but there was one place where the earth had been newly turned, and blades of young grass were beginning to creep through the clay. She felt sure that her mother must be sleeping there. So she sat down on the grave and began to knit. It was a clear, bright day, the sheep were crying on the hills, and the sea far off was like a glass; and it was strange to think her mother was lying down there, so near to her, with her face up to the sky. Eiradh began wondering how deep she was lying and whether she was still dressed in white. Her thoughts made her afraid, and she looked all around her. Though it was daytime, she could not bear to stay any longer, for she had heard about ghosts. As she walked home on her crutch, she looked round her very often, fancying she heard some one at her back.

Though Eiradh Nicraonail was a sickly girl, she was clever and quick, and she soon began to take a pleasure in the house. The neighbor-woman helped about the place and taught Eiradh many things—how to cook, how to make cakes of oatmeal on the brander, and how to wash clothes. She was so quick and willing, and longed so much to please her father and brothers, that they said, "Eiradh is as good as a woman in a house, though she is so young." Then Eiradh brightened, full of pride, and ever after that kept the home clean and pleasant, and forgot her griefs.

There was a man in Canna, a little old man with a club foot, who got his living in many ways, for he could make shoes and knew how to mend nets, and besides, he was a learned man, having been taught at a school in the south. Some of the children used to go to him in the evenings, and he taught them how to read; but he was so sharp and cross that sometimes he would have nothing to say to them, though they came. Now and then, Eiradh went over to him, and he was gentler with her than with the rest, because she had a trouble of the body like himself. He learned her her letters, and afterward, with a wooden trunk for a desk, made her try to write. Often, too, he came over to her in the house, and smoked his pipe while she knitted; but if her father, or any of her brothers came in, he gave them sharp answers and soon went away, while they laughed and said, "It is a pity that his learning does not make him more free." He was a strange old man, and believed in ghosts and witches. Eiradh liked to sit and listen to his tales. He told her how the bagpipes played far off when any one was going to die. He told her of a young man in Skye, who could cause diseases by the power of the evil eye, and of a woman in Barra, who used to change into a hare every night and run up to the top of the mountains to meet a spirit in black by the side of a fire made out of the coffins fo those who died in sin. He had seen every loophole in Skipness Castle full of cats' heads, with red eyes, and every head was the head of a witch. He believed in dreams, and thought that the dead rose every night and walked together by the side of the sea. Often in the dark evenings, when Eiradh was sitting at his knee, he would take his pipe out of his mouth and tell her to listen; if she listened very hard in the pauses of the wind, she would hear something like a voice crying, and he told her that it was the spirit of the poor lady who died in the tower, walking up and down, moaning and wringing its hands.

As Eiradh grew older she had so much to do in the house that she thought of these things less than before. But when she sat by herself knitting, and the day's work was over, voices came about her that belonged to another land, and she grew so used to them that their presence seemed company to her, and she was not afraid. By the time that she was seventeen years of age God's strength had come upon her, and she could walk about without her crutch. She had red hair, her face was white and well-favored, and her eyes were the color of the green sea.

One night, when her father and brothers were sleeping with her in the house, Eiradh Nicraonail had a dream. She thought she was standing by the sea, and it was full of moonlight and the shadows of the stars. While she stood looking and listening, there came up out of the sea a black beast like a seal, followed by five young ones, and they floated about in the light of the moon with their black heads up, listening to a sound from far away like the music of a harp. All at once the wind rose and the sea grew rough and white, and the lift was quite dark. In a little time the distant music grew louder and the wind died away. Then Eiradh saw the beast floating about alone in the white moonlight, and bleating like a sheep when robbed of its lamb; and at last it gave a great cry and stretched itself out stiff and dead, with its speckled belly shining uppermost and the herringsyle playing round it like flashes of silver light. With that she awoke, and it was dark night; the wind was crying softly outside, and she could hear her father and brothers breathing heavy in their sleep.

The next day, when her father and brother sat mending their nets at the door, she told them her dream. They only laughed, and said it was folly put into her head by the old man who taught her to read. But she saw that they looked at one another, and were not well pleased. All that day the dream troubled her at her work, and whenever she heard the sheep bleat from the hill-side she felt faint. The next night she said a long prayer for her father and brothers, and slept sound. The dream did not come again, and in a few days the trouble of it wore away. But when the news came that they were catching herring in Loch Scavaig, and the fisherman and his sons began preparing their boat to sail over and try their chance, all Eiradh's fears came back upon her twenty-fold. It was changeful weather early in the year; there were strong winds and a great sea.

The day before the boat went away Ian had the rheumatic trouble so sore in his bones that he could not rise out of his bed; and he was still so sick next day that he told the young men to go away alone, for fear of missing the good fishing. They went off with a light heart—four strong men and a tall lad.

Ian Macraonail never saw his sons any more. Three days afterward, news was brought that the boat had laid over and filled in a squall, and that every one on board had been drowned in the sea.-

Then Eiradh knew that her strange dream had partly come true, but that more was to come true yet. The water cried at the door. Ian sat like a frozen man in the house, and when Eiradh looked at him her tears ceased—she felt afraid. He scarcely said a word, and did not cry, but he paid no heed to his meat. He looked like the man on the hill-side when the voice of God came out of the burning bush.

Again and again Eiradh cried, "Father!" and looked into his face, but he held up his hand each time to warn her away. A thread ran through her heart at this, for she had always known he loved her brothers best, and now he did not seem to remember her at all. She went outside the house, and looked at the crying water, and hated it for all it had done. Her heart was sad for her five brothers who were dead, but it was saddest of all for her father who was alive.

The priest came, and prayed for the dead. Ian prayed, too, with a cold heart. Afterward the priest took him by the hand, looking into his eyes, and said, "Ian, you have suffered sore, but those the Lord loves are born to many troubles." Ian looked down, and answered in a low voice, "That is true; I have nothing left now to live for." But the priest said, "You have Eiradh, your daughter; she is a good girl." Ian made no answer, but sat down and smoked his pipe. Eiradh went out of the house, and cried to herself.

Now, that day Ian Macraonail put on his best black gear and the black hat with the broad crape band. The black clothes made him look whiter. He took his staff, and went up over the hill on to the cliffs, over the place where the black eagle builds, and stood close to the edge, looking over at Loch Scavaig, where the lads were drowned. While he stood there, a shepherd that knew him came by, and, seeing him look so wild, fancied that he meant to take the short road to the kirkyard. So the man touched him on the shoulder, saying, "He sleeps ill that rocks himself to sleep. We are in God's hands, and must bide his time." Ian knew what the shepherd meant, and shook his head. "I have been a well-doing man," he said, "and mine has been a well-doing house. I have drunk a bitter cup, but the Lord forbid that I should do the sin you think of." So the shepherd made the sign of the blessed cross, and went away.

After that Ian wore his black gear every day, and every day he went up on the high cliffs to walk. He ate his meat quite hearty, and he was gentle with Eiradh in the house; but he stared all around him like a man at the helm in a thick mist, and listened as the man at the helm listens in the mist for the wind that is coming. It was plain that he took little heart in his dwelling, or in the good money he had saved. One day he said, "When I go again to the herring-fishing, I must pay wages to strangers I cannot trust, and things will not go well." The day after that, at the mouth of lateness, they found him leaning against a stone, close over the place where the black eagle builds; and his heart was turned to lead, and his blood was water, and there were no pictures in his eyes.

Now Eiradh Nicraonail was alone in the whole world.

II.

When Ian was in the narrow house where the fire is cold and the grass grows at the door, Eiradh sold the boats and the nets, and all but the house she lived in; and when she counted the good money, she found there was enough to keep her from hunger for a little time. In these days she had little heart to work in the house and in the fields, and every time she thought of those who were lying under the hill she felt a salt stone rise in her throat. In the long nights, when she was alone, voices came out of the sea, and eyes looked at her—she heard the wind calling, and the ghost of the lady crying up in the tower—and she thought of all the strange things the old man had told her when she was small. Often her heart was so troubled that she had to run away to the neighbors, and sit among them for company. She often said, "I would rather be far away than here, for it is a dull place;" and she planned to take service on some farm across the water.

The women bade her wait and look out for a man, but Eiradh said, "The man is not born that would earn meat for me." She was dull and down-looking in these days, speaking little, but her bodily trouble was all gone, and she was clean-limbed and had a soft face. More than one lad looked her way, and would have come courting to her house at night, but she barred the door and would let no man in. One night, when a fisher lad got in, and came laughing to her bedside, he was sore afraid at the look of her face and the words of her mouth, though she only cried, "Go away this night, for the love of my father and mother. I am sick and heavy with sleep."

These were decent and well-doing lads, shepherds earning good wages, but Eiradh had a face to frighten them away.

The winter after Ian Macraonail died, Calum Eachern, the tailor, came north to Canna. The folk had been waiting for him since long, and there was much work to be done—so that Calum was busy morning and night in one house or another; but though he had been busier, his tongue could never have kept still. Every night people gathered in the place where he worked, and those were merry times. He was like a full kist, never empty; his tales were never done. He had the story of the king of Lochlan's daughter, and how Fionn killed the great bird of the red beak, and many more beside. He loved best to tell about the men of peace, with their green houses under the hillside, and about the changeling bairns that play the fairy pipes in the time of sleep, and about the ladies with green gowns, that sit in the magic wells and tempt the herdboys with silver rings. He had that many riddles they were like the limpets on the sea-shore. He knew old songs, and he had the gift of making rhymes himself to his own tune. So the coming of Calum Eachern was like the playing of pipes at a wedding on a summer day.

Calum was little, narrow in the shoulders, and short in the legs. His face was like a china cup for neatness. He had a little turned-up nose, and white teeth, and he shaved his beard clean every day. He had a little twinkling eye like a fox's, and when he talked to you he cocked his head on one side, like a sparrow on a dyke.

One night, he was at work in a neighbor's house, and Eiradh went in with the rest. Calum sat on his board, and some were looking on and listening to his talk. When Eiradh went in, he put his head on one side and looked at her, and said in a rhyme—

> "What did the fox say?
> 'Huch! huch! huch!' cried the fox;
> 'Cold are my bones this day—
> I have lent my skin to cover the head
> Of the girl with the red hair.'"

All the folk laughed, and Eiradh, laughed, too. Then she sat down on the floor by the fire, and hearkened with her cheek on her hand. Calum Eachern was like a bee in the time of honey. He stitched, and sang, and told tales about the men of peace, and the land where jewels grew as thick as chuckie-stones, and gold is as plenty as the sand of the sea. Whenever Eiradh looked up, he had his head on one side, and his eyes were laughing at her. By and by he nodded, and said:

> "What did the sea-gull say?
> 'Kriki! kriki!' cried the sea-gull;
> 'Hard it is to hatch my eggs this day—
> I have lent my white breast
> To the girl with the red hair.'"

Then he nodded again, and said:

"What did the heron say?
'Kray! kray!' said the heron;
'Poor is my fishing in the loch this day—
I have lent my long, straight leg
To the girl with the red hair.'"

With that, he flung down the shears and laughed till the tears were in his eyes. Eiradh felt angry and ashamed, and went away.

But for all that, she was not ill pleased. Listening to Calum Eachern had been like sitting out of doors on a bright, sunny day. It made her heart light. All the night long she thought of his talk. She had never heard tales like those before—all about brightness and a pleasant place. When she went to sleep, she dreamed she was in an enchanted castle, all made of silver mines and precious stones, and that Calum Eachern was showing her a fountain full of gold fish, and the fountain seemed to fall in rhyme. All at once, Calum laughed so loud that the castle was broken into a thousand pieces, and when she woke up it was bright day.

The day after that, who should come into the house but Calum Eachern. "A blessing on this house!" said he, and he sat down beside the fire. Eiradh was putting the potatoes in the big pot, and Calum pointed at the pot, and said:

"Totoman, totoman,
Little black man,
Three feet under
And bonnet of wood!"

Eiradh laughed at the riddle. Then Calum, seeing she was pleased, began to talk and sing, putting his head on one side and laughing. All at once he said, looking quite serious, "It's not much company you will be having here, Eiradh Nicraonail."

"That's true enough," said Eiradh. "It's a dull house that is without the cry of bairns, I'm thinking."

"And that's true, too," said Eiradh.

"Then why don't you take a man?" said he, looking at her very sharp.

Eiradh gave her head a toss, and lifted up the lid of the pot to look in.

"Your cheek is like a rose for redness," said Calum. "Are ye ashamed to answer?"

At that Eiradh lifted up her head and looked him straight in the face.

"The man is not born that I heed a straw," said she.

Calum laughed out loud to hear her say that, and a little after he went away.

Eiradh did not know whether she was pleased or angry, and all that night she had little sleep. She did not like to be laughed at, and yet she could not be rightly angry with such a merry fellow as Calum. It seemed strange to her that he should come to the house at all.

It seemed stranger, the next night, when Calum came in again, and sat down by the fire.

"How does the Lord use you this night, Eiradh Nicraonail?"

"The Lord is good," answered Eiradh.

"Can you read print?" he said, smiling.

"Ay," answered Eiradh, "print, and writing too."

"And that's a comfort," said Calum. "But I've brought you somebody to sit with ye by the fire in the long nights."

"And what's he like?" asked Eiradh, thinking Calum meant himself.

"He's not over fine to look at, but he's mighty learned. He's a little old man with a leather skin, and his name written on his face, and the marks o' thumbs all over his inside."

"And where is he this night?"

"This is him, and here he is, and many a merry thing he'll teach you, if you attend to his talking," said Calum; and he gave her a little book in the Gaelic, very old, and covered with black print; and soon after that he went away.

When he was gone, Eiradh sat down by the fire and turned over the leaves of the book that he had given her, and it seemed like the voice of Calum talking in her ear. There were stories about the fairies and the men of peace, and shieling songs of the south country, and riddles for the fireside in the south country on Halloween. Eiradh read till she was tired, and some of the stories made her laugh afterward, as she sat by the fireside with her cheek on her hand. She could not help thinking that it would be fine to live in the south country, where there was corn growing everywhere, and gardens full of flowers, and no sea.

After that Calum Eachern came often to the house, and Eiradh did not tell him to stay away. Some of the folk said: "Calum Eachern has a bad name," and bade Eiradh beware, because he had a false tongue. Eiradh laughed, and said: "I fear the tongue of no man." Every night she read the printed book, till she knew it from the first page to the last, and when she was alone, she would sing bits of the songs to Calum Eachern's tunes. Sometimes she would stand on the seashore, and look out across the water, and wonder what like was the country on the other side of the Rhu. In those days she was sick of Canna, and thought to herself: "If I was living in the south country, I should not be afraid of them that are dead;" and she remembered Calum's words: "It's not much company you will be having here, Eiradh Nicraonail."

One night there was a boat from Tyree in the harbor, and when Calum came in late, Eiradh knew that he had been drinking with the Tyree men. His face was red, and his breath smelt strong of the drink. He tried hard to get his will of her that night, but Eiradh was a well-doing girl, and pushed him out of the house. She was angry, and fit to cry, thinking of the words: "Calum Eachern has a bad name." That night she had a dream. She thought she was walking by the side of the sea, on a light night, and she had a bairn in her arms, and she was giving it the breast. As she walked, she could hear the ghost of the lady crying in the tower. Then she felt the babe she carried as heavy as lead, and it spoke with a man's voice, and had white teeth; and when she looked at its face, it was Calum's face, laughing, all cocked on one side. With that she woke.

When she saw Calem next, he hung down his head, and looked so strange and sad that she could not help laughing as she passed by. Then he ran after, and she turned upon him full of anger. But Calum had a smooth tongue, and she soon forgot her anger listening to one of his tales. She liked him best of all that day, for he was quiet and serious, and never laughed once. Eiradh thought to herself: "The man is no worse than other men, and drink will change a wise man into a fool."

Calum never tried to wrong her again, but one night he spoke out plain, and asked her to marry him, and go home with him in a Canna boat to the south. It was a long while ere Eiradh answered a word. She sat with her cheek on her hand, looking at the fire, and thinking of the night her mother died, and of her father and brothers that were drowned, and of the voices that came to her out of the sea. It was a rough night, and the wind blew sharp from the east, and she could hear the water at the door. Then she looked at Calum, and he had a bright smile, and held out his hand. But she only said: "Go away this night;" and he went away without a word. All night long she thought of his words: "It's a dull house without the cry of bairns," and she remembered the days when her mother used to nurse her, and her father cut her the crutch of wood with his own hands. Next morning the sea was still, and the light was the color of gold on the land beyond the Rhu. That day the folk seemed sharp and cold, and more than one mocked her with the name of Calum; so that she said to herself, "They shall not mock me without a cause;" and when Calum came to her the next night, she said she would be his good wife.

Soon after that Calum Eachern and Eiradh Nicraonail were married by the priest from Skye; and the day they married they went on board a Canna smack that was sailing south. An old man from Tyree was at the helm, and she sat on her kist close to him. Calum sat up by the mast with the men, who were all Canna lads, and as they all talked together, Calum whispered something and laughed, and all the lads looked at her and laughed too. Calum was full of drink. He had a bottle of whisky in the breast of his coat, and as the boat sailed out of the bay, he waved it to the folk on shore, and laughed like a wild man.

Now Eiradh felt sadder and sadder as she saw Canna growing farther and farther away; for she thought of her father and mother, and of the graveyard on the hill. The more she thought, the more she felt the tears in her eyes and the stone in her throat. Going round the Rhu she had the sea-sickness, and thought she was going to die. Though she had dwelt beside the sea so many years, she had never sailed on the water in a boat.

III.

Where Calum Eachern lived, the folk had strange ways, and many of them had both the Gaelic and the English. Their houses were whitewashed, and roofed with slate, and there was a long street, with shops full of all things that man could wish, and there was a house for the sale of drink. The roads were broad, and smooth as your hand, and on the sides of the hills were fields of corn and potatoes. The sea was twenty miles away, but there was a burn, on the banks of which the women used to tread their clothes. Eiradh thought to herself, "It is not as fine a country as Calum said."

Calum's house was the poorest house there. It had two rooms, and in the front-room Calum worked; the back-room was a kitchen, with a bed in the wall. Eiradh had brought with her some of the furniture from her father's house, and plenty of woolen woof made by her mother's own hands; and she soon made the place pleasant and clean. They had not been home a day when the laird came in for the back rent that was due, and Eiradh paid the money out of her own store. She had the money in a stocking inside her kist, and some of it was in copper and silver, but there were pound notes, quite ragged and old with being kept so many years.

It would take me a long winter's night to tell all that Eiradh thought in those days. She was like one in a dream. She felt it strange to see so many people coming and going in and out of the shops and houses, and the crowds on market-days, and the great heap of sheep and cattle. The folk were civil and fair-spoken, but most of the men drank at the public-house. There was a man next door who would get mad-drunk every night he had the money, and it was a sad sight to see his wife's face cut and bruised, and the bairns at her side crying for lack of food. Many of the men were weavers, and walked lame, as Eiradh used to do, and had pale, sickly faces, black under the eyes. The Gaelic they had was a different Gaelic from that the folk had in Canna, and sometimes Eiradh could not understand it at all.

Now, it was not long ere Eiradh found that Calum had a bad name in the place for drinking; and besides, he had beguiled a servant lass the year before, under the promise of marriage. Eiradh thought of the night when he had come drunk to the house, but she said nothing to Calum. She would sit and watch him for hours, and wonder she had thought him so bright and free; for she soon saw he was a double man, with a side for his home and another for strangers; and the first side was as dull as the second was bright. He never raised his hand to her in those days, and was sober; but he would sit with a silent tongue, and sometimes give her a strange look. Eiradh thought to herself, "Calum is like the south country, and looks brightest to them that are farthest away."

A year after they had come to the south country, Calum turned his front room into a shop, and made Eiradh look after it while he was at work. The goods were bought with her own good money, and were tea, sugar, tobacco, and meal. The first month Eiradh got all her money back. It was pleasant to sit there and sell, and know that she made a profit on each thing she sold; and Calum was light and merry, when he saw that his idea had turned out well. Eiradh's health was not so good in those days, and she had no children.

After that came days of trouble, for Calum grew worse and worse. He would take the money that Eiradh had earned, and spend it in the public-house; and when he came home in drink, he raised his hand to her more than once. Then Eiradh thought to herself, "My father did not love me, but he never struck me a blow; there is not a man in Canna who would lift his hand to a woman." After that she took no pleasure in trade, but would sit with a sick face and a silent tongue, thinking of Canna in the sea. Calum liked her the less because she did not complain. One day he told her he did not marry her for herself, but for the money she had saved; and this was a sore thing to say to her; but though the tears made her blind, she only looked at him and did not answer a word. There was some of the money left in her kist, but she never cared to look at it after what Calum had said.

After the day he married Eiradh, Calum had never left his home to work through the country as he once did. But one night late in the year he said he must go south on business, and in the morning he went away. Eiradh never saw him again on this side the narrow house. He went straight to the big city of Glasgow, and there he met the lass he had beguiled the year he married Eiradh, and the two sailed over the seas to Canada. The news came quick to Eiradh by the mouth of one who saw them on the quay.

One would need the tongue of a witch to tell all Eiradh's thoughts in those days. The first news seemed like the roar of the sea the time her brothers died, and the words stopped in her ears like the crying of the water day and night. She felt ashamed to show herself in the street, and she could not bear the comfort of the good wives; for they all said, "Calum had ever a bad name," and she remembered how the folk in Canna had used the same words. She would sit with her apron over her face, and greet* for hours with no noise. It seemed dreadful to be there in the south country, without friend or kindred, and the folk having a different Gaelic from her own. She felt sick and stupid, just like herself when she would cry night and day from the cradle, without strength to run upon her feet. She thought to herself, "I may cry till my heart breaks now, but no one heeds;" and the thought brought up the picture of her mother lying in the bed all white, and made her cry the more. Now, in those days voices came about her that belonged to another land, and the faces of her father and mother went past her like the white breaking of a wave on the beach in the night. She had dreams whenever she slept, and in every one of her dreams she heard the sough of the sea.

But Eiradh Eachern was a well-doing lass, and had been bred to face trouble when it came. Her first thought was this: "I will go back to Canna in the sea, and work for my bread in the fields." But when she looked in the kist, she found that Calum had been there and taken away all the good money out of the stocking, and a picture beside of the Virgin Mary, set round with yellow gold and precious stones the color of blood. Now, this grieved Eiradh most. She did not heed the money so much, but the picture had belonged to her mother, and she would not have parted with it for hundreds of pounds. She felt a sharp thread run through her heart, and she was sick for pain.

* Weep.

It is a wonder how much trouble a strong man or woman in good health can bear when it comes. Eiradh thought to herself at first, "I shall die;" but she did not die. The Lord was not willing that she should be taken away then. He spared her, as he had spared her in her sickness when a bairn at the breast.

One day a neighbor came in and said, "Will you not keep open the shop the same as before? You have always paid for your goods, and those that sent them will not press for payment at first." Now, Eiradh had never thought of that, and her heart lightened. That same day she got the schoolmaster to write a letter, in the English, to the big city, asking goods. The next week the goods came.

Then Eiradh thought, "God has not forsaken me," and worked hard to put all in order as before. Many folk came and bought from her, out of kindness at first, but afterward because they said she was a just woman, and gave full value for their money. All this gladdened her heart. She said, "God helps those that are fallen," and every penny that she earned seemed to have the blessing of God.

In those times she would lock up the house when the day was done, and walk by herself along the side of the burn; for the sound of the water seemed like old times; and when the moon came out on the green fields, they looked for all the world like smooth water. Voices from another land came to her, and spirits passed before her eyes; so that she often thought to herself, "I wonder how Canna looks this night, and whether it is storm or calm?"

I might talk till the summer came, and not tell you half of the many thoughts Eiradh had in the south country. She loved to sit by herself, as when she was a child; and the folk thought her a dull woman, with a white face. The women said, "Calum Eachern's wife has the greed of money strong in her heart, but she is a just-dealing woman." It was true that Eiradh found pleasure in trade, and would not sell to those who did not come to buy money in hand. Every piece she saved she put in the stocking in the old kist, and every week she counted it out in her lap.

So the time passed, and sometimes Eiradh could hardly call up right the memory of Calum's face. It seemed like a dream. These were the days of her prosperity, and every week she saved something, and every second Sabbath she saw the priest. Now, the folk in those parts had a religion of their own, and did not believe in the Virgin Mary or the Pope of Rome. Some of them were worse than that, and did not believe in the Lord Jesus Christ. All the children had the English as well as the Gaelic; and the preachings were in the English, and the English was taught in the school. But all the time she lived in the south Eiradh could not speak a word of that tongue. It seemed to her like the chirping of birds, with little meaning and a heap of sound.

All the years Eiradh sat in the shop, the Lord drew silver threads in her hair, and made lines like pencil-marks over her face; and when she was thirty-five years of age her sight failed her, and she had to wear glasses. She had little sickness, but she stooped in the shoulders, and had a dry cough. In those days she did not go out of the house at night, but sat over the fire reading the book Calum had given her long years before. The leaves of the book were all black and torn, and many of the pages were gone. Every time she looked at it she thought of old times. She had little pleasure in the tales and riddles of the south country—all about brightness and a pleasant place; for she thought to herself, " The tales are all lies, and the south country looks brightest far off, and the folk do not believe in the Virgin Mary or the saints." For all that, she liked to look at the old book; and let her thoughts go back of their own accord, like the flowing of water in a burn. Best of all, she loved to count the bright money into her lap, and think how the neighbors praised her as a just-dealing woman who throve well.

IV.

The years went past Eiradh Eachern like the waves breaking on the shore, and the days were as like each other as the waves breaking, and she could not count them at all. She was like the young man that went to sleep on the Island of Peace, and had a dream of watching the fairy people, and when he woke he was old and frail upon his feet. Eiradh was fifty years of age when she counted the money in her kist for the last time, and found that she had put by a hundred and twenty pounds in good money. That night she sat with the heap of money in her lap, and the salt tears running down her cheeks, and her bottom-lip quivering like the withered leaf on the bough of a tree.

Now, all these years Eiradh had one thought, and it was this: "Before I die, I will go back to Canna in the sea." Every day of her life she fancied she saw the picture of the green cliffs covered with goats and sheep, and the black scarts sitting on the weedy rocks in a row, and the sea rising and falling like the soft breasts of a woman in sound sleep. Every night of her life she had a dream of her father's house by the shore, and the water crying at the door. It seemed ever calm weather to her thoughts, and the sea was kinder and sweeter than when she was a child. Eiradh often thought to herself, " The water took away my five brothers, and close to the water my father and mother closed their eyes;" and the more she thought of them sleeping, the less she was afraid.

So when she had saved one hundred and twenty pounds in good money, she felt that she could abide no longer in the south country. The more she tried to stay a little longer, the more voices from another land came to her, saying, "Eiradh, Eiradh! go back to Canna in the sea." At last she had a dream; and she thought she was lying in her sowe* in a dark land, waiting to be laid in the earth. All at once she felt herself rocking up and down, and heard the sound of the sea crying, and when she put out her hand at

---

* Shroud.

her side it was dripping wet. Then Eiradh knew that she was drifting in a boat, and the boat was a coffin with the lid off, and though there was a strong wind she floated on the waves like a cork. All night long she floated and never saw land; only a light shining far, far off, over the dark water. When she woke she was sore troubled, and said to herself, "It is my wraith that I saw, and unless I haste I may never see my home again."

After that she never rested till she had sold the trade of her shop in the south country, and all she kept to herself was the old kist full of her clothes and the money she had saved. But she made a pouch of leather with her own hands, and put the money in it, and fastened the pouch to her waist underneath her clothes, and the only thing in the pouch beside the money was the old book in the Gaelic Calum had given her when she was a young woman.

I have told you that the place was twenty miles from the sea. One day she put her kist in a cart that was going that way, and the day after she took the road. It was a fine morning, early in the year. When she got to the top of the hill, and saw the place below her where she had lived so long, all asleep and still, with the smoke going straight up out of the houses, and not a soul in the street, it seemed like a dream. As she went on, the country was strange, but it looked finer and bonnier than any country she had ever seen. Now, her heart was so light that day that she could walk like a strong man. The sun came out, and the birds sang, and the land was green, and wherever she went the sheep cried. Eiradh thought to herself, "My dream was true after all, and the south country is a pleasant place."

For all that she was wearying to see Canna in the sea, and wondering if it was the same all those years. She counted on her fingers the names of the folks she knew, and wondered how many were dead. Every one of them seemed like a friend. She was keen to hear her own Gaelic again after so many years in a foreign land.

She walked twelve miles that day, and slept at a farm by the road at night. The next day she saw the sea.

It was good weather, and the sea was covered with fishing-boats and ships. She could hear the sough of the water a long way off, and it seemed like old times. There was a bit village on the shore, full of fisher-folk, and the houses minded her of those where she was born. There were skiffs drawn up on the shore, and nets put out to dry, and the air was full of the smell of fish.

She slept in the house of a fisher-woman that night, and the next day a fishing-boat took her out to catch the big steamboat to Tobermory. It was the first time that Eiradh had seen a boat like that, and it seemed to her like a great beast panting and groaning, and swimming through the water with fins and tail. It was full of the smell of fish, and the decks were covered with herring-barrels, and where there were no herring-barrels there were cattle and sheep. In one part of the boat there was a long box like a coffin, covered over with a piece of tarpaulin to keep it dry; and one of the sailors told Eiradh that it held the dead body of an old man from Skye, who had died on the Firth o' Clyde, and was being carried home to be buried with his kindred at home. Eiradh said, "It is a sad thing to be buried far away from kindred;" and she thought to herself, "If I had died in the south country, there would have been no kin or friend to carry me to Canna in the sea."

Neither wind nor tide could keep the big steamboat back; so wonderful are the works of the hand of man, when God is willing. Late at night Eiradh landed at Tobermory in Mull, but the moon was bright, and she saw that the bay was full of fishing-boats at anchor. Eiradh wondered to herself if any of the boats were from Canna.

She got a lodging in the inn that night, and the next morning she went down to the shore. There were heaps of fishermen on the beach, and many of them passed her the sign of the day, but none of them seemed to have her own Gaelic. Then Eiradh said, "Is there a Canna boat in the bay?" and they said, "Ay," and pointed out a big smack with her sails up, and a great patch on the mainsail. The skipper of the smack was on shore, and his name was Alastair. He was a big black-whiskered man, with large silly eyes like a seal's. Eiradh minded him well, though he was a laddie when she left, and went up and called him by his name, but he stared at her and shook his head. Then Eiradh said, "Do you mind Eiradh Nicraonail, who dwelt in the small house by the sea?" and the man laughed, and asked after Calum Eachern. Eiradh told him her troubles, and got the promise of a passage to Canna that day.

In the afternoon it blew hard from the east, but Eiradh went on board the smack with her kist. They ran out of the Sound of Mull with the wind, and kept in close to the Rhu, for the sake of smooth water. Eiradh felt a heaviness and pain about her heart, and sat on the kist with her head leaning against the side of the boat. She had a touch of the sea-sickness, but that passed away.

Alastair steered the smack on the west side of Eig, and the squalls came so sharp off the Scaur that they had to take down the topsail. As they sailed in the smooth water on the lee side of Eig Eiradh asked about the Canna folk she had known, and most of them were dead and buried. Then she asked about the old man who had taught her to read and write, and he was dead too. Many of the young folk had gone away across the ocean, to work among strangers and wander in a foreign land.

The heart of Eiradh sank to hear the news; for she thought to herself, " Every face will be as strange as the faces in the south." Then Alastair, seeing she put her hand to her heart, said, " What ails ye, wife? are you sick?" Eiradh nodded, and leant her head over the boat, looking at the sea.

A little after that the smack rounded the north end of Rum, and Eiradh saw Canna in the sea, just as she had left it long ago. There was a shower all over the ocean, but the green side of Canna was shining with the light through a cloud. Eiradh looked and looked; for there was not an inch of the green land but she knew by heart.

The wind blew fresh and keen, and they had to

lower the peak of the mainsail running for the harbor. Eiradh saw the tower, all gray and wet in the rain, and she thought she heard the lady's voice calling as in old times. Then she looked over to the mouth of Loch Scavaig, thinking to herself, "There is the place where my brothers were lost!" and that brought up the picture of her father, sitting dead on the cliffs and looking out to sea. Eiradh's eyes were blind with tears, and she could not see Canna any more; but as they ran round into the bay, her eyes cleared, and she saw her home close by the water-side, with the roof all gone, and the walls broken down, and a cow looking out of the door.

A little after that, when the anchor was down and the mainsail lowered, Alastair touched Eiradh on the arm, thinking she was asleep, for she was leaning back with her face in her cloak. Then he drew back the cloak and saw her face with a strange smile on it, and the eyes wide open. Though he was a big man, he was scared, and called out to his mates, and an old man among them said, "Sure enough she is dead." So they carried her body ashore in their boat, and put it in one of the houses, and sent word to the laird.

Eiradh Eachern had died of the same disease that killed her mother. She had o'er many thoughts to live long, and she knew the name of trouble. In her kist they found her grave-clothes all ready made and neatly worked with her own hands, and they buried her on the hill-side close to her father and mother. May the Lord God find her ready there to answer to her name at the Last Day!

CHAPTER IX.

NIGHT ON THE MINCH.

Gloomy Prophecies—Terrors of the Minch—The Viking—Hamish Shaw, the Pilot—Leaving Canna Harbor—Pictures of Skye and the Cuchullins—Remarks on Sir Walter Scott and his Poems—Afloat on the Minch—The Far-off Isles—Twilight—Hamish Shaw at the Helm—Summer Night—Talk about Ghosts and Superstitions—The Evil Eye—The Death-Cry—Wind Rising—Wind and Mist—Water-Snakes—Midnight—The Strange Ship—Peep o' Day—The Red Buoy—Anchorage in Loch Boisdale.

"She is a poor thing, a bit toy!" said the captain of the Lowland trader, regarding the *Tern* from the deck of his big vessel, while we lay in Canna harbor. "She's no' for these seas at all; and the quicker ye are awa' hame wi' her round the Rhu ye'll be the wiser. She should never hae quitted the Clyde."

Set by the side of the trader's great hull, she certainly looked a "toy"—so tiny, so slight, with her tapering mast and slender spars. To all our enumeration of her good qualities, the captain merely replied an incredulous "oomph," and assured us that, were she as "good as gold," the waters of the Minch would drown her like a rat, if there was any wind at all. Few yachts of twice her tonnage, and twice her beam, ever dared to show their sails on the outside of Skye, and the wiser they, thought the captain. Why, even he, in his great vessel, which was like a rock in the water, had seen such sights out there as had made his hair stand on end ; and he launched into a series of awful tales, showing how he had driven from the point of Sleat to Isle Ornsay, "up to his neck" in the sea ; how a squall off Dunvegan Head had carried away his topmast, broken his mainsail-boom, and swept his decks clean of boats and rubbish, all at one fell crash; and he added numberless other terrific things, all tending to show that we were likely to get into trouble. When he heard that we actually purposed crossing to Boisdale, and beating up along the shores of the Long Isles, as far as Stornoway, he set us down as madmen at once, and condescended to no more advice. After that, till the moment we sailed, he regarded us from the side of his vessel in a solemn sort of way, as if we were people going to be hung, and well deserving of our fate. You see, he was getting gray and cautious—his blood lacked phosphorus, his heart fire.

He frightened us a little, though. The Wanderer, who had planned the expedition, looked at the skipper, or the Viking, as we got into the habit of calling him, because he wasn't like one. The Viking, who had never before ventured with a yacht beyond the Clyde, was very pale, and only wanted encouragement to turn tail and fly. But Hamish Shaw, the pilot, setting his lips together, delivered himself so violently against flight, vowed so staunchly that, having come thus far, we must proceed, or be forevermore branded as pretenders, and finally swore roundly by his reputation as a seaman to carry us safely through all difficulties, that even the Viking shook his horrent locks, and became, for the instant, nearly as reckless as he looked. "Nothing," said the Viking, in a glow of intense ardor, "nothing gives me so much pleasure as tearing through the sea, with the wind blowing half a gale, and the boat's side buried to the cockpit-combing."

We had all great confidence in Hamish Shaw, for two very good reasons: first, because he had long been accustomed to sailing all sorts of boats in those waters; and second, because he was thoroughly plucky, steady as a rock, and cool as snow, in times of peril. Again and again, during the voyage, did we find reason to bless ourselves that we had such a man on board. He was fond of talk, and had much to say well worth listening to, but at critical moments he was like the sphinx, only rather more active. To see him at the helm, with his eye on the water, steadily helping the little craft through a tempestuous sea, bringing her bow up to the billows, and burying it in them whenever they would have drowned her broadside, or sharply watching the water to windward, with the great mainsail-sheet in his hand, shaking her through the squalls off a mountainous coast—these are things worth seeing, things that make one proud of the race. As for the Viking, although he had considerable experience in sailing in smooth water, and although he was a very handy fellow in the ship-carpenter's line, he was nowhere when it began to blow. The Wanderer could do a little in an emergency, but his nautical knowledge was very slight, just enabling him to distinguish one rope from another, if he was not particularly hurried in his movements. Now, the cook (as you have guessed from the beginning) was a lady, and, of course, could be of no use on deck in bad weather, although, as Hamish Shaw expressed it, she showed a man's spirit throughout the whole voyage.

In plain point of fact, there was only one thoroughbred sailor on board, only one man thoroughly competent to act on his own responsibility during a great emergency; and as he had only one pair of hands, and could not be everywhere at the same moment, 'twas a miracle that the *Tern* escaped destruction on more than one occasion. But (as the female novelists used to say) we anticipate.

As the distance from Canna to Loch Boisdale, the nearest point in the outer Hebrides, was about thirty miles, all quite open water, without the chance of any kind of harbor, and as the *Tern*, even with a fair wind, could not be expected to run more than five or six miles an hour *in a sea*, it was advisable to choose a good day for the passage. As usual in such cases, we began by being over-cautious, and ended by being over-impatient. This day was too calm, that day was too windy. We ended by doing two things which we had begun by religiously vowing not to to do—never to start for a long passage except at early morning; never to venture on such a passage without a fair wind. We weighed anchor at about two o'clock in the afternoon, with the wind blowing nothwest— nearly dead in our teeth.

But it was a glorious day, sunny and cheerful; the clouds were high and white, and the waters were sparkling and flashing far as the eye could see. The little *Tern* seemed to catch the glee. Directly the wind touched her white wings, she slipped through the harbor with rapid flight, plunged splashing out at the harbor mouth, and was soon swimming far out in the midst of the ocean, happy, eager, tilting the waves from her breast like a beautiful swimmer in his strength. Next to the rapturous enjoyment of having wings one's self, or being able to sport among the waves like a great northern diver, is the pleasure of sailing, during such weather, in a boat like the *Tern*. The blood is sparkling, but the brain is at work, beating steady as a pulse, under thoughts that come and go like the glimmer of foam and light.

Canna never looked more beautiful than that day— her cliffs were wreathed into wondrous forms and tinctured with deep ocean-dyes, and the slopes above were rich and mellow in the light. Beyond her was Rum, always the same, a dark beauty with a gentle heart. But what most fascinated the eye was the southern coast of Skye, lying on the starboard bow as we were beating northward. The Isle of Mist* was clear on that occasion, not a vapor lingering on the heights, and although it must be admitted that much of its strange and eerie beauty was lost, still we had a certain gentle loveliness to supply its place. Could that be Skye, the deep coast full of rich, warm under-shadow, the softly-tinted hills, " nakedly visible, without a cloud," sleeping against the " dim, sweet harebell-color" of the heavens? Where was the

---

* This name is purely Scandinavian—*Sky* signifying " cloud ;" whence, too, our own word "sky," the under, or vapor, heaven·

thunder-cloud, the weeping shadows of the cirrus, the white flashes of cataracts through the black smoke of rain on the mountain-side? Were those the Cuchullins—the ashen-gray heights turning to solid amber at the peaks, with the dry seams of torrents softening in the sunlight to golden shades? Why, Blaven, with its hooked forehead, would have been bare as Primrose Hill, save for one slight white wreath of vapor that, glittering with the hues of the prism, floated gently away to die in the delicate blue. Dark were the headlands, yet warmly dark, projecting into the sparkling sea and casting summer shades. Skye was indeed transformed, yet its beauty still remained spiritual, still it kept the faint feeling of the glamour. It looked like witch-beauty, wondrous and unreal. You felt that an instant might change it—and so it might and did. Ere we had sailed many miles away, Skye was clouded over with a misty woe, her face was black and wild, she sobbed in the midst of the darkness with the voice of falling rain and moaning winds.

Sir Walter Scott, in his notes made during a Highland tour, describes this western coast of Skye as "highly romantic, and at the same time displaying a richness of vegetation in the lower ground to which we have hitherto been strangers;" adding, "We passed three salt-water lochs, or deep embayments, called Loch Bracadale, Loch Einort, and Loch ——, and about eleven o'clock opened up Loch Scavaig. We were now under the western termination of the high range of mountains called Cuillen, or Quillin or Coolin, whose weather-beaten and serrated peaks we had admired at a distance from Dunvegan. They sank here upon the sea, but with the same bold and peremptory aspect which their distant appearance indicated. The tops of the ridge, apparently inaccessible to human foot, were rent and split into the most tremendous pinnacles. Toward the base of these bare and precipitous crags, the ground, enriched by the soil washed down from them, is comparatively verdant and productive." And he goes on, in the same gazetteer style, to describe Loch Scavaig and Loch Corruisk, just as if he were Brown or Robinson, and not the second name in the great roll of glorious creators. Nor is he much more felicitous in his treatment of the same theme in verse. This is his poetic description of Loch Corruisk, and it is quoted with enthusiasm in every guide-book:

> " Awhile their route they silent made,
>   As men who stalk for mountain-deer,
>   Till the good Bruce to Ronald said,
>   ' St. Mary! what a scene is here!
>   I've traversed many a mountain-strand,
>   Abroad, and in my native land,
>   And it has been my lot to tread
>   Where safety more than pleasure led.
>   Thus, many a waste I've wandered o'er,
>   Clomb many a crag, crossed many a moor,
>   But, by my halidome,
>   A scene so rude, so wild as this,
>   Yet so sublime in barrenness,
>   Ne'er did my wandering footsteps press
>   Where'er I happ'd to roam.'

XIV.

" No marvel thus the Monarch spake ;
For rarely human eye has known
A scene so stern as that dread lake,
　With its dark ledge of barren stone.
Seems that primeval earthquake's sway
Hath rent a strange and shattered way
　Through the rude bosom of the hill,
And that each naked precipice,
Sable ravine, and dark abyss,
　Tells of the outrage still.
The wildest glen, but this, can show
Some touch of Nature's genial glow ;
On high Benmore green mosses grow,
And heath-bells bud in deep Glencoe,
　And copse on Cruchan-Ben ;
But here—above, around, below,
　On mountain or in glen—
Nor tree, nor shrub, nor plant, nor flower,
Nor aught of vegetative power,
　The weary eye may ken.
For all is rocks at random thrown,
Black waves, bare crags, and banks of stone,
　As if were here denied
The summer sun, the spring's sweet dew,
That clothe with many a varied hue
　The bleakest mountain-side.

XV.

" And wilder, forward as they wound,
Were the proud cliffs and lake profound.
Huge terraces of granite black
Afforded rude and cumbered track ;
　For from the mountain hoar,
Hurled headlong in some night of fear,
When yelled the wolf, and fled the deer,
　Loose crags had toppled o'er ;

> And some, chance-poised and balanced, lay
> So that a stripling arm might sway
>   A mass no host could raise,
> In Nature's range at random thrown,
> Yet trembling like the Druid's stone
>   On its precarious base.
> The evening mists, with ceaseless change,
> Now clothed the mountains' lofty range,
>   Now left their foreheads bare,
> And round the skirts their mantle furled,
> Or on the sable waters curled,
> Or on the eddying breezes whirled,
>   Dispersed in middle air.
> And oft, condensed, at once they lower,
> When, brief and fierce, the mountain shower
>   Pours like a torrent down;
> And when return the sun's glad beams,
> Whitened with foam a thousand streams
>   Leap from the mountain's crown."

Bruce might swear himself hoarse "by his halidome" ere we could admit that the above was much more than the dryest verbiage. Yet the general features of the landscape are caught as in a photograph, with a bald fidelity which is characterestic of all Sir Walter's efforts in verse, and is noteworthy as having won for itself the special praise of Mr. Ruskin. We shall have something to say of Corruisk in good time, and it will not be difficult to deny that Walter Scott felt the spirit of the wild scenes at all—so totally out of harmony with nature is his verbose enumeration of details. Shakspeare, with his faultless vision, would not have failed to see Corruisk as it is, and to picture it in true emotional colors, but perhaps only Shelley, of all our poets, could have felt it to the true spiritual height and blended it into music, thought, and dream.

With the same felicity in prose and verse, Sir Walter, in the already-quoted extract from his journal, talks of the Coolins having a "*peremptory aspect*, which their distant appearance indicated" (we cannot construe this sentence), and in an easy, general way, speaks of the scenery of the neighborhood as "highly romantic." Is "peremptory," then, the adjective to apply to yonder peaks? Do the ghost-world, the strange dreams we have in sleep, the creeping thoughts we have in death-chambers, the whisperings we have from that "undiscovered country"—do all these things, any of these things, strike us as being "peremptory?" There is a perkish, commonplace, pretentious air about that word, as applied to beautiful mountains. Like that other word, "romantic," it should be cut out of the poetic vocabulary. The beadle is "peremptory," and the sensation scenes at metropolitan theaters are "highly romantic."

We were flying along quickly, and the breeze was heading us less and less. The sea still sparkled, far as the eye could see, a flashing surface—

"Dappled o'er with shadows flung
From many a brooding cloud;"

the wool-white cloud above, the soft shadow below. There was no danger, and the Viking was like a lion. All went merry as a marriage-bell. Picture after picture rose up, grew into perfect loveliness, and faded like a fairy palace into the air. Now it was MacLeod's Maidens, the three sister peaks on the western coast of Skye, linked together by a dim rainbow, and glimmering brightly through a momentary shower;

again, it was the far-off mouth of Loch Bracadale, rich in the darkest purple tints, with a real red-sailed fishing-boat in the foreground, to bring out the picture, just as Turner would have placed it on the canvas; and still again, it was the Cuchullins, already wreathed in mist, magnified to still more gigantic size by their own darkness, and looking as forlorn as if no sunlight had ever fallen on their livid brows.

But more frequently, with keener interest, with more anxious longing, our eyes were turned westward—to the far-off isles whither we were bound. We could see them better now, misted over by distance—part of the Barra highland, the three great hills of Uist, and, dimmest of all, the high hills of Harris. As the vapors shifted on the coast, the shape of the land changed; what had looked like mountains, drifted away before the wind; what had seemed a cloud, outlined itself darkly and more darkly; and, strange to say, the whole coast seemed, as we drew nearer, to retreat itself farther away, insomuch that when we had beaten ten or twelve miles of the actual distance to Loch Boisdale, the outer Hebrides looked as distant as ever, and we almost thought there must have been some mistake in our calculation of the number of miles across.

It was a strange feeling—riding out there in the open Minch in that little boat, and knowing that a storm, if it did catch us, would leave us little time to say our prayers. The vessel was too small and crank to "lie to," and, running before the wind, she would have drowned herself in no time. True, we had extemporized a kind of wooden scuttle for the cockpit, which might be of service in a sea, and did actually save us from some peril; but the boat, as Hamish Shaw expressed it, wanted "body," and would never live out bad weather in the open. It was a wonder Hamish ever accompanied us at all, he had such profound contempt for the *Tern*, quite agreeing with the skipper in Canna that she was merely a toy, a plaything. We suppose, however, that he had confidence in himself, and knew that if any one could save her at a pinch, he could.

We had started so late, that before we were halfway across it was growing quite dark. It promised to be a good night, however. The worst of our situation just then was that the wind was beginning to fail, and we were making very little way through the rough roll of the sea.

One certainly did not feel comfortable, tumbling out there in the deepening twilight, while the land on either side slowly mingled itself with the clouds. After taking our bearings by the compass, and getting a drop of something warm, we could do nothing but sit and wait for events. The Viking was beginning to feel unwell. Shivering, he looked to windward, seeing all sorts of nameless horrors. Twenty times, at least, he asked Hamish what kind of a night it promised to be. Twice he rushed down to examine the weather-glass, an aneroid, and, to his horror, it was slowly sinking. Then he got lights, and buried himself among the charts, feebly gazing at a blank space of paper labeled, "The Minch." At last, unable to disguise it any longer, he began to throw out dark hints that we were doomed; that it was madness sailing at night; that he had seen it from the beginning, and should not have ventured so far; that he knew from the color of the sky that we should have a storm that night; and that, only let him get safe back 'round the Rhu," no temptation on earth should 'lure him again beyond the Crinan Canal.

But Hamish Shaw was in his glory. He loved sailing at night, and had been constantly urging us into it. He had learned the habit as a fisherman—it was associated with much that was wildest and noblest in his life—and he was firmly persuaded that he could see his way anywhere in the waters, by night as well as by day. Owl-like, wakeful and vigilant, he sat at the helm, with his weather-beaten face looming through his matted ringlets, his black pipe set between his teeth, and his eye looking keenly to windward. He was not a sentimental man; he did not care much for " scenery ;" but do you think there was no dreamy poetry in his soul, that he had no subtle pleasure, concealed almost from himself, as the heaven bared its glittering breast of stars, and the water that darkened beneath reflected back the light, and the wind fell softly, till we could hear the deep breathing of the sea itself? What memories drifted across his brain!—of wild nights at the herring-fishing, of rain, snow, and wind, and of tender nights in his Highland home, when he went courting, in Highland fashion, to the lassie's chamber-door! He is a strange study, Hamish Shaw. To hear him speak directly of any scene he has visited, you would not credit him with any insight. But he sees more than he knows. His life is too full to take in separate effects, or to wonder anew. What light he throws for us on old thoughts and superstitions, on tender affections of the race! His speech is full of water and wind. He uses a fine phrase as easily as nature fashions a bud or a leaf. He speaks in natural symbols, as freely as he uses an oar. His clear, fresh vision penetrates even into the moral world, quite open and fearless even there, where the best of us become purblind.

We have tried again and again, for our own amusement, to reproduce a few specimens of Shaw's English. He is a true Gael, and speaks a foreign tongue, acquired in early youth. His language is at once remarkable for its obscurity and the frequent use of big words, and yet for a strange felicity of verbal touch. He attaches a certain meaning of his own to words, and tries hard to be explicit. For example, speaking once of the Gaelic speech, and becoming warm in its praise, "The Gaelic," he said, "is a kind of guttural language, a principal and positive language; a language, d'ye see? *full of knowledge and essence.*" It would be difficult to find anything obscurer than the beginning of the explanation, or more felicitous than its conclusion. The one word "essence" is perfect in its terse expression of meaning.

"I'm of the opinion," said Hamish, quietly surveying the heavens, "that the night will be good. Yon's a clear sky to windward, and there's nae carry. I would a heap sooner sail a craft like this by night than by day—the weather is more settled between gloaming and sunrise; and ye have one great advantage—the light is aye gaining on ye, instead o' the darkness."

"But, Shaw, man," cried the Viking, "we are creeping closer and closer to the land, and it will be a fearful business making it out in the mirk."

Shaw shrugged his shoulders.

"If we canna see it, we maun just smell it," he said. "It's useless to fash your head."

"A coast sown with rocks as thick as if they had been shaken out of a pepper-box! Reefs here, danger everywhere! And not a beacon nearer than Rhu Hunish lighthouse! O my God!"

And the Viking wailed.

By this time the summer night had quite closed in; Canna and Skye had long faded out of sight behind us, but we could still make out the form of the land ahead. The wind was rising again, and blowing gently on our quarter, so that we bade fair to make the coast of the Long Island sooner than was advisable. Still, it would have been injudicious to remain longer than was necessary out in the open; for a storm might come on by morning, and our fate be sealed. The best plan was to creep to within a couple of miles of the land, and hang about until we had sufficient daylight to make out our situation. It was even possible, if it did not get much darker, that we might even be able to distinguish the mouth of Loch Boisdale in the night.

The Viking plunged below to the charts, and, to while away the time, the Wanderer began talking to the steersman about superstition. It was a fine eerie situation for a talk on that subject, and the still summer night, with the deep, dreary murmur of the sea, powerfully stimulated the imagination.

"I say, Hamish," said the Wanderer, abruptly, "do you believe in ghosts?"

Hamish puffed his pipe leisurely for some time before replying.

"I'm of the opinion," he replied at last, beginning with the expression habitual to him, "I'm of the opinion that there's strange things in the world. I never saw a ghost, and I don't expect to see one. If the Scripture says true—I mean the Scripture, no' the ministers—there has been ghosts seen before my time, and there may be some seen now. The folk used to say there was a Ben-shee in Skipness Castle— a Ben-shee with white hair and a mutch like an old wife—and my father saw it with his own een before he died. They're curious people over in Barra, and they believe stranger things than that."

"In witchcraft, perhaps?"

"There's more than them believes in witchcraft. When I was a young man on board the *Petrel* (she's one of Middleton's fish-boats, and is over at Howth now), the winds were that wild there seemed sma' chance of winning hame before the new year. Weel, the skipper was a Skye man, and had great faith in an auld wife who lived alone up on the hillside; and without speaking a word to any o' us, he went up to bid wi' her for a fair wind. He crossed her hand wi' siller, and she told him to bury a live cat wi' its head to the airt wanted, and then to steal a spoon from some house and get awa'. He buried the cat, and he stole the spoon. It's curious, but, sure as ye live, the wind changed that night into the northwest, and never shifted till the *Petrel* was in Tobermory."

"Once let me be the hero of an affair like that," cried the Wanderer, "and I'll believed in the devil forever after. But it was a queer process."

"The ways o' God are droll," returned Shaw, seriously. "Some say that in old times the witches made a causeway o' whales from Rhu Hunish to Dunvegan Head. There are auld wives o'er yonder yet who hae the name of going out with the Deil every night in the shape o' blue hares, and I kenned a man who thought he shot one wi' a siller button. I dinna believe all I hear, but I dinna just disbelieve, either. Ye've heard o' the Evil Eye?"

"Certainly."

"When we were in Canna, 1 noticed a fine cow and calf standing by a house near the kirkyard, and I said to the wife as I passed (she was syning her pails at the door): 'Yon's a bonnie bit calf ye hae with the auld cow.' 'Aye,' said she, 'but I hope ye dinna look at them o'er keen'—meaning, ye ken, that maybe I had the Evil Eye. I laughed, and told her that was a thing that ne'er belong't to me or mine. That minds me of an auld wife near Loch Boisdale who had a terrible bad name for killing kye and doing mischief on corn. She was gleed,* and had black hair. One day, when the folk were in kirk, she reached o'er her hand to a bairn that was lying beside her, and touched its cheek wi' her finger. Weel, that moment the bairn (it was a lassie, and had red hair) began greeting, and turning its head from side to side, like folk in fever. It kept on sae for days. But at last anither

---

* She squinted.

woman, who saw what was wrang, recommended eight poultices o' kyedung (one every night) from the innermost kye i' the byre. They gied her the poultices, and the lassie got weel."

"That was as strange a remedy as the buried cat," observed the Wanderer; "but I did not know such people possessed the power of casting the trouble on human beings."

Hamish puffed his pipe, and looked quietly at the sky. It was some minutes before he spoke again.

"There was a witch family," he said at last, "in Loch Carron, where I was born and reared. They lived their lane,* close to the sea. There were three o' them—the mither, a son, and a daughter. The mither had great lumps all o'er her arms, and sae had the daughter; but the son was a clean-hided lad, and he was the cleverest. Folk said he had the power o' healing the sick, but only in ae way, by transferring the disease to him that brought the message seeking help. Once, I mind, a man was sent till him on horseback, bidding him come and heal a fisher who was up on the hill and like to dee. The warlock mounted his pony, and said to the man, 'Draw back a bit, and let me ride before ye.' The man, kenning nae better, let him pass, and followed ahint. They had to pass through a glen, and in the middle o' the glen an auld wife was standing at her door. When she saw the messenger riding ahint the warlock, she screeched out to him as loud as she could cry—'Ride, ride, and reach the sick lad first, or ye're a dead man.'

* *Their lane*—alone.

At that the warlock looked black as thunder, and galloped his pony; but the messenger being better mounted, o'ertook him fast, and got first to the sick man's bedside. In the night the sick man died. Ye see, the warlock had nae power of shifting the complaint but on him that brought the message, and no' on him, if the warlock didna reach the house before the messenger."

Here the Viking emerged with the whisky-bottle, and Hamish Shaw wet his lips. We were gliding gently along now, and the hills of Uist were still dimly visible. The deep roll of the sea would have been disagreeable, perhaps, to the uninitiated, but we were hardened. While the Viking sat by, gazing gloomily into the darkness, the Wanderer pursued his chat with Shaw, or, rather, incited the latter to further soliloquies.

"Do you know, Hamish," he said, slyly, "it seems to me very queer that Providence should suffer such pranks to be played, and should entrust that marvelous power to such wretched hands. Come, now, do you actually fancy these things have happened?"

But Hamish Shaw was not the man to commit himself. He was a philosopher.

"I'm of the opinion," he replied, "that it would be wrong to be o'er positive. Providence does as queer things, whiles,* as either man or woman. There was a strange cry, like the whistle of a bird, heard every night close to the cottage before Wattie Mac-

* At times.

leod's smack was lost on St. John's Point, and Wattie and his son drowned; then it stoppit. Whiles it comes like a sheep crying, whiles like the sound o' pipes. I heard it mysel' when my brither Angus died. He had been awa' o'er the country, and his horse had fallen and kickit him on the navel. But before we heard a word about it, the wife and I were on the road to Angus' house, and were coming near the burn that parted his house from mine. It was night, and bright moonlight. The wife was heavy at the time, and suddenly she grippit me by the arm, and whispered, 'Wheesht! do ye hear?' I listened, and at first heard nothing. 'Wheesht, again!' says she; and then I heard it plain—like the low blowing o' the bagpipes, slowly and sadly, wi' nae tune. 'O Hamish,' said the wife, '*wha* can it be?' I said naething, but I felt my back all cold, and a sharp thread running through my heart. It followed us along as far as Angus' door, and then it went awa'. Angus was sitting by the fire; they had just brought him hame, and he told us o' the fall and the kick. He was pale, but didna think much was wrang wi' him, and talked quite cheerful and loud. The wife was sick and frighted, and they gave her a dram; they thought it was her trouble, for her time was near, but she was thinking o' the sign. Though we knew fine that Angus wouldna live, we didna dare to speak o' what we had heard. Going hame that nicht, we heard it again, and in a week he was lying in his grave."

The darkness, the hushed breathing of the sea, the sough of the wind through the rigging, greatly deepened the effect of this tale; and the Viking listened intently, as if he expected every moment to hear a similar sound presaging his own doom. Hamish Shaw showed no emotion. He told his tale as mere matter-of-fact, with no elocutionary effects, and kept his eye to windward all the time, evidently looking out for squalls.

"For God's sake," cried the Viking, "choose some other subject of conversation. We are in bad enough plight already, and don't want any more horrors."

"What! afraid of ghosts?"

"No, dash it!" returned the Viking; "but—but— as sure as I live, there is storm in yon sky!"

The look of the sky to windward was certainly not improving; it was becoming smoked over with thick mist. Though we were now only a few miles off the Uist coast, the loom of the land was scarcely visible; the vapors peculiar to such coasts seemed rising and gradually wrapping everything in their folds. Still, as far as we could make out from the stars, there was no carry in the sky.

"I'll no' say," observed Hamish, taking in everything at a glance—"I'll no say but there may be wind ere morning; but it will be wind off the shore, and we hae the hills for shelter."

"But the squalls! the squalls!" cried the Viking.

"The land is no' so high that ye need to be scared. Leave you the vessel to me, and I'll take her through it snug. But we may as weel hae the third reef in the mainsail, and mak' things ready in case o' need."

This was soon done. The mainsail was reefed, and the small jib substituted for the large one; and after a glance at the compass, Hamish again sat quiet at the helm

"Barra," he said, renewing our late subject of talk, "is a great place for superstition, and sae is Uist. The folk are like weans, simple and kindly. There is a Ben-shee weel known at the head o' Loch Eynort, and anither haunts one o' the auld castles o' the great Macneil o' Barra. I hae heard, too, that whiles big snakes, wi' manes like horses, come up into the fresh-water lakes and lie in wait to devour the flesh o' man. In a fresh-water loch at the Harris there was a big beast like a bull, that came up ae day and ate half the body o' a lad when he was bathing. They tried to drain the loch to get at the beast, but there was o'er muckle water. Then they baited a great hook wi' the half o' a sheep, but the beast was o'er wise to bite. Lord, it was a droll fishing! They're a curious people. But do ye no' think, if the seas and the lochs were drainit dry, there would be all manner o' strange animals that nae man kens the name o'? There's a kind o' water-world—nae man kens what it's like—for the drown'd canna see, and if they could see, they couldna speak. Ay!" he added, suddenly changing the current of his thoughts, "ay! the wind's rising, and we're no far off the shore, for I can smell the land."

By what keenness of sense Hamish managed to "smell the land" we had no time just then to inquire, for all our wits were employed in looking after the safety of the *Tern*. She was bowling along under three-reefed mainsail and stormjib, and was getting just about as much as she could bear. With the rail under to the cockpit, the water lapping heavily against the cooming, and ever and anon splashing right over in the cockpit itself, she made her way fast through the rising sea. In vain we strained our eyes to discern the shore—

> "The blinding mist came down and hid the land
> As far as eye could see!"

All at once the foggy vapors peculiar to the country had steeped everything in darkness; we could guess from the helm where the land lay, but how near it was we were at a loss to tell. What with the whistling wind, the darkness, the surging sea, we felt quite bewildered and amazed.

The Wanderer looked at his watch, and it was past midnight. Even if the fog cleared off, it would not be safe to take Loch Boisdale without good light, and there was nothing for it but to beat about till sunrise. This was a prospect not at all comfortable, for we might even then be in the neighborhood of dangerous rocks, and if the wind rose any higher, we should be compelled to run before the wind, God knew whither. Meantime, it was determined to stand off a little to the open, in dread of coming to over-close quarters with the shore.

Hamish sat at the helm, stern and imperturbable. We knew by his silence that he was anxious, but he expressed no anxiety whatever. Ever and anon, he slipped down his hand on the deck to leeward, feeling how near the water was to the cockpit, and as there seemed considerable danger of foundering in the heavy sea, he speedily agreed with us that it would be wise to close over the cockpit hatches. That done, all was achieved that hands could do, save holding the boat with the helm steady and close to the wind—a task which Hamish fulfilled to perfection. Indeed, we were in no slight danger from squalls, for the wind was off the land, and nothing saved us, when struck by heavy gusts, but the firmness and skill of the helmsman. He had talked about smelling the land, but it is certain that he seemed to smell the wind; almost before a squall touched her, the *Tern* was standing up to it tight and firm, when ever so slight a falling off might have stricken us over to the mast, and perhaps (for the cockpit hatches were a small protection) foundered us in the open sea.

We will draw a veil over the sufferings of the Viking. He was a wreck by this time, too weak even to scream out his prophecies of doom, but lying anticipating his fate in the forecastle hammock, with the grog at his side and his eyes closed despairingly against all the terrors of the scene. The cook was lying in the cabin, very sick—in that happy frame of mind when it is a matter of indifference whether we float on or go to the bottom. The Wanderer, drenched through, clung close beside the pilot, and strained his eyes against wind and salt spray into the darkness. It would be false to say that he felt comfortable, but as false to say that he was frightened. Though dreadfully excitable by nature, he was of too sanguine a temperament to be overpowered by half-seen perils.

On the whole, though the situation was precarious, he had by no means made up his mind to be drowned; and there was something so stimulating in the brave conduct of the little ship, which seemed to be fighting out the battle on her own account, that at times he felt actually light-hearted enough to sing aloud a verse of his favorite "Tom Bowling." No man, however, could have sat yonder in the darkness, amid the rush of wind and wave, and failed to tremble at times, thinking of the power of God; so that, again and again, through the Wanderer's mind, with a deep sea-music of their own, rolled the verses of the Psalm—" They that go down to the sea in ships, that do business in great waters; these see the works of the Lord, and his wonders in the deep. For he commandeth, and raiseth the stormy wind, which lifteth up the waves thereof. They mount up to the heaven, they go down again to the depths; their soul is melted because of trouble. They reel to and fro, and stagger like a drunken man, and are at their wits' end. Then they cry unto the Lord in their trouble, and he bringeth them out of their distresses. He maketh the storm a calm, so that the waves thereof are still. Then are they glad because they be quiet; so he bringeth them unto their desired haven. Oh that men would praise the Lord for his goodness, and for his wonderful works to the children of men!"

It was now so dark that we could see nothing on any side of us, save the glitter of the crests of the waves, and the phosphorescent glimmer of the beaten water behind the keel. The wind was pretty steady, and the squalls not too frequent. We were running through the darkness at considerable speed, burying our bowsprit in every wave, and washing our decks as clean as salt water could make them. So low was the *Tern's* rail, and so close to the sea, even on the weather side, that it was almost like being dragged through the water bodily with the chilly waves lapping round one's waist.

Suddenly, out of the darkness ahead, shot a sharp glimmer of light; then there was a loud sound like the creaking of cordage and noise of sails; and then, before we could utter a cry, a large brig dashed across our bows, running with a free sheet before the wind. Ghostly and strange she looked in the mist, driving at tremendous speed, and churning the sea to sparkling foam. With a loud oath, Hamish shoved the helm hard-a-port, and brought the head of the *Tern* up to the wind. We had narrowly escaped a collision. With fascinated eyes we watched the brig dash on until it was swallowed up in the darkness, and when it was quite gone, drew a heavy breath of relief.

"Lord, that was a close shave!" muttered Shaw, drawing his cuff across his mouth, as is his manner when agitated. "Wha would hae thought o' meeting strange craft hereabouts? We'd may-be better rig out the mast-head lantern, in case o' mair accidents."

This was soon done, and although the lantern burnt blue and dim, we felt more secure. After so narrow an escape, what reasonable creature would have refused to drink his own health in the water of life? The grog-bottle was passed round, and never was a " nip of the screech " received with more affectionate unction.

It was a weary work, that waiting in the darkness. The wind sang, the water sobbed, the sail moaned, until the Wanderer began to get sleepier and sleepier, and at last, wet as he was, sank off into a doze, wherein he was just half conscious of the boat's motion through the water, and half dreaming of things far away. Suddenly he was startled by a roar in his ear, and rubbed his eyes wildly, listening. It was Hamish Shaw saying quietly:

"It's beginning to get light. I see the loom o' the land."

Shivering like a half-drowned rat in the cold, damp air of the dawn, and dashing the wet hair out of his weary eyes, the Wanderer stared all round him, and saw, when his obfuscated wits were able to concentrate themselves, that it was nearly daybreak, though all was dark above. A dim, silvern, misty glimmer was on the sea, and about two miles to the westward the land lay black in a mist like the smoke nearest the funnel of a new-coaled steamer. The Viking was poking his head through the cabin-hatch, and gazing shoreward.

"Can ye mak' out the shape o' these hills?" he asked of the pilot. "Loch Boisdale should be hereabouts."

Hamish shook his head.

"We maun creep in closer to mak' certain," he replied. "It's o'er dark yet. Yon bit place yonder—where you see a shimmer like the gleam o' herring-scales—looks like the mouth of the loch, but we maun creep in cannie and get mair light."

Although Shaw had been herring-fishing on the

coast for many years, he was not so familiar with the coast as might have been expected. He knew its general outline, but had not made close observation of details. With the indifference peculiar to the fishers, he had generally trusted to Providence and his own sagacity, without making any mental note of his experiences. So it was not until we had twice or thrice referred to the chart that he remembered that just south of Boisdale, about half a mile from shore, there was a dangerous reef called Mackenzie Rock, and that above this rock there was a red buoy, which, if descried in the dim light, would be a certain index to the whereabouts of the mouth of the loch.

"Tam Saunders put the *Wild Duck* on that rock when I was up here in the *Gannet*," said Hamish; "but she was as strong as iron—different frae this wee bit shell o' a thing—and they keepit her fixit there till the flood, and then floated her off wi' scarce a scratch. We'll just put her about, and creep in shore on the other tack."

Though the day was slowly breaking, it was still very misty, and a thin, cold "smurr" was beginning to dreep down in the sea. The wind was still sharp and strong, the sea high, and the squalls dangerous; but we knew now that the worst of our troubles must be over. As we approached closer to the shore, we noticed one great bluff, or headland, from which the land receded on either side, leaving it darkly prominent; and a reference to the chart soon convinced us that this headland was no other than the Rhu Hordag, which lies a few miles to the south of Loch Boisdale. So we put about again, and slipped up along the land, lying very close to the wind. It was soon clear that the dawn, although it had fully broken, was not going to favor us with a brilliant exhibition, nor to dispel the dangerous vapors in which the shore was shrouded. The whole shape of the land was distorted. One could merely conjecture where solid earth ended and mist began—all was confusion. No sun came out—only the dull glimmer through the miserable "smurr" betokened that it was day.

Suddenly, with a shriek of joy, the Viking discovered the buoy, and pointed it out through the rain. Yes, there it was, a red spot in a circle of white foam, about a quarter of a mile on the weather-quarter. With this assistance, it was decided that the spot which Shaw had compared to the "gleam of herring-scales" was indeed the mouth of the loch. Never did voyagers hail the sight of haven with greater joy!

It was a run of nearly a mile up to the anchorage, and the passage was by no means a safe one; but Hamish, once in the loch, knew every stone and shallow perfectly. When we cast anchor, the thin "smurr" had changed into a heavy rain, and all the scene around was black and wild. But what cared we? The fire was lighted in the forecastle, Hamish put on the kettle, and the kettle began to sing. Then, after donning dry clothes, we sat down as merry as crickets. The Wanderer dozed smilingly in a corner. The Viking swore roundly that it had been the "jolliest night" he had ever spent, and that such experiences made him in love with sailing. Hamish Shaw, to whom all the glory of the night belonged, first lit his black cutty pipe, and rested his head against the side of the forecastle, and then, in an instant, dropped off, heavy as a log, worn out with fatigue, and still gripping the cutty firmly between his teeth as he slept.

CHAPTER II.

THE FISHERS OF THE LONG ISLAND.

Loch Boisdale—The *Tern* at Anchor—The Inn and the Population—Rain—Boisdale in the Herring-Season—Fishing-boats and Camps—A Night in a West-Country Smack—Herring-gutters—Habits of East-Country Fishermen.

THE *Tern's* first anchorage in the Outer Hebrides was at Loch Boisdale, and it was there that the dreary landscape of the Long Island began to exercise its deep fascination over the Wanderer's mind. We lay at the usual place, close to the pier and inn, in the full enjoyment of the ancient and fish-like smell wafted to us from the curing-places ashore. The herring-fishers had nearly all departed, save one or two native crews, who were still laboring leisurely; but they had left their *débris* everywhere—skeletons of huts, piles of peat, fish-bones, scraps of rotten nets, even broken pots and dishes. One or two huts, some entirely of wood, stood empty, awaiting the return of their owners in the following spring. The whole place was deserted—its harvest-time was over. When we rowed ashore in the punt, the population—consisting of two old men and some dirty little boys—received us in grim amazement and silence, until the advent of the inn-keeper, who, repressing all outward symptoms of wonder, bade us a sly welcome, and showed us the way to his establishment. The obvious impression was that we were insane; the tiny craft in which we had come over, our wild and haggard appearance, and, above all, the fact that we had actually come to Loch Boisdale for pleasure (a fact unprecedented in the mind of the oldest inhabitant), all contributed to strengthen this belief. The landlord was free and inquisitive, humoring us cunningly, as keepers do mad people, receiving all our statements calmly and without contradiction, answering all our questions in the easy manner found useful in dealing with idiots and infants, never thinking it worth while to correct us when we were wrong. As he sat chatting with us over a glass of whisky, in a mildewy room of the inn, the inhabitants dropped in one by one; first, the two old men, then a little boy, then a tipsy fisherman, and so on, till the room was full of spectators, all with their mouths wide open, and all, without sign of ordering or drinking anything, staring at the strangers. This volley of eyes became at last so unbearable that it was thought advisable to direct it elsewhere by ordering "glasses round;" an act of generosity which, however grateful to the feelings, was received without enthusiasm, though the mouths and eyes opened still wider in amaze. The advent of the whisky, however, acted like a charm, and the company burst into a torrent of Gaelic.

The result of a long conversation with the populace—which in number and appearance bore about the same relation to a respectable community that a stage "mob" in "Julius Cæsar" would bear to the real article—was not particularly edifying. These gentlemen were cynical on the merits of Loch Boisdale; its principal beauties, in their opinion, being ague, starvation, and weariness. For any person to remain there, ever so short a time, who could by any possibility get out of it, was a thing not to be credited by common sense. The inn-keeper, however, tried to convey to us his comprehension that we had come there, not for pleasure, but " on a discovering manner," by which mystical Celticism he meant to say that we were visitors come to make inquiries, possibly with a view to commerce or statistics. He shook his head over both country and people, and seemed to think our expedition was a waste of time.

For three days after that, it rained as it can rain only in the Long Island; and when at last, tired out of patience, we rushed ashore, our friend the innkeeper received us with a deprecating smile. With keen sarcasm, we demanded if it were always " that sort of weather " in Loch Boisdale; but he replied quite calmly, " Ay, much aboot." But when we sat down over usquebaugh, and the rain, still plashing darkly without,

" With its twofold sound,
The clash hard by, and the murmur all round !"

showed that the weather was little likely to abate that day, the landlord seemed to think his credit at stake, and that even Loch Boisdale was appearing at a disadvantage. To console him, we told him that story of the innkeeper at Arrochar which poor Hugh Macdonald used to retail with such unction over the toddy. An English traveler stayed for some days at Arrochar, and there had been nothing but rain from morn to night. The landlord tried to keep up his guest's spirits by repeated prophecies that the weather was "about to break up;" but at last, on the fifth day, the stranger could endure it no longer. "I say, landlord, have you ever—now, on your honor—have you ever any other sort of weather in this confounded place?" The landlord replied humbly, yet bitterly, "Speak nae mair, sir, speak nae mair. I'm just perfectly ashamed of the way in which our weather's behaving!" But the Loch Boisdale landlord seemed to think the tale too serious for laughter.

As we have noted above, the herring harvest was over. Twice in the year there is good fishing—in the spring and in the autumn; but the autumn fishing is left quite in the hands of a few native boats. The moment the spring-fishing ends, Loch Boisdale subsides into torpor. All is desolate and still; only the fishy smell remains, to remind the yawning native of the glory that is departed.

A busy sight, indeed, is Loch Boisdale or Stornoway in the herring season. Smacks, open boats, skiffs, wherries, make the narrow waters shady; not a creek, however small, but holds some boat in shelter. A fleet, indeed!—the Lochleven boat from the east coast, with the three masts and the three huge lugsails; the Newhaven boat, with its two lugsails; the Isle of Man "jigger;" the beautiful Guernsey runner, handsome as a racing-yacht, and powerful as a revenue cutter; besides all the numberless fry of less noticeable vessels, from the fat west-country smack, with its comfortable fittings, down to the miserable Arran wherry.* Swarms of seagulls float everywhere, and the loch is so oily with the fishy deposit that it requires a strong wind to ruffle its surface. Everywhere on the shore and hillsides, and on the numberless islands, rises the smoke of camps. Busy swarms surround the curing-houses and the inn, while the beach is strewn with fishermen lying at length, and dreaming till work-time. In the afternoon, the fleet slowly disappear, melting away out into the ocean, not to re-emerge till long after the gray of the next dawn.

Did you ever go out for a night with the herring-fishers? If you can endure cold and wet, you would enjoy the thing hugely, especially if you have a boating mind. Imagine yourself on board a west-country smack, running from Boisdale Harbor with the rest of the fleet. It is afternoon, and there is a nice, fresh breeze from the southwest. You crouch in the stern, by the side of the helmsman, and survey all around you with the interest of a novice. Six splendid fellows, in various picturesque attitudes, lounge about the great, broad, open hold, and another is down

---

* The Arran wherry, now nearly extinct, is a wretched-looking thing, without a bowsprit, but with two strong masts. Across the foremast is a bulkhead, and there is a small locker for blankets and bread. In the open space between bulkhead and locker birch tops are thickly strewn for a bed, and for covering there is a huge woolen waterproof blanket ready to be stretched out on spars. Close to the mast lies a huge stone, and thereon a stove. The cable is of *heather rope*, the anchor *wooden*, and the stock a *stone*. Rude and ill-found as these boats are, they face weather before which any ordinary yachtsman would quail.

in the forecastle boiling coffee. If you were not there, half of these would be taking their sleep down below. It seems a lazy business, so far; but wait! By sunset the smack has run fifteen miles up the coast, and is going seven or eight miles east of Rhu Hunish lighthouse; many of the fleet still keep her company, steering thick as shadows in the twilight. How the gulls gather yonder! The dull plash ahead of the boat was caused by the plunge of a solan goose. That the herrings are hereabout, and in no small numbers, you might be sure, even without that bright, phosphorescent light which travels in patches on the water to leeward. Now is the time to see the lounging crew dart into sudden activity. The boat's head is brought up to the wind, and the sails are lowered in an instant.* One man grips the helm, another seizes the back rope of the net, a third the "skunk" or body, a fourth is placed to see the buoys clear and heave them out, the rest attend forward, keeping a sharp look-out for other nets, ready, in case the boat should run too fast, to steady her by dropping the anchor a few fathoms into the sea. When all the nets are out, the boat is brought bow on to the net, the "swing" (as they call the rope attached to the net) secured to the smack's "bits," and all hands then lower the mast as quickly as possible. The mast lowered, secured, and made all clear for hoisting at a moment's notice, and the candle lantern set up in the

---

* There is fashion everywhere. An east country boat always shoots *across* the wind, of course carrying some sail; while a west-country boat shoots *before* the wind, with bare poles.

iron stand made for the purpose of holding it, the crew leave one look-out on deck, with instructions to call them up at a fixed hour, and turn in below for a nap in their clothes; unless it so happens that your brilliant conversation, seasoned with a few bottles of whisky, should tempt them to steal a few more hours from the summer night. Day breaks, and every man is on deck. All hands are busy at work, taking the net in over the bow, two supporting the body, the rest hauling the back rope, save one who draws the net into the hold, and another who arranges it from side to side in the hold to keep the vessel even. Tweet! tweet!—that thin, cheeping sound, resembling the razor-like call of the bat, is made by dying herrings at the bottom of the boat. The sea to leeward, the smack's hold, the hands and arms of the men, are gleaming like silver. As many of the fish as possible are shaken loose during the process of hauling in, but the rest are left in the net until the smack gets on shore. Three or four hours pass away in this wet and tiresome work. At last, however, the nets are all drawn in, the mast is hoisted, the sail set, and while the cook (there being always one man having this branch of work in his department) plunges below to prepare breakfast, the boat makes for Loch Boisdale. Everywhere on the water, see the fishing-boats making for the same bourne, blessing their luck or cursing their misfortune, just as the event of the night may have been. All sail is set, if possible, and it is a wild race to the market. Even when the anchorage is reached, the work is not quite finished;

for the fish have to be measured out in "cran" baskets,* and delivered at the curing-station. By the time that the crew have got their morning dram, have arranged the nets snugly in the stern, and have had some herrings for dinner, it is time to be off again to the harvest-field. Half the crew turn in for sleep, while the other half hoist sail and conduct the vessel out to sea.

Huge, indeed, are the swarms that inhabit Boisdale, afloat or ashore, during the harvest; but, partly because each man has his business on hand, and partly because there is plenty of sea-room, there are few breaches of the peace. On Sunday night, the public-house is crowded, and now and then the dull roar ceases for a moment, as some obstreperous member is shut out summarily into the dark. Besides the regular fishermen and people employed at the curing station, there are the herring-gutters—women of all ages, many of whom follow simply the fortunes of the fishers from place to place. Their business is to gut and salt the fish, which they do with wonderful dexterity and skill.

Hideous, indeed, looks a group of these women, defiled from head to foot with herring garbage, and laughing and talking volubly, while gulls innumerable float above them, and fill the air with their discordant screams. But look at them when their work is over, and they are changed indeed. Always cleanly, and generally smartly, dressed, they parade the roads and wharf. Numbers of them are old and ill-favored,

---

* A cran holds rather more than a herring-barrel, and the average value of a cran-measure of herrings is about one pound sterling.

but you will see among them many a blooming cheek and beautiful eye. Their occupation is a profitable one, especially if they be skillful; for they are paid according to the amount of work they do.

It is the custom of most of the east-country fishers to bring over their own women—one to every boat, sleeping among the men, and generally related to one or more of the crew. We have met many of these girls, some of them very pretty, and could vouch for their perfect purity. Besides their value as cooks, they can gut herrings and mend nets; but their chief recommendation in the eyes of the canny fishermen is that they are kith and kin, while the natives are strangers "no' to be trusted." The east-country fisherman, on his arrival, invariably encamps on shore, and the girl or woman "keeps the house" for the whole crew.

For the fisherman of the east coast likes to be comfortable. He is at once the most daring and the most careful. He will face such dangers on the sea as would appall most men, while at the same time he is as cautious as a woman in providing against cold and ague. How he manages to move in his clothes is a matter for marvel, for he is packed like a patient after the cold-water process. Only try to clothe yourself in all the following articles of attire: pair of stockings, pair of stockings over them half up the leg, to be covered by the long fishing-boots; on the trunk, a thick flannel, covered with an oilskin-vest; on the top of these, an oilskin-coat; next, a mighty muffler to wind round the neck, and bury the chin and mouth; and last of all, the sou'wester! This is the usual costume of an east-country fisherman, and he not only breathes and lives in it, but manages his boat, on the whole, better than any of his rivals on the water. He drags himself along on land awkwardly enough; and on board, instead of rising to walk, he rolls, as it were, from one part of the boat to the other. He is altogether a more calculating dog than the west-country man, more eager for gain, colder and more reticent in all his dealings with human kind.

On our arrival at Loch Boisdale in the *Tern*, there was nothing to redeem the cheerless gloom of the place. We lingered only a few days, during which it blew a violent gale; and then, slipping out of the harbor with the first light, began to work northward along the coast.

CHAPTER XI.

GLIMPSES OF THE OUTER HEBRIDES.

First Glimpse—The Uists and Benbecula—Their Miserable Aspects—Hamish Shaw—Solemnity of the People—Brighter Glimpses—The Western Coast of the Island—Winter-Storm—The Sound of Harris—The Norwegian Skipper—The Fjords—Kelp-burners—View from Kenneth Hill, Loch Boisdale—A Sunset—The Lagoons—Characteristics of the People—Civilized and Uncivilized—Miserable Dwellings—Comfortable Attire—Their Superstitions and Deep Spiritual Life.

A DREARY sky, a dreary fall of rain. Long, low flats, covered with their own damp breath, through which the miserable cattle loomed like shadows. Everywhere lakes and pools, as thickly sown amid the land as islands amid the Pacific waters. Huts, wretched and chilly, scarcely distinguishable from the rock-strewn marshes surrounding them. To the east, the Minch, rolling dismal waters toward the far-off heads of Skye; to the west, the ocean, foaming at the lips, and stretching barren and desolate into the rain-charged clouds.

Such was the first view of Ultima Thule, and such, indeed, are the Outer Hebrides during two or three days out of the seven. Theirs is the land of Utgard-Loke, a lonely outer region, not dear to the gods. There are mountains, but they do not abound, and are unadorned with the softer colors which beautify the inner and more southerly isles. There are no trees, and few flowers. Two-thirds of the herbage lacks the exquisite softness of the true pasture. The peat-bog supplies the place of the meadow, the gray boulders strew the hills in lieu of red heather. The land is torn up everywhere into rocky fjords and desolate lagoons. Where the sea does not reach in an arm, the fresh water comes up and deepens in countless lakes and pools. There are few song-birds, even the thrush being rare; but the wild-goose screams overhead, and the ice-duck haunts the gloaming with its terribly human "Calloo! calloo!"

The islands of Uist, with Benbecula between, extend from the Sound of Harris as far south as Barra, and appear to have originally formed one unbroken chain; and still, indeed, at low ebbs, a person might almost walk dryshod from Loch Boisdale to Loch Maddy. On the eastern side, and here and there in the interior, there are high hills, such as Hecla and Ben Eval; and everywhere on the eastern coast reach long arms of the sea, winding far into the land, and sometimes, as in the case of Loch Eport, reaching to the very fringe of the Western Ocean. The land is, for the most part, low and unfertile, but there are a few breezy uplands and fine moors. All along the western side of the islands stretches a blank coast-line, unbroken by loch or haven, however small; and above it rises a broad tract of hillocks, composed of snow-white sand and powdered sea-shells, and covered by dry green pasture. Washed and winnowed out of the deep bed of the ocean, driven in and piled up by the great waters, the sands and shells gather year after year, and, mixing with the moister soil of the interior, yield an arable and fertile soil.

To the mind of Hamish Shaw, who has been here many a year herring-fishing, these features of the land are quite without interest or excuse. "It's a poor, miserable country," he avers; " little use to man ! " And this, by the way, is the standard by which Shaw measures all the things of this world—their greater or less utility to the human. He has a sneer for every hill, however high, that will not graze sheep. A seagull or a hawk he would destroy pitilessly, because it cannot be converted into food. He is angry with the most picturesque fjords, until it can be shown that the herring visit them, or that the hill-burns that flow into them afford good trout. All this is the more remarkable in a man so thoroughly Celtic, so strangely spiritual in his reasonings, so pure with the purity of the race. There is a fresh life grafted on his true nature. Inoculated early with the love for commerce, he most admires cultivated land-scenery of any kind but that original nature which delights in the wild and picturesque is still unconsciously nourished by the ever various sea whereon he earns his bread.

Hamish Shaw's charge against the Long Island is substantial enough; the country is poor, and neither fat nor fertile. The harvest is very early and very poor. There is an excellent shield against cold, in the shape of beds of excellent peat, sometimes twenty feet in depth, and there is a certain provision against famine in the innumerable shell-fish which cover the numberless shores. The tormentil, properly pounded and prepared, furnishes a first-rate tan for cow or horse leather, of which the people make shoes. The land is, for the most part, little better than waste land, but there is good pasturage for sheep.

The people, on the first view, seem slow and listless, overshadowed, too, with the strange solemnity of the race. There is no smile on their faces. Young and old drag their limbs, not as a Lowlander drags his limbs, but lissomly, with a swift, serpentine motion. The men are strong and powerful, with deep-set eyes and languid lips, and they never excite themselves over their labor. The women are weak and plain, full of a calm, domestic trouble, and they work harder than their lords. "A poor, half-hearted people!" says the pilot; "why don't they till the land and fish the seas?"

Here, again, the pilot has his reasons. The people are half-hearted—say, an indolent people. They do no justice to their scraps of land, which, poor as they be, are still capable of great improvement; but their excuse is that they derive little substantial benefit from improvements made where there is only yearly tenure. They hunger often, even when the fjords opposite their own door are swarming with cod and ling; but it is to be taken into consideration that only a few of them live on the seashore or possess boats. They let the ardent east-country fishermen carry off the finest hauls of herring. Their work stops when their mouths are filled, and yet they are ill-content to be poor.

All this, and more than this, is truth, and sad truth. Hamish has a strong bill against both country and people. But there is another and finer side to the truth. The watery wastes of Uist gather powerfully on the imagination, and the curious race that inhabit them grow upon the heart.

At the first view, as we have said, all is dreary —sky, land, water; but, after a little time, after the mind has got the proper foreground for these new prospects, the feeling changes from one of total depression into a sense of peculiar magic. Instead of dull, flat pools, the lagoons assume their glory of many-colored weeds and innumerable water-lilies; out of the dreary peat-bog rise delicate vapors that float in fantastic shapes up the hill-side; the sun peeps out, and the mossy hut sends its blue smoke into the clear, still air; all changes, and every nook of the novel prospect has a beauty of its own.

His must be a strange soul who, wandering over these hillocks, and gazing westward and seaward in calm weather, is not greatly awed and moved. There is no pretense of effect, no tremendousness, no obtrusive sign of power. The sea is glassy smooth, the long swell does not break at all, until, reaching the smooth sand, it fades softly, with deep, monotonous moan. Here and there, sometimes close to land, sometimes far out seaward, a horrid reef slips its black back through the liquid blue, or a single rock emerges, tooth-like, thinly edged with foam. Southward loom the desolate heights of Barra, with crags and rocks beneath, and although there is no wind, the ocean breaks there with one broad and frightful flash of white. The sea-sound in the air is faint and solemn; it does not cease at all. But what deepens most the strangeness of the scene, and weighs most sadly on the mind, is the pale, sick color of the sands. Even on the green heights, the wind and rain have washed out great hollows, wherein the powdered shells are drifted like snow. You are solemnized as if you were walking on the great bed of the ocean, with the serene depths darkening above you. You are ages back in time, alone with the great forces antecedent to man; but humanity comes back upon you creepingly, as you think of wanderers out upon that endless waste, and search the dim sea-line in vain for a sail.

Calm like this is even more powerful than the storm. Under that stillness you are afraid of something—nature, death, immortality, God. But at the rising of the winds rises the savage within you: the blood flows, the heart throbs, the eyes are pinched close, the mouth shut tight. You can resist now as mortal things resist. Lifted up into the whirl of things, life is all; the stillness—nature, death, God—is naught.

Terrific, nevertheless, is the scene on these coasts when the storm-wind rises,

"Blowing the trumpet of Euroclydon."

Westward, above the dark sea-line, rise the purple-black clouds, driving with a tremendous scurry eastward, while fresh vapors rise swiftly to fill up the rainy gaps they leave behind them. As if at one word of command, the waters rise and roar, their white crests, towering heavenward, glimmering against the driving mist. Lightning, flashing out of the sky, shows the long line of breakers on the flat sand, the reefs beyond, the foamy tumult around the rocks southward. Thunder crashes afar, and the earth reverberates. So mighty is the wind at times that no man can stand erect before it; houses are thrown down, boats lifted up and driven about like faggots. The cormorants, ranged in rows along their solitary cliffs, eye the wild waters in silence, starving for lack of fish, and even the nimble seagull beats about, screaming, unable to make way against the storm.

These are the winter gales—the terror alike of husbandmen and fishers. The west-wind begins to blow in October, and gradually increases in strength, till all the terrors of the tempest are achieved. Hail-storms, rain-storms, snow-storms alternate, with the terriffc wind trumpeting between; though the salt sea-breath is so potent, even in severe seasons, that the lagoons seldom freeze and the snow will not lie. The wild, wandering birds—the hooper, the beangoose, the gray-lag, all the tribes of ducks—gather together on the marshes, sure of food here, though the rest of the north be frozen. The great Arctic seal sits on Haskier and sails through the Sound of Harris. Above the wildest winds are heard the screams of birds.

Go, in December, to the Sound of Harris, and on some stormy day gaze on the wild scene around you; the whirling waters, sown everywhere with isles and rocks—here the tide foaming round and round in an eddy powerful enough to drag along the largest ship—there a huge patch of seaweed staining the waves, and betraying the lurking reef below. In the distance loom the hills of Harris, blue-white with snow, and hidden ever and anon in flying mist. Watch the terrors of the great sound—the countless reefs and rocks, the eddies, the furious, wind-swept waters; and pray for the strange seaman whose fate it may be to drive helpless thither. Better the great ocean, in all its terror and might. Yet, through that fatal gap, barks, though unpiloted, have more than once driven safely. Into Loch Maddy, while we were lying there, dashed a water-logged vessel, laden with wood, from Norway. Caught by tempests off the Butt of Lewis, she had run down the western coast of the Outer Hebrides, and was in dire distress, when, as a last resource, it was determined to take the Sound. No man on board knew the place, and it was impossible to send on shore for a pilot. On they drove, the skipper working with his men, the lead-line constantly going, the watches at bow and at masthead singing out whenever any dangerous spot loomed in view. All along the coast gathered the island people, expecting every moment to see the vessel dashed to pieces; and to the skipper's frenzied eye they were *wreckers* watching for their prey. For a miracle, the vessel went safely through, without so much as a scratch. The skipper, with bleeding hands and tearful eyes, brought his ship into Maddy. All his stores were gone, save a few barrels of gin, and these he contrived to exchange for common necessaries. Though it was still wild weather, and though his vessel was quite unseaworthy, he was bent on pushing forward to Liverpool. Off he went, and after a day's absence returned again, wild and anxious. He had beaten as far as Barra Head, and being checked there by a gale from the southwest, had been compelled to return as he had come. Again he drove forth, and disappeared; and again he reappeared, wilder than ever, but as indomitable. The wind had once more checked him off Barra, and hurled him back to Loch Maddy. He started a third time, and did not return. It is to be hoped that he reached his destination in safety, and that when he next goes afloat, it will be in a better vessel.

To the mind of a seaman, such coasts as that of the Long Island can scarcely look attractive or kindly; for his quick eye perceives all the danger, all the ghastly plotting against his life. Yet in the summer-time the broad and sandy western tracts are very beautiful in their luxuriant vegetation, covered with daisies, buttercups, and the lesser orchids, brightly intermingled with the flowers of the white clover. They are quite pastoral and peaceful, despite their proximity to the great waters.

Indeed, the place is full of attractions, directly the vulgar feeling is abandoned, and the mind, instead of waiting to be galvanized by some powerful effect, quietly resigns itself to the spirit of the scene. Sight-seeing is like dram-drinking, and the sight-seer, like the dram-drinker, is not particular about the quality, so long as the dose of stimulant is strong and stiff.

The typical tourist, who goes into ecstasies over the Trossachs, and crawls wondering under the basaltic columns of Staffa, would not, perhaps, be particularly stimulated at first by a pull up one of the numberless fjords which eat their winding way into the eastern coasts of the Outer Hebrides. The far-off hills around

Skiport and Maddy are not tall enough for such a modern, and the sea is dull, not being sensational, but old-fashioned. We, on the other hand, who find it unnecessary to rush far for wonders, and who are apt to be blind to nature's more obtrusive beauties, have a greater liking for these quaint old fjords than for the showy Trossachs or the splendid Glencoe. To float through them alone, in a small boat, on a quiet summer gloaming, is marvellously strange and eerie; for they are endless, arm growing out of arm just as the bourne seems reached; winding and interwinding, sometimes only a few feet in depth, at others broad and deep—and at every point of vantage there is something new to look upon. Some idea of the windings of the tides may be gained from the statement that Loch Maddy in North Uist, although covering only ten square miles, possesses a line of coast which, measuring all the various islands, creeks, and bays, has been calculated to ramify over three hundred miles. For picturesque sea depths, swarming with rare aquatic plants, and for variety of strange sea-birds, these fjords are unmatched in Britain; and they are characterized by wonderful effects of sun and mist, rainbow apparitions, fluent lights and shadows. Pleasant it is, in still weather, to lean over the boat's side and watch the crystal water-world in some quiet nook, vari-colored with rocks, weeds, and floating tangle, and haunted by strange images of life. You are back in the great crustacean era, when man was not. Innumerable shell-fish, many of rare beauty, surround you; wondrous monsters, magnified by the water, stare at you with their mysterious eyes, till Humanity fades out of sight. When you raise your head, you are dazzled, and almost tremble at the new sense of life.

Ever and anon, in the course of these aquatic rambles, you meet a group of kelp-burners gathered on a headland or promontory; and a capital study it would make for an artist with some little Rembrandtish mastery over the shadows. Clouding the background of cold, blue sky, the thick smoke rises from their black fire, and the men move hither and thither, in and out of the vapor, raking the embers together, piling the dry seaweed by armsful on to the sullen flames. As they flit to and fro, their wild Gaelic cries seem foreign and unearthly, and their unkempt hair and ragged garments loom strangely through the foul air. On the hill slope above them, where a rude road curves to the shore, a line of carts, each horse guided by a woman, comes creaking down to the wood-strewn beach to gather tangle for drying. The women, with their coarse serge petticoats kilted high and colored handkerchiefs tied over their heads, stride like men at the horses' heads, and shriek the beasts forward.

Standing on Kenneth Hill, a rocky elevation on the north side of Loch Boisdale, and looking westward on a summer day, one has a fine glimpse of Boisdale and its lagoons, stretching right over to the edge of the Western Ocean, five miles distant. The inn and harbor, with the fishing-boats therein, make a fine foreground, and thence the numerous ocean fjords, branching this way and that like the stems of seaweeds, stretch glistening westward into the land. A little inland, a number of huts cluster, like beavers' houses, on the site of a white highway; and along the highway peasant men and women, mounted or afoot, come wandering down to the port. Far as the eye can see the land is quite flat and low, scarcely a hillock breaking the dead level until the rise of a row of low sandhills on the very edge of the distant sea. The number of fjords and lagoons, large and small, is almost inconceivable; there is water everywhere, still and stagnant to the eye, and so constant is its presence that the mind can scarcely banish the fancy that this land is some floating, half-substantial mass, torn up in all places to show the sea below. The highway meanders through the marshes until it is quite lost on the other side of the island, where all grows greener and brighter, the signs of cultivation more noticeable, the human habitations more numerous. Far away, on the long black line of the marshes, peeps a spire, and the white church gleams below, with school-house and hovels clustering at its feet.

A prospect neither magnificent nor beautiful, yet surely full of fascination; its loneliness, its piteous human touches, its very dreariness, win without wooing the soul. And if more be wanted, wait for the rain—some thin, cold "smurr" from the south, which will clothe the scene with gray mist, shut out the distant sea, and brooding, over the desolate lagoons, draw from them pale and beautiful rainbows, which come and go, dissolve and grow, swift as the colors in a kaleidoscope, touching the dreariest snatches of water and waste with all the wonders of the prism. Or if you be a fair-weather voyager, afraid of wetting your skin, wait for the sunset. It will not be such a sunset as you have been accustomed to on English uplands or among high mountains, but something sullener, stranger, and more sad. From a long, deep bar of cloud, on the far-off ocean horizon, the sun will gleam round and red, hanging as if moveless, scarcely tinting the deep, watery shadow of the sea, but turning every lagoon to blood. There will be a stillness as if Nature held her breath. You will have no sense of pleasure or wonder—only hushed expectation, as if something were going to happen; but if you are a saga-reader, you will remember the death of Balder, and mutter the rune. Such sunsets, alike yet ever different, we saw, and they are not to be forgotten. Then most deeply did the soul feel itself in the true land of the glamour, shut out wholly from the fantasies of mere fairyland or the grandeurs of mere spectacle. The clouds may shape themselves into the lurid outlines of the old gods, crying

   Suinken i Gruus er
   Midgards stad !

the mist on the margins of the pools may become the gigantic witch-wife, spinning out lives on her bloody distaff, and croaking a prophecy; but gentler things may not intrude, and the happy sense of healthy life dies utterly away.

 Pleasant it is, after such an hour, to wander across the bogs and marshes, and come down on the margin of a little lake, while the homeward passing cattle low in the gloaming. You are now in fairyland. With young buds yellow, and flowers as white as snow, floating freely among the floating leaves, the water-lilies gather, and catch the dusky silver of the moon. The little dab-chick cries, and you see her sailing, a black speck, close to shore, and splashing the pool to silver where she dives. The sky clears, and the still spaces between the lilies glisten with stars whose broken rays shimmer like hoarfrost and touch with crystal the edges of leaves and flowers. You are a child at once, and think of Oberon.

Neither more nor less than we have described them are the Outer Hebrides; a few mountains, endless stretches of peat bogs and small lagoons, a long tract of shell-sand hillocks, all environed, eaten into, and perpetually shapened afresh by the never resting sea—

> "Hebrid isles,
> Set far amid the melancholy main."

Like all such children of the sea, they flit from mood to mood, sometimes terrible, sometimes miserable, peaceful occasionally, but never highly gay. Half the year round they are misted over by the moist oceanic rains—in winter the sea strews them anew with sea-weeds, shells, and drift timber—and for a few days in the year they bask in a glassy sea and behold the midsummer sun.

The rafters of most of the dwellings on the seashore are composed of the great logs of drift-wood which find their way over the ocean to the western coasts— mighty trees, with stumps of roots and branches still remaining, wafted from the western continents. Many of these trunks are covered with the foliage of seaweed, and adorned with barnacles—which, it is still popularly believed, are geese in the embryo. Others are the masts and yards of ships.

As has before been noted, the people of these isles are very poor. Their chief regular occupation, not a very profitable one now, is the manufacture of kelp; but they work during a portion of the year at the cod, ling and herring fisheries. At certain seasons of the year, they reap an excellent harvest out of the cuddies, or young lithe, which appear on the coast in numbers nearly as great as the herring fry. They are taken by thousands in long bag nets tied to the end of a long pole. In hard times the people subsist almost entirely on shell-fish, such as cockles and mussels, which abound on the endless sea-coast. Most of them have small crofts, and a few of them are able to keep cows. Here and there reside wealthy tacksmen, who rent large farms, employ a good deal of labor, and people the wastes with cattle and sheep. These tacksmen rule the land with quite arbitrary sway. In their hands lies the welfare of the population. Many of them appear to be honest, kindly men, but there are evidences that some of them still keep their dependents as "scallags," in virtual slavery.

Walk from one end of the Uists to the other and you will not meet a smiling face. It is not that the people are miserable, though they might be happier; nor is it that they are apathetic, though they could be more demonstrative. With one and all of them life is a solemn business; they have little time for sport —indeed, their disposition is not sportive. You must not joke with them—they do not understand; not because they are stupid, not because they are suspicious of your good faith, but merely because their visions, unlike the visions of brilliant races, are steady rather than fitful—seeing the world and things under one changeless ray of light, instead of by wonderful flashes. From the beginning to the end they have the same prospect, without summer, without flowers. Wild mirth-making in such a world would look like mountebanking among graves.

Yet how tender they are! how exquisitely fresh and kind! They are the most home-loving people in the world; that is one of the chief reasons why they do not venture more on the water at greater distances from the family croft. One meal under the dear old roof, with the women and the little ones gathered aroundabout, is sweeter than a dozen at a distance or on board ship; hard fare and sorry sleeping in a hut on the waste, where the wife can rear her young and the old mother spin in the ingle, is to be preferred to fine service and good clothes anywhere else in the world. There is an old Gaelic saying common here, "A house without the cry of bairns is like a farm without kye or sheep." Next to this love of home, this yearning to be the center of a little circle, there dwells in the people of the islands a passionate fondness for localities. Uist is brighter to most than any promised land, however abundant the store of milk and honey. They know the place is bare and desolate, they know that it becomes a sore, sore pinch to live on the soil, but they know also that their fathers lived here before them, wedded here, died here, and (they fervently believe) went virtuously to heaven from here. True, some of the younger and livelier spirits express their willingness to emigrate, and do emigrate occasionally, exhibiting under the influence of liquor plentifully distributed all the signs of exhilaration; but such are exceptions, corrupted youngsters, caught too early by the yellow itch of gold. Nothing is more noticeable in these islands than the demoralizing influence of civilization on the race. The farther one recedes from the seaports, from the large farms of the wealthy tacksman, from the domain of the shopkeeper and the schoolmaster, the brighter do the souls of the cotters grow, the opener their hands, the purer their morals, and the happier their homes. Whenever the great or little Sassenach comes, he leaves a dirty trail like the slime of the snake. He it is who abuses the people for their laziness, points sneeringly at their poor houses, spits scorn on their wretchedly cultivated scraps of land; and he it is who, introducing the noble goad of greed, turns the ragged domestic virtues into well-dressed prostitutes, heartless and eager for hire. In the whole list of jobbers, excepting only the "mean whites" of the Southern States of America, there are few paltrier follows than the men who stand by Highland doors and interpret between ignorance and the great proprietors. They libel the race they do not understand, they deride the affections they are too base to cultivate, they rob and plunder, and would exterminate wholly, the rightful masters of the soil. They are the agents of civilization in such places as the Outer Hebrides; so that, if God does not help the civilized, it is tolerably clear that the Devil will.

In the islands, beware of the civilized. The cultivated islander, like the Sassenach, gives you nothing in kindliness, charges you double for everything, and sees you go without any grief save that of half-satisfied greed. Recollect, nevertheless, that he is doing well, tills his ground well, and by-and-by, perhaps, will keep a little store, going on from little to big trading, till he owns both land and boats. The poor, uncivilized islander, on the other hand, makes you welcome to his hearth, gives you "bite and sup" of the best, talks to you with free heart and honest sympathy, and is only hurt and pained if you try to repay hospitality with money. No matter how poor the hut, the stranger must have something—if not a drink of milk, the croft being too poor to support a cow, at least a draught of water in a clean basin. And the smile that sweetens such gifts is like Christ's turning water into wine. We shall not soon forget the pain and indignation of an old islander, while telling of his experience once in the Lowlands. He had been walking far, and was very thirsty, when he descried a snug cottage, with a clean, sonsy housewife standing on the threshold. "Good wife," he said, after the usual greeting, "I am very dry; can you give me a drink of milk?" "We have nae milk," was the reply. "A drink of water then," said the wanderer. "Aweel," said the woman, "if you like i'll show ye the *well*, but we *hae to fetch the water oursel's!*" "My father and my mother," said our informant, after recounting the anecdote—"my father and my mother would have risen screeching from their graves, had I greeted the stranger at their door with such a speech."

Such are some of the people's virtues—philoprogenitiveness (rather a doubtful virtue this in the eyes of some political economists!), honesty, hospitality. Note, too, a few of their faults, or, as some would say, their vices. Their stanchest friend cannot say that they are over-clean. They will sometimes litter like pigs, when by a little trouble they might live like human beings; and they do not always comb their hair. Then, again, they don't and won't go in for "improvements." The house their parents lived in is good enough for them—a herring-barrel is good enough for a chimney, clay is good enough for a floor. They would feel chilly in a bigger dwelling. They are used to the thick peat-smoke, the pig by the fire, the hens on the rafters—perhaps, too, in the season, the calf in a corner. A philosopher may say —" Why not ? "

One picture of a cottage may be as good as a dozen. Imagine, then, a wall, five or six feet thick, tapering inward, and thereon, springing about a foot within the outer edge of the wall, a roof of turf and thatch, held down by heather ropes set close together, and having at either ends great stones about twenty pounds in weight. The interior is divided by a wooden partition into two portions, the " but " and the " ben." The calf is in a corner, and the hens roost on the beams overhead. The floor is clay, baked hard with the heat of the peat fire. The roof is soot-black, having a hole in the top, with a herring barrel for a chimney. From the center descends a heavy chain, with a hook at the end whereon to hang the great black kettle. The mistress of the house squats on her hams at the door, and, leaning her cheek on her hands, watches you approach. The pig is paddling in the puddle close by. Perhaps, if the house is prosperous, the pony is grazing a short distance, with his forelegs tied to prevent his running away.

A stranger, wandering here, will be struck by the fact that, although the dwellings are so wretched, the dress of the poor inhabitants is remarkably good, showing few signs of poverty. Almost, all wear homespun, and as much of it as possible—stout, coarse tweeds for the men, and thick flannels for the women. Nearly every house has a spinning-wheel, many houses possess a loom; a few have both; and a busy sight it is to see the comely daughter working at the loom, while the mother spins at her side, and even the man knits himself a pair of stockings while he smokes his pipe in the corner. The men, as well as the women are excellent weavers.

Another point that will strike a stranger, in the Uists especially, is the enormous number of ponies. Where they come from, what they are useful for, we have been unable to find out; but they literally swarm, and must be a serious encumbrance to the population. We were offered a splendid little filly for thirty shillings.

Thus far nothing has been said of the deep, inner life of this people. Little as we have seen, and less as we understand, of *that*, we see and understand enough for great emotion. Put the spiritual nature aside in estimating capabilities, and you exclude all that is greatest and most significant. Now, directly the mental turn of the islanders is apprehended, it is clear at a glance why they must inevitably sink and perish in the race with the southerner or east-countryman. They are too ruminant by nature, too slow to apprehend new truths. They are saddened by a deep, clinging sense that the world is haunted. They have faith in witchcraft, in prophecy, in charms. If a stranger looks too keenly at a child, they pray God to avert " the evil eye." They believe that gold and gems are hidden in obscure corners of the hills, but that only supernatural powers know *where*. They have seen the " Men of Peace," or Scottish fays, with blue bonnets on their heads, pushing from shore the boat that is found adrift days afterward. Some of their old women retain the second sight. Strange sounds—sometimes like human voices, at others like distant bagpipes—are heard about their dwellings when any one is going to die. they tremble at the side of " fairy wells." They have the Gruagach, or Banshee. In short, they have a credulous turn of mind, not entirely disbelieving, even when they know the evidence to be very doubtful, for they aver that the world is fuller of wonders than any one man knows.* In their daily life, at births, at weddings, at funerals, they keep such observances as imply a deep sense of the pa-

---

* MacCulloch, writing in 1824 speaks of such superstitions as virtually extinct over all the Highlands. "The Highlanders," he says,"now believe as much as their Pictish and Saxon neighbors;" and he proceeds, in his usual silly fashion, to rake up all

thetic nature of human ties. The voices of winds and waters are in their hearts, and they passionately believe in God.

It is still the custom, in the Uists and in Barra, to gather together on the long winter nights, and listen to the strange stories recited by aged men and women. These stories have been handed down from generation to generation, and are very curious indeed, dealing with traditions obviously originating in pre-historic periods.* The listeners know all about Ossian and Fingal, and regard them almost as real beings. Here and there in the islands reside men famous for their good stories, of which they are very proud. Some of them are familiar with ancient poems, full of sea sounds and the cries of the wind. With these stories and poems—tales of enchanted lands and heavenly music—they keep their hearts up in a desolate and lonely world; but on all such subjects they are very silent to the stranger, until he has managed to win their confidence and disarm their pride.

the large names he can muster, for the purpose of showing that their superstitions were always plagiarisms of the most commonplace kind With his usual felicity in quoting at random, he throws no light whatever on the subject. We wonder if he ever came in contact with a Celt of the true breed. Doubtless; but, lacking insight, he saw no speculation in the visionary eyes. Even a long night's talk with Hamish Shaw would have had no effect on this queer compound of pedantry and skittishness—this man of prodigious Latinisms and elephantine jokes. Yet his letters were addressed to Walter Scott, who was doubtless much edified by their familiarity and endless verbiage.

* For a full feast of Highland legends of the traditional kind, consult Mr. Campbell's " Popular Tales."

With such a people, religion is naturally a vital thing, important as life itself. The poor women will travel miles on miles to hear mass, or (if Protestants) to take the communion. It is held an evil thing to miss religious ceremonial on the Sabbath. In all affairs of joy or sorrow, there is one straight appeal to the Fountain-Head—the Lord God who reigns in heaven. Dire is the suffering that can be borne when the sufferer is told by the priest that it is "God's will."

What dullness! what a civilization! How inferior are these benighted beings to their instructors—the petty tradesmen and the small factors! How blessed will the islands be when the present demoralizing influences are withdrawn, and the paupers possess in their place the huckster's scales and the grocer's tallow candle!

CHAPTER XII.

SPORT IN THE WILDS.

Sealguir thu mar a mharbhas thu Geadh a's Corr' a's Crotach.—"O sportsman, when killest thou goose, and heron, and curlew?"—*Highland Proverb.*

The Sportsmen and their Dog—The Hunter's Badge—The Weapons—Shooting in the Fjords—Eiders, Cormorants, Curlews—Duck-Shooting near Loch Boisdale—The *Tern* at Anchor in Lock Huport—Starvation—Wild-Goose Shooting on Loch Bee—The Shepherd's Gifts—Goose-Shooting on Loch Phlogibeg—The Melancholy Loch—Breeding-Places of the Wild-Fowl—Rain-Storm—"Bonny Kilmeny"—Short Rations—The Passing Ship—Red Deer, Salmon, and Eagles—Corbies and Ravens—Seal-Shooting in the Maddy Fjords—Reflection on Wild Sports in General.

IF the gentle reader be a sportsman of the usual breed, serious, professional, perfect in training, a dead shot at any reasonable distance, and at any object, from a snipe to a buffalo, it is with no respectful feelings that he will hear of our hunting raids through the Highland wilds. We were three—the Wanderer, Hamish Shaw, and the dog Schneider, so named in a fit of enthusiasm, after seeing Mr. Jefferson's "Rip Van Winkle." The Wanderer would have been a terrible fellow in the field if he had not been short-sighted, and in the habit of losing his spectacles. As it is, he was at least terribly in earnest, and could contrive to hit a large object, if he did not aim at it with any particular attempt to be accurate. Hamish Shaw was not great at flying game, but he was mightily successful in sneaking up for close shots at unsuspecting and *sitting* conies, and his eye was as sharp as a backwoodsman's in picking up objects at a distance. The third member of the party, Schneider, the dog, was of the gentler sex, wayward, willful, for the lack of careful training during her infancy, apt to take her own way in hunting matters, until brought to a due sense of decorum by a vigorous application of the switch. She was, in fact, a noble specimen of the species Briggs, having been trained by the Wanderer himself, with the usual triumphant result in such cases; so that, if no sheep caught her eye, and a keen watch was kept upon her movements, she could be depended on for a stalk or a chase quite as much as either of her masters. Though she could not point or set, she was a tolerable retriever, and few dogs of any kind could match her for long and steady labor in the water.

Now, it was the fixed determination of the Wanderer, on again roaming northward, once and forever to prove his title to the hunter's badge, by killing, according to the requirements of the old Highland formula, a red deer, a salmon, an eagle, a seal, and a wild-swan, every one of which he religiously swore to skin and stuff as eternal credentials, testifying unmistakably that he was a man of prowess in the field. All these, of course, had to be slain single-handed, unaided by any more complicated weapons of destruction than the rifle, the fowling-piece, and the rod. Cunningly enough, he had fixed on Uist and the adjacent islands as an excellent place to begin his labors, and perhaps achieve the crowning honors of them all. The red deer, he knew, were certainly not numerous there; but the system of stalking them places the possibilities strongly in favor of the hunter, who lies securely hidden, close to one of the paths the game is sure to take when driven by boatmen from the adjacent small islands where they feed. Salmon were plentiful in the great lochs communicating with the sea, and in some of the larger rivers. The lesser seals swarmed at all times, while during winter even the great Arctic monster brooded on Haskeir, and played splashingly at leapfrog through the Sound of Harris. Here and there, hovering over the inaccessible peaks, poised the eagle, in all the glory of his freedom, while the ravens croaked jealously on the shadowy crags below. As for the hoopers, solitary specimens had been known to alight on the lonely lochans even during the sunny season, and in winter the huge migratants landed in swarms—no very difficult mark for the hunter's bullet or "swan-post."

These were the mighty game, the hierarchy of the hunter's heaven—beautiful, distant, not readily to be won, until drawn down by the music of the whizzing ball. But the Wanderer was not proud; he had an eye to lesser game, and being inoculated at that time with the least bit of the naturalist's enthusiasm, he longed greedily for additions to his museum. Wherefore the eider-duck, and the merganser, and the grebe, and all the various tribes of sea-birds and land-birds, were carefully marked for addition to the list of specimens culled by that steadfast hand. Then there was the cabin-table to be catered for; and rapturously was it noted that wild-ducks, and plovers, and moor-fowl, and conies were numerous in all the islands, and that the monster wild-goose, a still more noble quarry, was breeding in seeming security in the hearts of all the greater moorland lochs.*

* In that curious and scarce little book on the Western Hebrides, published by the Rev. John Lane Buchanan, in 1793, there is a marvelous account of the ornithological treasures to be found in the islands. The naïveté with which the reverend gentleman retails his wonders is very comical:

"The species of land and sea-fowls over all this country," he begins, "are too many to be mentioned in so limited a work as this. Tarmachans, plovers, blackbirds, starlings (or dimddan), red muir cocks and hens, ducks and wild-geese by thousands, particularly on the plains of South Uist, and elsewhere; woodcocks, snipes, ravens, carrion-crows, herons, bats, owls, all kinds of hawks and eagles, so large and strong, that they carry off lambs, kids, fawns, and the weaker kind of sheep and foals. They have been known to attack even cows, horses, and stags; and their nests are frequently found to be plentifully supplied with fish, which, in what are called plays of fish, they pick up from the surface of the sea.

" A species of robbery, equally singular and cruel, was lately practised in this country very commonly, and sometimes at this day, in which the eagles are the principal actors. The thieves, coming upon the eaglets in their nests, in the absence of their dams, sew up the extremity of the great gut; so that the poor creatures, tortured by obstructions, express their sense of pain in frequent and loud screams. The eagle, imagining their cries to proceed from hunger, is unwearied in the work of bringing in fresh prey, to satisfy, as he thinks, their craving appetites. But all that spoil is carried home by the thieves at night, when they come to give a momentary relief to the eaglets, for the purpose of prolonging, for their own base ends, their miserable existence.

These were the weapons: a Snider rifle, a double-barrel breech-loader, good for stopping small game on the hillsides; and a long shoulder duck-gun, Big Benjamin by name, good for any or every thing at a hun-

This infernal practice is now wearing fast away, being strictly watched by the gentlemen, and severely punished. Mr. MacKenzie, for every eagle killed in Lewis, gives a half-crown. One of those large eagles was taken in the Isle of Herries, at Tarbert, together with a large turbot, in which the animal had fastened its talons, when asleep at the surface of the water, so as not to be able to disengage them. The eagle, with his large wings expanded like sails, drove before the wind into the harbor, where he was taken alive (his feet being entangled in the turbot) by the country people.

"Birds of passage, of several kinds, are seen over all the isles. Swans, cuckoos, swallows, lapwings, plovers, etc., and wild-fowls of several kinds, rendered tame, are often seen about the yards, dunghills, and doors of houses, among the poultry.

"The *Bishop Carara*, or *Bunubbuachil*, is larger than any goose, of a brown color, the inside of the wing white, the bill long and broad. It dives quicker than any other bird. It was never known to fly, the wings being too short to carry a weight seldom under but often above, sixteen pounds.

"The black cormorant is not held in much estimation by the islanders; but such as have white feathers in their wings, and white down on their bodies, are famous for making soup or broth of a delicate taste and flavor.

"The Western Hebrides abound in solan-geese, seagulls, and singing-ducks, of a size somewhat less than that of common ducks. They are constantly employed, either in diving for sand-eels, which are of a speckled color, like leeches, or in sitting together in flocks, and singing, which is heard at the distance of half a mile, and is accounted very pleasing music.

"The duck called the Crawgiabh, is larger than a Muscovy duck, and almost tame—you may approach very near it before it takes wing—and is frequently kept by gentlemen among the other poultry.

dred yards, and certain, if loaded with the due amount of shot and powder, to stretch low the unwary shooter with its sharp recoil. Then there was the rod, a slight thing, but clever and pliant, besides being very portable, and the six or seven kinds of flies—the dark wild-drake's wing, with white tip, being found the

"*Rain-Goose.*—This fowl is always heard at a great distance before a storm; it is almost as large as a goose.

"*Drillechan,* or Water-Magpie.—This bird is larger than a land-magpie, beautifully speckled, with a long, sharp, and strong bill, red as blood. It never swims, but flies from place to place, following the ebb, picking up spout-fish. They are silent during the flow of the tide, and begin to whistle the moment it turns.

"*Starnags.*—This bird appears in spring on these coasts, about the size of a hawk, with long, sharp-pointed wings, extremely noisy and daring. They are speckled, but the prevailing color is white.

"*Fasgatar.*—This bird is of blackish-blue, as large as a hawk, and is constantly pursuing the starnags through the air, to force them to throw out of their mouths whatever they have eaten; and the vile creatures catch every atom of what the others throw out before it reaches the water. It will sometimes venture to sit on any boat, if the passengers have provisions, and throw out any, by way of encouraging its approaches.

"*Wild Doves.*—Every cave and clift is full of wild doves."

The above needs a little comment. The eagle story may be taken at its worth; but the rain-goose and the Bishop Carara fairly puzzle us—unless by the latter is meant the loon. The *drillechan,* which has a bill "as red as blood," and which whistles "at the turn of the tide," is, of course, the little seapie, or oyster-catcher. The *starnags* may be a species of gull, and the *fasgatar,* the herring-hawk, so hateful to honest fishers. As for the *singing-duck,* the only bird at all answering to the description is the *ice-duck,* whose strangely eerie cry is perhaps "pleasing," but, assuredly, very melancholy. "Calloo! calloo!" it moans aloud during windy weather, in a voice like the cry of a child in mortal pain.

finest for trout in all those gloomy waters. Besides these, there was the telescope, taken in preference to a binocular field-glass, as being at once more powerful and more sportsmanlike—but voted a bore in the sequel, always getting lost if carried in the hands, and when slung over the shoulders by a strap, constantly dangling forward in the way of the gun when the shooter stooped, or suddenly loosening at the critical moment, before firing, to scare the purposed victim away with a savage rattle!

There were two ways of hunting—on foot, over the moors, and on water, through the winding fjörds. Of the two, we preferred the latter—deeming it the more enjoyable, and less wearisome to the body.

Floating hither and thither with the lug-sail, a light air guiding the punt surely, though slowly, toward the victims, Hamish at the helm, Schneider fretting in the bottom, the Wanderer crouching with cocked gun in the bows, we soon accumulated specimens of the many species of ducks, the male and female eider, the black guillemot, the herring-hawk, the black scart and green shag, and the calloo. All and each of these birds we roasted and tasted after the skinning, having determined to give a fair trial to every morsel that fell to rod or gun; out of them all, the only eatable birds were the eiders, and to devour *them* with a relish would require an appetite. As for the scart, angels and ministers of grace defend us from that taste again! The rakings of greasiest ship's pantry, the scrapings of the foulest cook's colander, mingled with meat from the shambles and stinking fish from the seashore, could not surpass its savor!

Yet the fishermen praise it hugely, and devour it with greed. At St. Kilda, where the chief diet of the inhabitants consists of sea-fowl, and elsewhere over all the islands, the birds are prized as food exactly in proportion to their fishy and oily taste; the stronger the savor, the more precious the prize.

Of all common birds that fly, commend us to the curlew; for we are by no means of that tribe of sportsmen who like an easy prey, and in our eyes the more difficult the chase the more glorious the sport. The curlew has two noble qualities. Kept till the right minute, cooked to a turn, delicately basted, and served with sweet sauce, it equals any bird that flies, is more delicate than the grouse, richer than the partridge, and plumper than the snipe. Then, still better, it is, without any exception whatever, the most difficult of all English birds to catch unawares, or to entice by any device within shooting distance. It is the watchman of birds—the shyest, the most vigilant, the most calculating. It knows better than yourself how far your gun can carry; and with how mocking and shrill a pipe it rises and wheels away, just as you flatter yourself it is within gunshot! Poor will be your chance at the wild-duck on the shore, if the whaup be near; for his sharp eye will spy you out, as you crawl forward face downward, and at his shrill warning, "whirr" will sound the wings of the quacking flock, as they rise far over your head, and you rise shaking off the dirt and cursing the tell-tale. When a band of curlews alight, be sure that not one avenue of approach is unguarded; look with a telescope, and mark the outlying guards—one high up on a rock, another peering round the corner of a cliff, a third far up on the land, and a last straggler perhaps passing over your own head with a whistle to his brethren. In all our sporting experience—and it has been long, if not glorious—we have known only one of these birds to have been shot *sitting;* and this one was slain on a hillside by Hamish Shaw, who strapt his gun upon his back, and crawled through the heather on his stomach, like a snake!

Let the sportsman who has distinguished himself on the moors or among the turnip fields, and boasts loudly of his twenty brace, try his hand at a day's curlew shooting, and if on a first or second trial he bags enough dinner for a kestrel, we will call him the prince of shooters. In the breeding season only is it possible to shoot this bird easily, without an accurate knowledge of its habits, or much experience of its wary arts; but who destroys the bird-mother or her tender mate?

The Wanderer and Hamish Shaw slew many a whaup in the fjörds at Boisdale. Nowhere in the Highlands were these birds so plentiful—they gathered in great flocks, literally darkening the sky; but nowhere, also, were they shyer and wilder, for the numberless pairs of eyes told hugely against the shooter. A little was done by seeking concealed station, and having the birds driven as much as possible in that direction; but the most successful plan was to row the punt slowly to the spot where the birds thronged the rocks, with their heads and bodies all turned one way, and when they arose screaming, to run the chance of picking off solitary individuals at long distances. It was found that the culew always felt himself perfectly safe flying at eighty or ninety yards; and, with careful shooting and proper loading, Big Benjamin could do wonders at that distance at any tolerably-sized bird *on the wing*.

In the greater inland lochs of Boisdale, while the *Tern* was flying in the harbor, the wild-duck were plentiful, and they were vigorously hunted on two occasions by our sportsmen and the dog. It was not such easy work as duck-shooting often is, for all the shores of the lochs were covered with deep sedge and reeds, stretching out far into the water, and affording safe cover to innumerable coots and dabchicks, as well as to the ducks themselves. Schneider, however, performed famously, swimming and forcing his way through the green forest, till he startled many a bird to the open.

Enough of such ignoble chronicling of small beer. Whaups, wild-ducks dabchicks—these are to be found on every moor and lochan south, as well as north, of the Tweed. But what says the reader to the wild-goose? A more noticeable fellow surely, and well worthy of the sportsman's gun. Even far south in England, in severe weather, you have been startled by the loud "quack, quack, quack," above your head, and looking upward, you have seen, far up in the air, the flock flying swiftly, in the shape of a wedge, wending, God knows whither, with outstretched necks, in noble flight. The tame-goose, the fat, waddling, splay-footed, hissing gosling, all neck and bottom, is an eye-sore, a monstrosity, fit only for the honors of onion-stuffing and apple-sauce, at the Christmas season; but his wild kinsman is Hyperion to a satyr, noble as well as beautiful, winged like an eagle, powerful as a swan, not easily to be slain by Cockney gun, not easily to be surpassed in his grand flight by Cockney imagination. Now, we had long known that the wild-goose bred in the wilds of Uist, and we longed to take him in his lair; and pursue him we did at last, under circumstances most clearly warranting bird-slaughter, if ever such circumstances occurred in our chequered lifetime.

We had been storm-staid for a week in Loch Huport, a lonely sea-fjörd, about midway between Loch Boisdale and Loch Maddy, affording a snug anchorage in one of its numerous bays—Macpherson's Bay by name. So wild were the squalls for days that we could not safely get on shore with the punt, although we were anchored scarcely two hundred yards from land. Now, by sheer blockheadedness, having calculated on reaching Loch Maddy and its shops at least a fortnight before, we had run short of nearly everything—bread, biscuits, sugar, tea, coffee, drink of all kinds; and but for a supply of eggs and milk, brought off at considerable peril from a lonely hut a few miles away, we should have been in sore distress indeed. At last, the Wanderer and Hamish Shaw went off for a forage, with guns and dog, determined, if all else failed, and they could not purchase supplies, to do justifiable murder on a helpless sheep. Though the wind was still high, they sailed up Loch Huport with the punt and lug-sail, and having reached the head of the loch, and drawn the boat up high and dry, they set off on foot with Big Benjamin and the double-barrel.

About five hundred yards distant, and communicating with Loch Huport by a deep, artificial trench, nearly passable by a boat at high tide, lies another smaller loch of brackish water, which, in its turn, communicates, through reedy shallows, with a great loch reaching almost to the Western Ocean. Dean Monro, who visited the place long ago, speaks of the latter as famous for its red mullet—" ane fish the size and shape of ane salmont ; " and it still abounds in both fresh-water and ocean fishes :

> " For to this lake, by night and day
> The great sea-water finds its way,
> Through long, long windings of the hills,
> And drinks up all the pretty rills,
> And rivers large and strong." *

The smaller loch was only about half a mile broad, so the sportsmen determined to separate, each taking one of the banks; Hamish Shaw shouldering Big Benjamin, which was heavily charged with the largest dropshot, and the Wanderer the double-barrel. Shortly after the parting, the Wanderer saw an aged Celt, who was fishing for sethe with bait—coarse twine for a line, and a piece of cork for a float; and this worthy, after recovering from the shock of seeing an armed Sassenach at his shoulder, averred that there were plenty of " geeses " up the loch. " The geeses is big and strong, but she'll only just be beginning to flee awa' "—a statement which we interpreted to mean

* Wordsworth's " Highland Boy."

that the young birds were fully fledged, and able to rise upon their wings.

The shores of the Loch were boggy and covered with deep herbage, with great holes here and there as pitfalls to the unwary pedestrian; and the Wanderer stumbled along for about a mile without seeing so much as the glint of a passing wing. At last, he perceived a small and desolate island, over which two black-backed gulls hovered, screaming at the sight of the stranger. From a corner of this island rose a duck, and sped swiftly, out of gunshot, down the water. The Wanderer waded, sure that it must wheel; and wheel it did, after flying five hundred yards, and passed back close over its head. Down it came, plump as a stone. Alas! only a good duck, with its buff breast and saw-toothed bill; and a mother too, for out from the weedy point of the island, diving in unconcern, paddled her five young, earning their own living already, though they were only wingless little lumps of down. The wanderer bagged his bird disappointedly, for he had been on short rations for days, and had made sure of a mallard.

A cry from Hamish Shaw! He was standing across the water, pointing backward up the Loch, and shouting out a sentence, of which only one word—"geese!"—was audible. The Wanderer crept stealthily to the water's edge, and espied a number of large birds seated on the water a quarter of a mile away. The telescope soon proving the blissful truth that these were "the geese," it was hurriedly arranged in pantomime that Hamish should creep back and press the birds gently forward, without approaching so close as to compel them to rise, while the Wanderer, with his dog, crouched behind a rock on the water's edge, ready to attack the unwary ones as they swam past. "To heel, Schneider—down!" With burning eyes and panting breath crouched the dog; for, thank heaven! it was one of her good days, and not a sheep was nigh.

It was one of those periods of awful suspense known only to the man who shoots—a quarter of an hour of agony—the knees soaking in muddy weeds, the perspiration rolling down the cheeks—an unaccountable and fiercely resisted desire to sneeze suddenly taking possession of the nose—one eye, in an agony, glaring command on the animal, the other peering at the approaching game. And now, horror of horrors! it is beginning to mizzle. The spectacles get misted over every minute, and they are wiped with a hand that trembles like an aspen leaf. Suppose the piece, at the last moment should refuse to go off? A bad cartridge, on this occasion, means no less than semi-starvation! There they are— little more than a hundred yards away—a mighty gander, gray headed and jaunty, leading the way, a female a few yards behind, then another gander and his wife, and lastly four fat young geese, nearly as big as their parents, but duller in their attire and far less curious in their scrutiny of surrounding objects. Hush! the first gander is abreast of us—we have to hold down the dog by main force. We do not fire, for our hearts are set on the young brood; they will be tender—papa will be tough. Perdition! Schneider, driven to frenzy, and vainly trying to escape, utters a low and hideous whine—the old ganders and geese start in horror—they flutter, splash, rise—and there is just time to take rapid aim at one young goose, just dragging itself into the air, when the dog plunges into the water, and the whole portly covey are put to rout.

As the smoke of the gun clears away, all the geese are invisible but one, which lies splashing on the surface, mortally wounded; him Schneider approaches to secure, but, appalled by a hiss, a beat of the wings, a sudden sign of showing fight, turns off and would retreat ignominiously to shore. She has never tackled such a monster since a certain eventful day when she was nearly murdered by another wounded bird, also a goose, but of a different kind—a solan, or a gannet. Dire is the language which the Wanderer hurls at her head, fierce the reproaches, bitter the taunting reminiscences of other mishaps by flood and field; till at last, goaded by mingled shame and wrath, the dog turns, showing her teeth, despatches the foe with one fell snap, and begins trailing him to shore. Meanwhile, the Wanderer hears a loud report in the distance—crash! roar!—unmistakably the voice of Benjamin, adding doubtless to the list of slain.

Flushed with triumph, for at least one meal was secure, the Wanderer slung the spoil over his shoulder, patted the dog in forgiveness of all sins, and made his way over to the other side as rapidly as possible. Arrived there, he looked everywhere for Hamish, but saw no sign of that doughty Celt. At last his eye fell on something white lying among the

heather; and lo! an aged gander, blood-stained,
dead as a stone. Then, emerging from the deep
herbage, rose the head of Shaw—a ghastly sight;
for the face was all cut and covered with blood. An
old story! Held in hands not well used to his ways,
Big Benjamin had taken advantage of the occasion,
and, uttering his diabolical roar, belging forwards
and kicking backwards, had slain a gander, and
nearly murdered a man at the same time.

A little water cleared away the signs of battle,
but Hamish still rubbed his cheek and shoulder,
vowing never to have any more dealings with such
a gun so long as he lived. After a rest and a drop
of water from the flask, tracks were made homeward,
and just as the gloaming was beginning, the fruit of
the forage was triumphantly handed over to the cook
on board the yacht.

Blessings do not come singly. By the side of the
yacht, and nearly as big as herself, was a boat from
shore, offering for sale new potatoes, fresh milk, and
eggs. On board were a shepherd and his wife, who,
living in an obscure bay of the loch, had only just
heard of the yacht's arrival. The man was a little
red-headed fellow, wiry and lissome; his wife might
have passed for a Spanish gipsy, with her straight
and stately body, her dark, fine features and glittering black eyes, and the colored handkerchief
setting off finely a complexion of tawny olive.
Kindly and courteous, hearing that a "lady" was
on board, they had brought as a present to her
two beautiful birds—a young male kestrel and a
young hooting owl, which from that day became

members of the already too numerous household on board the *Tern*. The kestrel lives yet—a nautical bird, tame as possible, never tired of swinging on a perch on the deck of a ship; but the owl, christened "The Chancellor," on account of his wig, disappeared one day overboard, and was in all probability drowned.

The shepherd was a mountaineer, and was well acquainted with the ways and haunts of birds. He knew of only one pair of eagles in that neighborhood, and from his vague description, translated to us by Hamish Shaw, we could not make out to what precise species of eagle he referred. He had harried the nest that spring, but the young had died in his hands, and he was afraid the old birds would forsake the mountain. In answer to our questions about sport, he said that the small lochans close by attracted a large number of birds, but if we wished a genuine day of wild-fowl-hunting, we must go to Loch Phlogibeg, two miles in the interior, where the geese were legion. He recommended us to get the punt carried across the hills—a feat which might speedily be achieved by vigorous work on the part of four strong men.

As it was still too windy next morning to think of lifting anchor and urging the yacht farther on her journey up the open coast, the punt was taken to shore at an early hour by Hamish and the Wanderer; and an aged shepherd and his son, living in a cottage on the banks of the fjörd, were soon persuaded to assist in carrying the boat overland. It was warm work. The hills were steep and full of great holes between the heather, and the earth was sodden with rain which had fallen during the night. Fortunately, however, there intervened, between the sea and Loch Phlogibeg, no less than four smaller lochs, over which the punt was rowed successively, thus reducing the land journey from two miles to little more than half a mile. And lovely, indeed, were these little lochans of the hills, nestling among the hollows, their water of exquisite limpid brown, and the water-lilies floating thereon so thickly that the path of the boat seemed strewn with flowers. Small trout leaped at intervals, leaving a ring of light that widened and died. From one little pool, no larger than a gentleman's drawing-room, and appareled in a many-colored glory no upholsterer could equal, we startled a pair of beautiful red-throats—but the guns were empty, and the prize escaped. There were ducks also, and flappers numberless—stately herons, too, rising at our approach with a clumsy flap of the great black wings, and tumbling over and over in the air, when out of the reach of danger, in awkward and unwieldy play.

What is stiller than a heron on a promontory? Moveless he stands, arching his neck and eyeing the water with one steadfast gaze. Hours pass—he has not stirred a feather; fish are scarce; but sooner or later, an eel will slip glittering past that very spot, and be secured by one thrust of the mighty bill. He will wait on, trusting to Providence, hungry though he is. Not till he espies your approach does he change his attitude. Watchful, yet still, he now stands sidelong, stretching out his long neck with a serpentine motion, till, unable to bear the suspense any longer, he rises into the air.

At last, all panting, we launched the punt on Phlogibeg. Delicious, indeed, at that moment, would have been a drop of distilled waters, but the last whisky-bottle had been empty for days, and was not to be replenished in those regions. Having despatched the Highlanders homeward, with a promise from them to aid in the transport of the boat on the return journey next day, the Wanderer and his henchman prepared the guns and set off in search of sport.

Loch Phlogibeg is a large and solitary mere, in the heart of a melancholy place. Around it the land undulates into small hills, with bogs and marshes between, and to the southeast, high mountains of gneiss, with crags and precipices innumerable, rise ashen gray into the clouds. All is very desolate— the bare mountains, the windy flats, the ever-somber sky. There is not a tree or shrub; instead of underwood, stones and boulders strew the waste. The mere itself is black as lead; small islands rise here and there, heaped round with rocks and stones, and covered inside with deep, rank grass and darnel. Everywhere in the water jut up pieces of rock—sometimes a whole drift-reef, like a ribbed wall; and at the western end are the ruins of a circular tower, or dune, looking eerie in the dim twilight of the dull and doleful air.

But now we are afloat, pulling against a chill, moist wind. Hark! The air, which was before so still, is broken by unearthly screams. The inhabitants of the lonely place are up in arms, yelling us away from their nests and young. Look at the terns, pulsing up and down in the air with that strange, spasmodic beat of the wings, curving the little black head downward, and uttering their endless *creaking croak.* Why, that little fellow, swift as an arrow, descended almost to our faces, as if to peck out our eyes; we could have struck him with a staff! Numberless gulls, large and small, white and dark, all hovering hither and thither, above our heads, now unite in the chorus; and two of the large, black-backed species join the flying band, but, unlike the rest, voice their indignation only at long intervals. The din is frightful! all the fiends are loose! Yet numerous as are the criers in the air, they are only a fraction of the swarms visible in the loch—flocks of them sitting moveless on the island shores, solitary ones perching on the straggling rocks where they protrude through the water, others floating and feeding far out from land. See yonder monster gull, perched on a stone; she looks huge as an eagle, with back as black as ebony, breast as white as snow, and large and glistening eyes; she does not move as we approach, but her frantic mate hovers above us and tries to scream us away. Though sorely tempted to secure so magnificent a bird, we spare her, partly for the sake of her young, partly (and more selfishly) for fear of frightening from the loch other and more precious game. Note the smaller and darker plumaged birds, paddling swiftly here and there close to the rocks; they are young gulls, recently launched out on the great water of life.

All this life only deepens the desolation of the

mere. There is a hollow sadness in the air, which the weird screech of the birds cannot break.

But the geese—where are they? Not one is visible as yet; we have not even heard a quack. Is it, indeed, to be a wild-goose chase, but only in the figurative sense, not literally? No—for Hamish, with his lynx-like eye, has picked out the flock afar away; he points them out again and again—there! and there!—but the Wanderer, wipe his spectacles as he will, can see nothing. With the telescope, however, he at last makes them out—a long line upon the water, numberless heads and necks. What a swarm! Surely all the geese of Uist have gathered here this day to discuss some solemn business! It is the very parliament of geese—grave, traditional—beginning and ending, like so many of our own parliaments, in a "quack." Hush! Now to steal on them slowly with muffled oars. Some, the older birds, will rise, but surely out of all that mighty gathering a few will be our own!

As we approach, the geese retreat—they have spied us already, and wish to give us a wide berth. Two or three have risen, and winged right over the hill. Never mind! push forward. So swiftly do they swim, that the boat does not gain a foot upon them, but they cannot pass beyond the head of the loch up yonder, half a mile away, and there, at least, we shall come upon them. Hark! they are whispering excitedly together, and the result of the conference is that they divide into two great parties, one making toward a passage between some islands to the left, the other keeping its straight course up the mere. Conscious of some deep-laid scheme to baulk us, we

follow the band that keep straight forward—forty
ganders, geese, and goslings, flying swiftly for life.
Faster! faster! we are gaining on them, and by the
time they reach that promontory, we may fire. Now
they are beginning to scatter, some diving out of
sight, and many rising high on wing to fly round the
land. They have rounded the promontory, doubtless
into some secret bay—not a bird is visible. Yes, one!
For a miracle, he is swimming straight this way. His
dusky plumage and crestless head prove him a juve-
nile; and surely nature, when she sent him into this
world of slayers and slain, denied him the due proportion of goose's brains. Is he mad, or blind, or does
he want to fight? He is only fifty yards away, and
rising erect in the water, he flaps the water from his
short wings and gazes about him with total unconcern.
A moment afterward, and he is a dead gander.

Not a moment is to be lost; quick—round the
promontory—or the flock will be heaven knows
where. Too late! Not a bird is to be seen. We
are close to the head of the loch, with a full view of
all the corners; not a solitary feather. They cannot all be diving at the same time. Yet we can
swear they did not rise on the wing; had they done
so, we could not have failed to perceive them. Two
score geese suddenly invisible, swallowed up in an
instant, without so much as a feather to show they
once were! Hamish Shaw scratches his head, and
the Wanderer feels awed; both are quite unable to
account for the mystery.

You see, it is their first real Wild-Goose Day, and
being raw sportsmen, actually accumulating their

12*

knowledge by personal experience, and utterly rejecting the adventitious instruction of books, they are unaware that the young wild-goose, when sore beset on the water, has a sly knack of creeping in to shore, and betaking himself for the time being to the shelter of the thick heather, or the deep, grassy boghole. But now the mystery is clear; for yonder is the last of the stragglers, running up the bank as fast as its legs can carry it, and disappearing among the grass above. Tallyho! To shore, Schneider, and after it! The dog plunges in, reaches the bank, and disappears in pursuit. Running the boat swiftly in to shore, we land and follow with the guns. Half running, half flying, screaming fiercely, speeds the goose, so fast that the dog scarcely gains on her, and making a short, sharp turn, rushes again to the water, plunges in, dives, and reappears out of gunshot. But his companions—where are they? Gone, like the mist of the morning. Though we search every clump of heather, every peat-hole, every water-course, and though Schneider, seeming to smell goose at every step, is as keen as though she were hunting a rat in his hole, not a bird do we discover. Can they have penetrated into some subterranean cave, and there be quacking in security? Forty geese—vanished away! By Jupiter, we have been befooled!

Somewhat tired, we rest for a time on the waterside. The mere is silent again, untroubled by the screaming birds or the murderous presence of man. A drift-mist is passing rapidly against the upper parts of the mountains yonder, and the crags look terrific through its sickly smoke, and the wind is getting higher. Hark! Is that distant thunder? or is it the crumbling down of crags among the heights? It is neither. It is the hollow moan of the western ocean, beating in on the sands that lie beyond these desolate flats. One feels neither very wise nor very grand, caught by such a voice in the wilderness, caught— hunting geese. Had it been a red deer, now, or an eagle, or even a seal, that we were pursuing; but a goose—how harmonize *it* with the immensities? Of course, it is merely association; for, in point of fact, the wild-goose is a thoroughly noble bird, a silence-lover, a high soarer, an inhabitant of the lonely mere and desolate marsh, a proud haunter of the weedy footprints of the sea.

Yes, the wind is rising. Dark clouds are driving up to westward, and the surface of the mere begins to whiten here and there with small, sharp waves. It looks like the beginning of a spindrift gale, but the weather is very deceptive in these latitudes, and it may mean nothing after all. It will be better, however, to be making tracks over the hills.

Up goes the lugsail, and we drive down the loch with frightful speed. Down with it; for the water is sown with rocks, and if we touch a stone while going at that speed, the punt's side will be driven into splinters. We fly fast enough now, without sail or oar. Ha! yonder are the geese round that point, all gathered together again, and, doubtless, conversing excitedly about their recent terrific adventures. Before they can scatter much, we have rounded the point and are down upon them. Bang goes Big Benjamin! Bang! bang! goes the double-barrel. Four fine young birds are secured, two of them due to Ben the monster. We have just dragged them into the boat, when the rain begins to come down, while the wind is still flogging the water with pitiless blows.

And so, wet and weary, we drew up the punt in a sheltered creek, and turned her over. Hard by were some rude huts, built of peat turfs and wood—the summer abodes, or shielings, of the shepherds, who bring their flocks over here for the pasture; and in one of these we left our oars, mast, sail, and other articles. Then shouldering our spoil, we put our backs to the wind and rain, and dashed along, through bog and over ditch, till we arrived at the shepherd's hut on the side of Loch Huport.

There, on the threshold, greeting us with a smile, was a Highland lass, in the clean short-gown and colored petticoat, with hair snooded carefully and bare feet as white as alabaster. She was, without doubt, the sweetest maiden that we had yet met in our Highland rambles. Like her of whom Wordsworth sung—

"A very shower
Of beauty was her earthly dower;"

and it was ghostly beauty, the spiritual sweetening the earthly. The features were not faultless; the nose was perhaps a little inclined to heaven, but the eyes! What depth they had? What limpid serenity and far-searching thought! They were sorrowful eyes—had doubtless been washed with many tears. What struck us most about this creature was her strange whiteness and purity—her linen was literally like snow. her face was pale, her bare arms and legs were like marble—it was cleanliness almost oppressive, giving to her a wild, fantastic influence, finely in keeping with those eerie wilds. If an artist could have seen this maiden, painted her in her habit as she lived, and written beneath, " Bonnie Kilmeny," he would have been hailed as a great ideal painter. Jamie Hogg would have screamed and run, at seeing the heroine of his superb poem so incarnated, so sent to grace the wilds with witch-beauty :

> " Als still was her luke, and als still was her ee,
> Als the stillness that lay on the emeraut lee,
> Or the mist that sleips on a waveless sea. . . .
> And oh . her beauty was fayir to see,
> But still and steadfast was her ee!"

Yet we just now called her a maiden. Maid she was none, as we afterward discovered, but a mother— the shepherd's daughter-in-law. Whence, then, that maiden whiteness, so coldly spiritual ? that alabaster body, so " purified from child-bed taint ?" They were not of this earth ; the woman's soul, like Kilmeny's, was in the "land of thocht," and morning and even was washing the body clean in the delicate dews of dream.

Unfortunately, Kilmeny, as we mean to call her till the world's end, " had no English," and Hamish Shaw had to interpret for her pensive lips; but, after all, those deep eyes needed no interpreters; they told their own strange tale. It was very commonplace, of course—would we have some milk? and had we had good sport ? and was the Wanderer an Englishman ? and whence had the yacht come? But the wretched hut, the thick peat-smoke—nay, even the ragged urchin in the corner—could not shake us out of a dream, such power had one exquisitely expressive face in startling the wayworn spirit and making it tremble. There was a message of some sort, a sudden light out of another world—what message, what light? was another question—but it was beautiful!

> "She met me, stranger, upon life's rough way,
> And lured me toward sweet death, as night by day
> Winter by spring, or sorrow by sweet hope
> Led into life, light, peace. An antelope,
> In the suspended impulse of its lightness,
> Were less ethereally light ; the brightness
> Of her divinest presence trembles through
> Her limbs, as underneath a cloud of dew
> Embodied in the windless heaven of June,
> Amid the splendor-wingéd stars, the moon
> Burns inextinguishably beautiful."

Yes, that was it; she "lured toward sweet death." When the Wanderer thinks of her now, it is often with a cold chill—as of one *laid out*, in a snowy winding-sheet, prinked with white lilies from the lochans. It is only a fancy, but the eyes still haunt him. Perhaps the woman is dead.

"Who is the goose now?" we hear the reader exclaim ; and perhaps he is right. It was, at all events, a strange ending to our Wild-Goose Day. The shepherd, with some difficulty, for the wind was high, rowed us in his clumsy skiff to the yacht, where we soon turned in, and dreamed about Kilmeny.

Two wild days of rain and wind had to pass away ere we could get across to Loch Phlogibeg for the punt. At last, however, we went over, shot a few moor-geese, and brought the punt back through a drenching mist. It only remains to be added that, with the assistance of Schneider and the hawk, we ate up every goose we slew, and if we had had something to swallow with the same, even a crust of bread or a biscuit, would have found the flesh delicious. But man cannot live on goose alone, however young, however tender. How did we crave a scrap of bread, and a drop of whisky, or tea to wash it down!

Though we had goose galore, and eggs, and milk, that was all Loch Huport could do for us; and, really, it might have been much worse, and we were ungrateful beings to crouch frowningly and mutter about starvation. Hamish Shaw was the bitterest, for he was out of tobacco, and to him, as to many another water-dog, life without tobacco was accursed torture. He had tried tea, till that was quite exhausted. Then he attempted a slice of boot-leather, and rather liked it—only, if he had persisted in smoking that kind of stuff, he would soon have had to go barefoot. The Wanderer recommended *peat*, but the idea was rejected with indignation.

Just as the weather was beginning to clear, a large ship put into the loch, for a rest after weeks of bad weather, and by boarding her we procured a few supplies—a little tea, some tobacco, and a number of weeviled biscuits. Now, the presence of a large vessel acts like magic in a solitary place. No sooner had the ship entered the loch than the region, which had previously seemed uninhabited, became suddenly populous, and numerous skiffs rowed out laden with natives. The skipper did what the Yankees would call a "smart" thing with the natives on that occasion. Having need of hands to get in his anchors, which had dragged, he paid them off in biscuits of the finest quality, telling them to return next day, and (if they pleased) he would take in exchange for biscuits any quantity of *dried fish* they liked to bring. The natives were of course delighted, and the skipper secured a splendid lot of fish for the southern market. But conceive the disgust of the poor deluded Celts on examining their prize of dearly-coveted bread—for the biscuits were full of weevils, and worth scarcely a penny a pound.

"All this far you have been digressing!" cries the impatient reader. "We have heard more than we want to hear about ducks and geese, and hunger and thirst; but what of the red deer, the eagle, the salmon, the hooper, the seal?" Well, as to the red deer, we may or may not have been the death of many a forest king—their antlers may or may not be hanging over the chimney-piece in our smoking-room—but we did not get so much as a glimpse of a deer in the wilds of the Long Island. The salmon had not yet ascended the rivers, and the wild swans were rearing that year's young in the distant north. More than one eagle we beheld, floating among the mountain peaks on the eastern coast, and dwarfed by distance to the size of a wind-hover; but mighty would have been the hunter who could reach and slay the sky-loving birds in their glory. Indeed few have ever killed an eagle in its full pride of strength and flight. It is the sickly, half-starved, feeble bird that inadvertently crosses the shepherd's gun, and yields a lean and unwholesome body to the stuffer's arts.

Such an one we saw low down on the crags of Ben
Eval, passing with a great heavy beat of the wing
from rock to rock, now hovering for an instant over
some object among the heather, then rising painfully
and drifting along on the wind. We had no gun
with us that day, or we think that, by cautiously
stalking among the heights, we might have made
the bird our own ; and, indeed, our hearts were sad
for the great bird, with that fierce hunger tearing at
his heart, while, doubtless, the yellow eyes burnt
terribly through the gathering films of death. Out
of the hollow crags gathered six ravens, rushing with
hoarse shrieks at the fallen king, and turning away
with horrible yells whenever he turned towards them
with sharp talon and opened beak ; attracted by the
noise, flocked from all the surrounding pastures the
hideous hooded crows, with their sick gray coats and
sable heads, cawing like devils ; and these, too, rushed
at the eagle, to be beaten back by one wave of the
wrathful wings. It was a sad scene—power eclipsed
on the very throne of its glory, taunted and abused by
carrion,

"Sick in the world's regard, wretched and low,"

yet preserving the mournful shadows of its dignity
and kingly glory. Every movement of the eagle
was still kingly, nor did he deign to utter a sound ;
while the crows and ravens were detestable in every
gesture—mean, groveling, and unwieldy—and their
cruel cries made the echoes hideous. Round the
shoulder of the hill floated the king, with the
imps of darkness at his back. We fear his day of

death, so nigh at hand, was to be very sad. Better that the passing shepherd should put a bullet through his heart and carry him away to deck some gentleman's hall, than that he should fall spent yonder, insulted at his last gasp, torn at by the fiends, seeing the leering raven whet his beak for slaughter, and the corby perched close by, eager to pick out the golden and beautiful eyes.

> "By too severe a fate,
> Fallen, fallen, fallen, fallen,
> Fallen from his high estate,
>   And welt'ring in his blood ;
> On the bare earth exposed he lies,
>   With not a friend to close his eyes."

We were not loathe to see him go. It would have required a hard heart to take advantage of him, in the last forlorn moments of his reign.

Just as he passed away, there started out from the side of a rock a ghastly apparition, glaring at us with a face covered with blood, and looking as if it meant murder. It was only a sheep, and for the moment it amazed us, for it seemed like the ghost of a sheep, horrid and forbidding. Alas! though it glared in our direction, it could not see; its poor, gentle eyes had just been destroyed, the red blood from them was coursing down its cheeks; and it was staggering, drunken with the pain. It was the victim of the hoody or the raven, ever on the watch for the unwary, ready in a moment to dart down on the sleeping lamb or the rolling sheep, and make a meal of its eyes; then, with devilish chuckle, to track the blind and tottering victim hither and thither, as it feels its feeble way among the heights, until, standing on the edge of some high rock, it can be startled, with a wild beat of the wings and a hoarse shriek, right down the fatal precipice to the rocks beneath ; and there the murderer, while a dozen others of his kind gather around him in carnival, croaks out a discordant grace, and plunges his reeking beak into the victim's heart.

Though we slew a raven and a half a dozen corbies, having after that night sworn a savage vendetta against the murderous kind, no eagle died by our hand ; neither eagle, nor red deer, nor hooper, nor salmon. So far the search for the hunter's badge in Ultima Thule was a wretched failure, ending only in humiliation and despair. But we have at least taken one step in the right direction ; for we can avow, by Diana and by Nimrod, or (if the reader likes it better) by the less classic shade of Colonel Hawker, that we killed a seal, and did so under circumstances which may, we fancy, be quite as well worth relating as any other sporting matter recorded in these pages.

It was up among the fjörds of Maddy that the seal began to attract our attention. They were floating about in considerable numbers, coming quite close to the yacht at times, but always keeping well aloof whenever there was the slightest smell of powder. So one day the punt was got ready, Big Benjamin and the rifle put on board, and the Wanderer and his henchman started off up the fjörds.

There was a stiff breeze from the east, and the little boat shot swiftly with the lugsail through the island waters. Every now and then the head of a seal popped up out of gunshot, floated for some minutes exactly like an oscillating leather bottle, and then was drawn slowly out of sight—still like a bottle, with the neck (or snout) upwards. The creeks were full of female eider and gool-ducks, each female followed by five or six fluffs of down in various stages of development; and on one headland, which smelt as strongly of stale fish as a herring-boat, a whole covey of cormorants, sitting bolt upright, like parsons in black coats and dingy neckcloths, were basking in the sunlight. The sea-larks twittered everywhere, the oyster-catchers whistled, the curlews screamed; and the gulls, scattered all around as thick as snowflakes, completed the chorus with their constant cries.

There was a rocky point, well up the principal fjörd, which we had ascertained to be a constant resort of the seals, and on which, only the day before, an eye-witness had seen no less than forty, old and young, taking their noonday siesta all at once. Toward this point we ran with the fresh breeze, not firing a shot on the passage, but watching warily ahead; and at last, when in full view of the rocks and about a quarter of a mile distant, we hauled down the lugsail and "lay to" reconnoitering. Hamish Shaw's quick eye discovered seals at once, and the telescope soon showed that he was right. There they were, three or four at least in number, sunning themselves snugly on the very outermost rocks of the promontory, ready, on the slightest alarm, to slip like eels into the water. What was to be done? Shooting them from the boat was impossible: a nearer approach on the water would soon scatter them to the deeps. However, by careful stalking, a good shot might be had from the land. About a hundred yards behind the siesta, rise knolls of deep grass, intermingled with great boulders, and among these there must be many a capital point of vantage. Luckily, the knolls were well to leeward of the seals, and there was no chance of the wind playing traitor. Be it noted, that a seal, although not particularly sharp-sighted, has as fine a nose as a stag for any foul scent—such as that exuded, as Dean Swift vowed and as delicate monsters know, by the murderous monster man.

Leaving Hamish in charge of the punt, the Wanderer shouldered the rifle and made a long detour inland, not venturing to turn his face until he was well to leeward of his quarry. Then, strapping the rifle on his back in backwoodsman fashion, and throwing himself down on his hands and knees, he began crawling slowly toward the hidden point. Ah, my Grub Street friends, how little do ye think of the discomforts of the wilds! The ground was squashy as a sponge, and full of horrible orifices, where the black rain-water gathered and grew stagnant. The Wanderer's knees were soon soaking, and ever and anon he plunged up to the elbows in a puddle, treacherously covered with green. Be sure he muttered no blessings Again and again he was on the point of rising erect, but was checked by the reflection that it was now impossible to mend matters, and that so much might be achieved by pushing on.

He was soon close to the knolls, which, instead of

affording such good cover as he had anticipated, lay pretty well exposed to the view of the black gentlemen on the promontory. Ha! there they were, their tails cocked up in the air like a Yankee's legs, but resting on nothing. It was immediately quite clear that, to get within shot of all or any of them, the Wanderer must learn something from his ancient enemy, the snake, and do the rest of the stalking on his stomach.

Did you ever try to perform this feat—to lie straight down on your face, keep your whole body and legs stiff, and wriggle yourself forward with your elbows and breast, just as you have seen the clown in the pantomime when he has designs on the pasteboard leg of mutton in the flat? If you are fat, don't attempt it; it is fatiguing if you are lean. But add to the difficulties of the feat the inconveniences of doing it in a place as wet as a sponge, and thereby drenching your whole person with the green water of the damp morass, and you have some idea of the Wanderer's situation. Nothing daunted, however, he oozed—literally oozed—through the long grass, brushing the dirt with a dip of his nose, and glaring through his spectacles at the prey. Satan himself could not have managed better. The Wanderer had his reward, for the seals, unsuspicious of danger, remained as motionless as stones.

Five were visible—three very large, two smaller—all seated less than a hundred yards away. Creeping behind a large rock, which afforded a tolerable rest for the rifle, the Wanderer breathed a space, for he was quite exhausted with his labor, and then prepared to fire. He trembled very much, partly with fatigue, partly with terror, lest he might miss; but getting two in line, and aiming as steadily as his nerves would allow, he pulled the trigger. A sharp crack, and all was over. The smoke curled up from the muzzle of the gun, and for a minute he thought that he had missed. But no! all the monsters had disappeared but one, which was floundering wildly among the rocks, and making for the sea. The Wanderer rushed down, ready to finish the work with the butt end of his rifle, but before he could reach the spot the seal had plunged into the sea. Forgetting, in his excitement, to load again, he saw it rise and sink with short, painful dives, and, at last, with a deep breath, it turned over on its back, floundered, and sank in the bubbles of its own dying breath. By the time that Hamish came round with the punt no seal was there; and, indeed, the rascal seemed to receive with a look of incredulity the news that any one had even been hit at all. He rowed over the spot indicated, looking down for the white gleam of the seal's belly, but the water was very deep, and the slain one was lost beyond all hope of recovery.

That, reader, was the seal we slew. We certainly did not "bag" him, but we nevertheless accredit ourselves with the glory of his death; and no taunts of the ill-disposed shall make us change our opinion.

Having cleared the state-lounge of its occupiers, and sought in vain for other loungers on shore, we determined to drift about, in the hope of getting chance shots from the boat. The water was full of seals, and the black heads were still coming and going in all directions. Now, it was a fixed and determined superstition of Hamish Shaw that the seal, being fond of music, can often be lured within gunshot by whistling; and it was a pretty sight, finely illustrating the pleasures of the imagination, to see the Wanderer and his henchman, guns in hand, whistling softly to attract the attention of some black head oscillating out of range. Neither being very musical, but producing a sound like the grating described by Milton on

"Scrannel pipes of wretched straw,"

their melody did not seem to have much effect; until suddenly, about fifty yards away, a gray old fellow popped his head through the water and stretched out his neck for a good stare in our direction. Shaw continued softly whistling, and both took aim and fired. There was a great splash in the water, and the seal was gone.

It is the opinion of a capital writer on field-sports, Mr. John Colquhoun of Bute, that "all swimming seals, if hit at all, are shot through the head, and immediately spread out on the surface, giving ample time to row up and seize a flipper," and that consequently all stories of seals shot swimming, and suddenly submerged in deep water, are at the best exceedingly doubtful. It does, indeed, seem reasonable to avow that only the head of a swimming seal can be hit, the head being the only part visible; but the bullet may not necessarily reach the brain, and death may not be immediate.

Thus ended, not gloriously, our sport in the Wilds. None of the great trophies were won, though keen had been the chase, but something better had been gained—the fresh sense of new life. Cold and exposure, damp and hunger, rain and wind, daily acted as tonics to exhausted nature; and the Wanderer, who had swallowed enough iron to make a gun-barrel and enough strychnia to poison a boarding-school, was renewed like Æson by the rough process of nature herself. To the weary and exhausted, he recommends such a cure with confidence Fight with the elements from morn to night, fear neither cold nor wet, defy the elements—and the cure will come of itself. Nerve-exhaustion (nervousness is another thing, and means merely weak-mindedness) is the one thing that must not be coddled and humored.

There is another question, however, raised by the benevolent—the cruelty of sport as blended with the sorrow of things that feel. Now, we are not among those enthusiasts who avouch that the fox and hare enjoy being hunted, and that nothing is more glorious to a red deer than being shot on the hillside; and we will yield to no man in love for dumb things—we hold them so dear, and have so many of them around us, that we are laughed at by all our friends. Sport, be it granted, is a savage instinct, yet it is none the less a natural one. All true sportsmen love animals better than men who do not love sport. Well, as to wild-shooting. It has, in our eyes, this grand recommendation—it combines a maximum of hard labor and skill with a minimum of slaughter;

for, in the eyes of the wild-shooter, a prize is precious precisely in proportion to the difficulty of capture. Pheasant-shooting is like shooting in a hen-house; partridge-shooting is mere murder of the innocents; grouse-shooting is sometimes as bad; all these have for their main object the filling of an enormous bag. But in wild-shooting, not only are you forced to contend with mountainous difficulties, and taken into scenes of extraordinary excitement, but you are amply satisfied with little or nothing as a recompense. One precious ornithological prize is "bag" enough for a fortnight. You cannot help admitting that some of your feelings and deeds are savage, but you have the satisfaction of knowing that the odds are always twenty to one against you, and that whatever you win is secured by a drudgery quite out of proportion to the value of the capture.

CHAPTER XIII.

COASTING SKYE.

Effects of Cruising on Yacht and Voyagers—Re-crossing the Minch—Northwest Coast of Skye—Becalmed off Loch Snizort—Midnight—Lights of Heaven and Ocean—Dawn—Columns of the North Coast—The Quirang—Scenery of the Northeast Coast—The Storr—Portree Harbor.

DEVIOUS, yet persistent as a crow which flies wearily homeward against pitilessly beating rain and wind—now staggering along a good mile, now drifting backward, overcome by some blast of more than common fury—the little yacht made her way along the rock-sown coast of the Long Island. All the elements seemed leagued against her, and we flitted along, from anchorage to anchorage, in a dense and rainy mist—literally, "darkness visible." Such a tiny, stubborn, desolate, rain-bedraggled, windstraw of a vessel never before ventured into so inhospitable a region ; for the wild sea-weed grew upon her and trailed around her in slimy masses ; her sails were torn by the sharp teeth of the wind ; her ropes rotted by the insidious and mildewy slime ; her once bright pennon was a rag—and altogether, but for the exquisitely delicate contour, which no dirt or raggedness could spoil, she might have been taken for some miserable wherry of the isles. But the whirlwind spared her, the waves melted their wrath against her, and the beating rain only tightened her timber; and, not to be daunted by damp, whirlpool, hurricane, or any other of the powers of that eerie region, she persisted in her explorations as devotedly as any little lonely lady in Wonderland. As for the voyagers, they had long since abandoned all attempts to look civilized. Their clothes hung upon them like those suits with which Jews tempt seafaring-men in Whitechapel. Hamish Shaw's black, corkscrew ringlets were wildly matted together, and his face was bristling all over. Even Schneider, the dog, looked disreputable; for the salt water and sea air had taken all the gloss and curl out of her coat, and her poor eyes were closed up with a sort of influenza. Not without pleasure, at last, did we turn homeward, leaving the Long Island to its loneliness and gloom.

Our first intention had been to cruise along the coast of the Outer Hebrides as far as Stornoway; but we had spent so much time in navigating the southern parts of the Long Island that we paused at Loch Maddy, and, after spending a week in examining the surrounding fjörds and islands, thought it high time to recross the Minch It was now late in August, and the gales of wind were daily becoming more frequent in occurrence, longer-lasting, and stronger while they lasted. One morning, therefore, we left Loch Maddy, with a brisk breeze from the north, and, lying close to the wind, steered straight across the Minch, in the direction of the northern cliffs of Skye. Dim in distance, Skye loomed before us—the northern crags, the great heights of Dunvegan, Macleod's Maidens, and the shadowy Cuchullins—and far away eastward, the faint outline of the mainland was traceable for many a mile. The day was gray and dreamy, the wind steady as could be, the waves rising and falling with a deep, slumbrous murmur, most assuring to the mariner. One had nothing to do but steer the boat, and let her work her way lightly and steadily over the easy waters, as they broke in dark, foam-edged masses to the south.

Although there seemed little perceptible speed on the vessel, she gained mile after mile swiftly enough, and the mouth of Loch Maddy, with its rocky islands, began rapidly to mingle with the gray line of sea, while Skye grew darker and darker as we approached, the sleepy masses of mist gathering on all its heights as far as eye could reach.

Early in the afternoon, we passed Dunvegan Head, and then Vaternish Point; but by this time the breeze had grown very faint indeed, and when we were in the middle of the great mouth of Loch Snizort, the wind ceased altogether. For hours we rolled about on a most uncomfortable sea, till the sun sank far away across the Minch, touching with red light the hazy outline of the Long Island. Then, all in a moment, as it were, the eyes of heaven opened, very dim and feeble, and the night—if night it could be called—came down with a chilly sprinkle of invisible dew. All round the yacht the sea burnt, flashed and murmured, lit up by innumerable lights. Wherever a wave broke there was a phosphorescent gleam. The punt astern floated in a patch as bright as moonlight; and every time the counter of the yacht struck the water, the latter emitted a flash like sheet-lightning. The whole sea was alive with millions of miraculous creatures, each with a tiny light to pilot him about the abysses. Here and there the medusa moved luminous, devouring the minute creatures that swarmed around it, terrible in its way as the Poulp that Victor Hugo has caricatured so immortally;* and other creatures of volition, to us nameless, passed mysteriously; while ever and anon a shoal of tiny sethe would dart to the surface, and hover in millions around the yacht. Though there was no moon, the waters and the sky seemed full of moonlight. The silence was profound, only broken by a dull, heavy sound at intervals—whales blowing off the headland of Dunvegan.

Midnight, and no breeze came. The sky to the north unfolded like a flower blossoming, and the Northern Lights flitted up from the horizon, flashing like quicksilver, and filling the sight with a peculiar thrill of mesmeric sensation. Lights gleaming on the ocean, the eyes of heaven glittering, the Aurora flashing and fading—with all these the sense seemed overburthened. Now and then, as if the pageant were incomplete, a star shot from its sphere, gleamed, and disappeared.

There was nothing for it but to roll about on the shining sea till the wind came. Leaving Hamish at the helm, the Wanderer crept into the cabin, and was soon fast asleep, in spite of the lurching of the yacht.

* "Les Travailleurs de la Mer."

He was awakened by the familiar sound of the water rushing past a vessel under sail; and, without opening his eyes, he knew that the yacht had got a breeze. Creeping out into the cockpit, he saw the waters quite black on every side; darkness everywhere, save where the first cold sparkle of day was beginning to peep above the far-off mountains of the mainland.

We were in luck; for the breeze was from the northwest, and just enough for us to carry. When day broke, red and somber, we were off Hunish Point, and saw on every side of us the basaltic columns of the coast flaming in the morning light, and behind us, in a dark hollow of a bay, the ruins of Duntulm Castle, gray and forlorn. The coast views here were beyond expression—magnificent. Tinted red with dawn, the fantastic cliffs formed themselves into shapes of the wildest beauty, rain-stained and purpled with shadow, and relieved at intervals by slopes of emerald, where the sheep crawled. The sea through which we ran was a vivid green, broken into thin lines of foam, and full of innumerable medusæ, drifting southward with the tide. Leaving the green, sheep-covered island of Trody on our left, we slipt past Aird Point, and sped swift as a fish along the coast, until we reached the two small islands off the northern point of Loch Staffin—so named, like the island of Staffa, on account of its columnar ridges of coast. Here we beheld a sight which seemed the glorious fabric of a vision—a range of small heights, sloping from the deep green sea, every height crowned with a columnar cliff of basalt, and each rising over each, higher and higher, till they ended in a cluster of towering columns, minarets, and spires, over which hovered wreaths of delicate mist, suffused with the pink light from the east. We were looking on the spiral pillars of the Quirang. In a few minutes the vision had faded; for the yacht was flying faster and faster, assisted a little too much by a savage puff from off the Quirang's great cliffs; but other forms of beauty arose before us as we went. The whole coast from Aird Point to Portree forms a panorama of cliff-scenery quite unmatched in Scotland. Layers of limestone dip into the sea, which washes them into horizontal forms, resembling gigantic slabs of white and gray masonry, rising, sometimes, stair above stair, water-stained, and hung with many-colored weed; and on these slabs stand the dark cliffs and spiral columns, towering into the air like the fretwork of some Gothic temple, roofless to the sky; clustered sometimes together in black masses of eternal shadow; torn open here and there, to show glimpses of shining lawns sown in the heart of the stone, or flashes of torrents, rushing in silver veins through the darkness; crowned in some places by a green patch, on which the goat feed, small as mice; and twisting frequently into towers of most fantastical device that lie dark and spectral against the gray background of the air. To our left, we could now behold the island of Rona, and the northern end of Raasay. All our faculties, however, were soon engaged in contemplating the Storr, the highest part of the northern ridge of Skye, terminating in a mighty insulated rock or monolith, which points solitary to heaven, two thousand three hundred feet above the sea, while at its base, rock and crag have been torn into the wildest forms by the teeth of earthquake, and a great torrent leaps foaming into the sound. As we shot past, a dense white vapor enveloped the lower part of the Storr, and towers, pyramids, turrets, monoliths were shooting out above it, like a supernatural city in the clouds.

Weary and exhausted as we were, we gazed on picture after picture with rapt eyes, looking little at Raasay, which was closing us in upon the left. At every hundred yards, the coast presented some new form of perfect loveliness. We were now in smooth water. The red dawn had grown into a dull-gray day, and the wind was coming so sharp off the land that we found it necessary to take in a reef. We had scarcely beaten into Portree, in the teeth of the most severe squalls, when the bad weather began in earnest, with some clouds from the northwest, charged like mighty artillery with wind and rain. Snug at our anchorage, we smiled at the storm, and heartily congratulated ourselves that it had not caught us off the perilous heads of Skye.

Portree is the capital of Skye, and, like all Highland capitals, is dreary beyond endurance, and without a single feature of interest. After lingering a day to rest our weary bodies, we left the harbor on a rather black-looking forenoon, with the intention of slipping down to Loch Sligachan, a distance of only some eight or nine miles, and of lying for a little time in the immediate neighborhood of the wonderful Cuchullins. The little *Tern* had carried her mainsail nearly all the journey in the open, and now, for the first and second time, we lashed down the boom and put on the "trysail"—just for the purpose of shifting comfortably down to Sligachan. Fortunate for us, as the event proved, that we did so—for we left without a pilot, and were destined to be blown on somewhat sharply by the mighty Cuchullins.

The wind was ahead, and had fallen so much that the beating down was very slow work indeed; and we had, therefore, full leisure to examine all the fine "glimpses" in the narrow sound—the mighty cliffs of Skye, piled up above us on the starboard side, the undulating isle of Raasay to the left, the gigantic Storr astern, and Ben Glamaig rising darkly over the starboard bow. Nothing could be wilder and more fantastic than some of the shapes assumed by the Skye cliffs, nothing finer than some of their shadowy tints. Contrasted with them, Dun-Can, of Raasay, on the top of which the oracular Doctor and Boswell danced a *pas de deux*, looked like a mere earthen sugar-loaf beaten flat at the top. All under Dun-Can stretched a brown and rocky country, pastoral and peaceful enough in parts, and having even green slopes and bright heathery glades, together with fine pieces of artificial woodland, through which glittered the waterfall—

"A silver pleasure in the heart of twilight!"

Strange looked the Storr behind us, rising solitary into the sky, with its satellite pinnacles and towers lying underneath in the dark-blue shade.

Our eyes turned with most eagerness, however, toward Ben Glamaig, now scarcely visible in a thick, purple mist. Cloud after cloud was settling on his summit, sinking lower and lower, to mantle him from forehead to feet; and the long, thread-like film of the falling rain was drawn down his darkness with faint gleams of light; yet the sea about us was quite quiet, and the wind was ominously still. Hamish Shaw cocked his eye up at the giant in true sailor style, but delivered it as his judgment that "the day would be a fine day, tho' we micht may-be hae a *shower ;*" and Hamish had reason on his side, for the giants of Skye sometimes look very threatening when they mean no harm, and very friendly when they are drawing a great breath into their rocky lungs, preparatory to blowing your boat to the bottom of the sea.

Altogether, it was with not quite comfortable feelings that we drew nearer and nearer to the mouth of Sligachan. The place bore an ugly name—there was danger above and danger under—rocks below and squalls above. Right across the mouth of Loch Sligachan stretches a dangerous shoal, leaving only a passage of a few yards, and to sail through this at all it is necessary to have the tide in your favor. Then, as you enter, you must look out for "Bo Sligachan"—a monster lying in wait, just under water, to scrunch your planks behind his weedy jaws. Then, again, beware of *squalls!* Down the almost perpendicular sides of Ben Glamaig, down the beds of the torrents, inaudible till it has sprung shrieking upon you, comes the wind. Talk about wind! You know nothing whatever on that subject, unless you have been in a boat among these mountains. Huge skiffs have been lifted out of sheltered nooks made expressly for their reception—lifted up, twirled rapidly in the air like straws, and smashed to fragments in an instant. If a hen ventures to open her wings sometimes, up she goes in the air, whisks round and round for a moment, and comes down with the force of a bullet—dead. The mail-gig, which runs at the foot of Ben Glamaig, on a road well sheltered from the worst fury of the blast, has sometimes to stand to face the wind for minutes together, knowing that it would certainly be upset if the squalls caught it broadside. Not very long ago, a great schooner was capsized and foundered at anchor here, by a sudden gust, just because she happened to have one or two empty herring-barrels piled upon her deck. Next to Loch Scavaig, for fury of sudden squalls, comes Loch Sligachan. In the latter you have only the breath of Glamaig, but at Scavaig, you must prepare for the combined blasts of all the Cuchullins—all the giants gathering together in the mist, and manifesting a fury to which Polypheme's passion against Ulysses was a trifle.

But it was summer-time, and we anticipated nothing terrific, otherwise we should certainly not have ventured yonder in so frail and tiny a thing as the *Tern*. We had already falsified all the dire predictions which greeted us on setting forth, and followed us throughout our journey—we had crossed and recrossed the Minch, penetrated into the wild fjörds of the Long Island, beaten round the northeast coast of Skye in the open sea—all in a poor little crank craft not seven tons burden, seven feet beam, rigged for racing, and intended only for river-sailing in very mild weather. Our good fortune, instead of turning our brains, had made us more cautious than when we set forth. Many perils escaped had explained to us the real danger of our attempt. We had certainly no anticipation of meeting in the narrows the fate which we had escaped so often in the open sea.

What with the slight wind, and the weary beating down the Sound, we did not sight Sconser Lodge, which lies just at the mouth of Loch Sligachan, until the sunset. By this time the clouds had somewhat cleared away about Glamaig, and glorious shafts of luminous silver were working wondrous chemistry among the dark mists. We put about close to Raasay House, a fine dwelling in the midst of well-cultivated land, and feasted our eyes with the f ntastic forms and colors of the Skye cliffs to the westward, grouped together in the strange, wild illumination of a cloudy sunset; domes, pinnacles, spires, rising with dark outline against the west, and flitting from shade to light, from light to shade, as the mist cleared away or darkened against the sinking sun; with vivid patches between of dark-brown rocks and of green grass washed to glistening emerald by recent rain. It was a scene of strange beauty— Nature mimicking with unnatural perfection the mighty works of men, coloring all with the wildest hues of the imagination, and revealing beyond, at intervals, glimpses of other domes, pinnacles, and spires, flaming duskily in the sunset, and crumbling down, like the ruins of a burning city, one by one. What came into the mind just then was not Wordsworth's sonnet on a similar cloudy pageant, but those wonderful stanzas of a wonderful poem by the same great poet on the eclipse of the sun in 1820 :

> " Awe-stricken she beholds the array
> That guards the temple night and day ;
> Angels she sees that might from heaven have flown,
> And virgin saints, who not in vain
> Have striven by purity to gain
> The beatific crown—
>
> " Sees long-drawn files, concentric rings,
> Each narrowing above each ; the wings
> The uplifted palms, the silent marble lips,
> The starry zone of sovereign height—
> All steeped in the portentous light !
> All suffering dim eclipse !"

It is difficult to tell why these lines should have arisen in our mind at that moment—for no stronger reason, perhaps, than that which caused the figures themselves to rise before Wordsworth by the side of Lugano. He had once seen the Cathedral at Milan, and when the eclipse came, he could not help following it thither in imagination. These faint associations are the strangest things in life, and the sweetest things in song. Portentous light ! dim eclipse ! These were the only words truly applicable to the scene we were gazing upon at that moment ; and those few words were the chain of the association— the magical charm linking sense and soul—bringing Milan to Skye, filling the sunset picture with the wings, uplifted palms, and silent lips of angels and virgin saints—

> " All steeped in the portentous light !
> All suffering dim eclipse !"

It was just as we were contemplating this wonder that the water blackened to windward, and we were laid over with the first squall from Glamaig. What a screaming in the riggings! what a rattling of dishes and buckets in the forecastle! What a clutching at spars and ropes on deck! It was gone in a moment, and the *Tern* dashed buoyantly forward. The wind had freshened suddenly, and we were bowling along at five or six miles an hour, carrying trysail, foresail, and the second jib. We were still a good two miles from Sconser Lodge, so that the squalls, when they reached us, had lost much of their force. Squall second was even softer than the first; we laughed as it whizzed through the rigging, just putting the bulwarks under, and we were still further encouraged by a sudden brightening of the Ben. Fools! that brightening should not have beguiled us. Hamish, who was at the helm, had just made the remark that he thought "the nicht would be a good nicht," and we were about half a mile off the mouth of Loch Sligachan, when *squall third*, coming sheer down the sides of Glamaig, smote us like a thunderbolt, and with a terrific shriek laid the *Tern* clean upon her broadside. It was a trying moment; the trysail trailed in the water, and the water, covering all the decks to leeward, poured in a light-green stream into the cockpit, and even through the hatches into the cabin. The cook screamed from below amid an awful clatter of rubbish, and those on deck shivered and looked pale. "Off wi' the foresail!" screamed Hamish; and it was done in an instant. For a moment it seemed as if the little craft would never right, but slowly she emerged from her bath and was shaken up in the wind, shivering like a half-drowned bird. All breathed hard after the escape. After such a warning it was considered advisable to exchange the big jib for the little storm one—which was done, and eased the boat very considerably.

Well, it is useless to go on with further details of our entry into Sligachan. So determined did the wind seem to oppose our passage and give us a ducking, that once or twice we actually thought of turning tail and running back to Portree. But we persevered, even without a local pilot, and the tide being nearly full, we passed over sunken dangers with comparative safety. At the narrowest part of the passage we could see the bottom, and actually grazed it with our keel. But the winds were the worst. The anchorage was right at the foot of Glamaig, so that the nearer we drew the fiercer and more sudden were the squalls. The people gathered on shore, evidently expecting to see us get into trouble. To their astonishment, however, we shook the little *Tern* through every blast, righted and saved her at each moment of peril, and finally dropped anchor safely before it was quite dark. How we should have fared on a really stormy day it is not difficult to guess. This was an ordinary evening, somewhat windy, but what the men of Sligachan called "good weather." So terrific, however, is the suction of the hills beyond, and so sheer the descent of Glamaig to the water, that winds which are mild elsewhere become furious here. Keep us from Sligachan after October, when the southwester begins to come with its mighty rain-clouds over the sea!

While we are on the subject of squalls, we may complete our report against Ben Glamaig by stating that on one occasion, during our stay in the loch, although we were only about two hundred yards from low-water mark, we could hold no communication with the shore for a night and a day, and were all that time watching anxiously lest the *Tern's* heavy mast should founder her at anchor. "Half a gale" of wind was blowing; and with many of the squalls the boat, though perfectly bare of canvas, lay over so much as to ship water into the cockpit. The wind came straight off Glamaig, and though there was no "fetch" whatever, there was scarcely a dark spot between us and the shore—all was churned as white as snow.

That night, shut up on board his little vessel, the Wanderer read again King Haco's Saga, and put it into new language for the English public. All through the voyage he had been thinking of Haco and his chiefs; and how they had haunted that coast in their strange ships, leaving everywhere the traditions of their race. Skye still rings with them. Portree is still "the King's Harbor;" "Kyleakin" remains the "Passage of King Hakon." How they fared among the perilous waters, is a tale worth telling, and most fittingly in the narrow inland sounds of Skye, where Haco the King and his invading fleet will never be forgotten.

CHAPTER XIV.

THE SAGA OF HACO THE KING.*

I.

KING ALEXANDER'S DREAM AND DEATH.

WHEN Haco the King ruled over Norway, King Alexander, son of William, sent from Scotland in the Western Sea two bishops to King Haco, begging him to give up those lands in the Hebrides which King Magnus Barefoot had unjustly taken from King Malcolm. King Haco answered, that Magnus had settled with Malcolm what districts the Norwegians should have in Scotland, or in the islands which lie near it, adding, moreover, that the King of Scotland had no rule in the Hebrides at the time when King Magnus won them from King Godfred, and also that King Magnus had only taken back his birthright. Then quoth the bishops, "Our master, the King of Scotland, would willingly purchase all the Hebrides, and we therefore entreat King Haco to

* Wherever, in the following translation, I have used a modern Scotch word, such as "speired" (inquired), "harried" (plundered), "kirk" (church), "bairns" (children), it is to be understood that the modern word is the same in form, sound, and meaning as the original Icelandic.—R. B.

value them in fine silver." But Haco laughed, saying he had no such lack of pence as to be compelled to sell his inheritance. With these words for an answer the bishops went their way.

Now, from this cause there speedily arose great coldness between the kings; yet, again and again, Alexander the King sent fresh messengers with new offers. But when he could not purchase those lands of King Haco, he took other measures in hand which were not princely. Collecting a host throughout all Scotland, he prepared for a voyage to the Hebrides, and vowed to win those islands under his dominion, vowing clear and loud before his subjects that he would not rest till he had set his flag on the cliffs of Thurso, and had gained all the provinces which the Norwegian monarch possessed west of the German Ocean.

In these days King Alexander sent word to John, Lord of the Isles, that he wished to speak with him. But King John would not meet the Scottish king till some earls of Scotland had pledged their honor that he should fare safely. When the king met the Scottish monarch he bade King John that he would give up Kiamaburgh into his power, and three other castles which he held of King Haco, as also the other lands which King Haco had given him. But John did well and uprightly, and said that he would not break his troth to King Haco. On this he went away, and stopped not at any place till he came quite north to the Lewis.

That summer, Alexander, King of Scotland, then

lying in Kiararey Sound, dreamed a dream. He thought that three men came to him; one of them was in royal robes, but very stern, ruddy in countenance, short and thick; another was of slender make, but active, and of all men most majestic; the third, again, was of a very great stature, but his features were wild and distorted, and he was unsightly to look upon. Now, these three spoke to Alexander in his dream, and speired whether he meant to harry the isles of the Western Sea. Alexander answered that he certainly meant to win back the isles under his crown. Then those three spirits bade him go back, and told him no other course would turn out to his good. The king told his dream, and many bade him to return. But the king would not, and a little after he fell sick and died. The Scottish army then broke up; and they bare the king's body to Scotland.

Now all men say that the three men whom the king saw in his sleep were—St. Olaf, King of Norway; St. Magnus, Earl of Orkney; and Columba, the Saint of Icolmkill.

II.

KING HACO GATHERS HIS HOST.

Then the Scottish people took for their king Alexander, the son of Alexander, who married the daughter of Henry, king of England, and became a meikle prince.

In the summer of 1262 there came to Haco, King of Norway, many letters from the kings of the Hebrides in the Western Seas, complaining sore of the ill-deeds of the Earl of Ross, Kiarnach, son of Mac-Camal, and other Scots. These same burned villages and kirks, and killed great numbers both of men and women. They had even taken the small bairns, and, raising them on the points of their spears, shook them till they slipped down to their hands, when they threw them away, dead, on the ground. The letters said, also, that the Scottish king would win all the Hebrides if life was granted him.

When King Haco heard these tidings they gave him much uneasiness, and he laid the case before his council. Then it was settled that King Haco should, in the winter season about Yule, issue an edict through all Norway, and order out both troops and food for an expedition. He bade all his forces meet him at Bergen early in spring.

King Haco came to Bergen on Christmas. He dwelt there during the spring, and made ready swiftly for war. After that a great number of barons and officers, and vassals, and a vast many soldiers came in daily unto him.

King Haco held a general council near Bergen, at Backa. There the meikle host came together. The king then cried that this host was to be sent against Scotland, in the Western Seas.

During this voyage King Haco had that great vessel which he had bade them build at Bergen. It was built all of oak, and had twenty banks of oars. It was decked with beads and necks of dragons beautifully overlaid with gold. He had also many other well-found ships.

In the spring, King Haco sent John Langlifeson

and Henry Scott west to the Orkneys, to get pilots for Scotland. From thence John sailed to the Hebrides, and told King Dugal that he might expect an army from the east. Word had got abroad that the Scots would harry in the islands that summer. King Dugal therefore spread a report that forty ships were coming from Norway. Some time before the king himself was ready he sent eight ships to the westward. The captains of these were Ronald Urka, Erling Ivarson, Andrew Nicholson, and Halvard Red.

When the king had built his ship, he went with all his host from the capital to Eidvags; afterwards he himself hied back to the city, and dwelt there some nights, and then set out for Herlover. Here came together all the troops, both from the north and the south.

King Haco lay with all his force at Herlover; it was a mighty and glorious host.

Three nights before the Selian vigils King Haco set sail for the German Sea with all his fleet. He had now been King of Norway six and forty winters. He had a good breeze, the weather was fair, and the fleet beautiful to behold sailing southward to the islands of the Western Sea.

III.

SAILING OF THE GREAT FLEET.

King Haco had a company chosen well for his own ship. There were, on the quarter-deck, Thorlife, Abbot of Holm, Sir Askatin, four priests, chaplains to the king, Andrew of Thissisey, Aslac Guss, the king's master of the horse, Andrew Hawardson, Guthorm Gillason and Thorstein his brother, Eirek Scot Gautson, with many others. There were on the main-deck: Aslack Dagson, Steinar Herka, Klomit Langi, Andrew Gums, Eirek Dugalson, the father of King Dugal, Einar Lang-Bard, Arnbjorn Suela, Sigvat Bodvarson, Hoskuld Oddson, John Hoglif, Arni Stinkar. On the fore-deck there were: Sigurd, the son of Ivar Rofu, Ivar Helgason of Lofloc, Erland Scolbein, Dag of Southeim, Briniolf Johnson, Gudleik Sneis, and most of the king's chamberlains, with Andrew Plytt, the king's treasurer. There were in the fore-castle: Eirek Skifa, Thornfin Sigvald, Kari Endridson, Gudbrand Johnson, and many of the cupbearers. There were four men on every half rower's seat. With King Haco, Magnus, Earl of Orkney, left Bergen, and the king gave him a good galley. These barons were also with the king: Briniolf Johnson, Fin Gautson, Erling Alfson, Erlend Red, Bard of Hestby, Eilif of Naustadale, Andrew Pott, and Ogmund Krekedants. Erling Ivarson, John Drotning, Gaut of Meli, and Nicholas of Giska, were behind with Prince Magnus at Bergen, as were several other officers who had not been ready.

King Haco, having got a gentle breeze, was two nights at sea, when he reached the harbor of Shetland, called Breydeyiar Sound, and from thence he sailed to Ronaldsvo with all his host.

While King Haco lay in Ronaldsvo, a great darkness drew over the sun, so that only a little ring was bright around; and it continued so for some hours.

IV.

KING HACO'S SAILING SOUTHWARD.

On the day of St. Laurence's wake, King Haco, after a cruise in the Orkneys, sailed with all his forces to a haven that is called Hasleviarvic, from that to Lewis, so on to Raasa, and from thence to that place in Skye Sound which is called Calliach Stone. Here he was joined by Magnus, King of Man, and by Erling Ivarson, Andrew Nicholson, and Halward. He next sailed south to the Sound of Mull, and then to Kiararey, where King Dugal and the other Hebrideans were assembled with their men.

King Haco had now more than one hundred vessels, for the most part large, and all of them well prepared both with men and weapons. While he abode at Kiararey he sent fifty ships south to the Mull of Kintire to harry. The captains of the same were King Dugal, Magnus, King of Man, Bruniolf, Johnson, Ronald Urka, Andrew Pott, Ogmund Krekedants, Vigleic Priestson. He sent, also, five ships for Bute under Erling Red, Andrew Nicholson, Simon Stutt, Ivar Ungi Eyfari, and Gutthorm the Hebridean.

Then did Haco the King sail south to Gudey before Kintire, where he anchored. There he met John, King of the Isles, whom King Haco in vain besought to follow him. But King John said he was pledged to the Scottish king, of whom he held more lands than of King Haco. He, therefore, entreated King Haco to dispose of all those estates which he had conferred upon him. King Haco kept him with him some time, vainly trying to win him back to his allegiance.

During King Haco's stay at Gudey, an abbot of Greymonks came to him, bidding him spare their cloister and Holy Kirk. The king granted them this, and gave them his own promise in writing.

Friar Simon had long lain sick, and he had died at Gudey. His corpse was carried to Kintire and buried in the Greymonks cloister. They spread a fringed pall over his grave and called him Saint.

In those days came men from King Dugal, and said that the lords of Kintire and others would surrender their lands to King Haco, and follow with their clansmen under his banner. Then the king said that he would not harry their lands if they yielded the next day; ere noon they took an oath to King Haco and gave hostages. The king laid a fine of a thousand herd of cattle on their estates. Thereupon Angus yielded up Isla also to the king, and the king granted it back unto him as liegeman to Norway.

Soon after this the king sailed south along Kintire with all his fleet, and anchored in Arran Sound. Thither often came barefooted friars from the King of Scotland to King Haco, seeking peace. Here King Haco freed his prisoner, King John, gave him many rich gifts, and bade him go in peace. Then did he swear to King Haco to labor at all times to make peace between him and the King of Scots. Thereafter King Haco sent Gilbert, Bishop of Hamer, Henry, Bishop of Orkney, Andrew Nicholson,

Andrew Plytt, and Paul Soor to King Alexander, who met them honorably, and sent envoys to King Haco in his turn. Now King Haco had writ down all the names of the Western Islands which he called his own, and King Alexander had named all those which he would not yield. These last were Bute, Arran, and the two Cumbras. But the Scots willfully held aloof from a settlement, because summer was ending and the foul weather was beginning. Seeing this, Haco the King sailed in under the Cumbras with all his host.

Thereafter King Haco sent as envoys a bishop and a baron, and to meet them came some knights and cloistermen. They spoke much, but could not agree, and late in the day so many Scots gathered together that the Norwegians feared treachery and drew away to their ships. Many now bade the king end the truce and harry, as food was scant. But Haco sent one Kolbein Rich to the King of Scots with peace letters, offering that the kings should meet, with all their host, and speak of peace. If peace, by God's grace, took place, it would be well; but if not, then should the kings fight with their whole host, and let him win whom God pleased. The King of Scots was not loath to fight, but said little in answer. Kolbein went back to his master, and thereupon the truce was over.

V.

THE KING'S FLEET MEETS WITH A GREAT STORM.

The king now sent sixty ships into Skipa-Fjörd (Loch Long). Their commanders were Magnus, King of Man, King Dugal, and Allan his brother, Angus, Margad, Vigleik Prieston, and Ivar Holm. When they came to the head of the Fjörd, they took their boats and drew them over the land to a great water which is called Loch Lomond. On the far side thereof was a rich earldom called Lennox, and in the center were many islands, well peopled, which the Northmen wasted with fire, destroying also all the buildings on the water side.

Allan, brother of King Dugal, marched far into the land, slew many men and took many hundred head of cattle. Thereafter the Northmen went back to their ships. They met with so great a storm that ten of their ships were wrecked in the Fjörd. It was now that Ivar Holm took that sickness of which he died.

King Haco still lay in the open. Michaelmas happened on a Saturday, and on Monday night after there came a great tempest with hailstones and rain. The watch on the forecastle of the king's ship called out that a transport vessel was driving against their cable. The men leapt up on deck, but the rigging of the transport caught the prow of the king's ship and carried away its figure-head. The vessel then fell so foul aboard that its anchor grappled the ropes of the king's ship, which straight began to drag its anchor. Whereupon the king bade them cut the transport's cable, which being done, she drove out to sea. The king's ship now rode safe till daylight. In the morning, at flood tide, the transport was cast ashore, together with a galley. The wind still rose, the king's men got more ropes and cast out a fifth anchor. The king himself rowed ashore in his boat to the isles and ordered mass to be sung. Meantime the ships dragged up the sound, and the storm was so fierce that some cut away their masts and others drove ashore. The king's ship still drove, though seven anchors had been cast out. They threw out an eighth, which was the sheet anchor. The ship still drove, but at last the anchors held fast. Five ships went ashore. So great was the storm that men said magic had done it, and the fall of rain was dreadful

Now when the Scots saw that the vessels had driven ashore, they gathered together and approached the Northmen, and threw at them. But the Northmen fought well and fiercely, sheltered by their ships; the Scots made several attacks at intervals, killing few men, but wounding many. Then King Haco sent boats with men to help them.

Lastly, the king, with Thorlaug Bosa, set sail for the shore in a barge. At his coming the Scots fled, and the Northmen passed the night ashore. But in the night the Scots entered the wrecked transport and bare off what they could. The morning after the king landed with many armed folk; he ordered the vessel to be lightened and towed out to the fleet.

VI.

THE BATTLE OF LARGS.

A little after that they saw the Scots, and they thought the King of Scotland was there himself, because the host was so great. Ogmund Krekedants stood on a height, and his men with him. The Scots attacked him with their van, and approached him in so great force that the Northmen begged the king to row out to his ships and to send them help. The king would stay on land, but they would not let him bide in such danger, and he rowed out in his boat to his fleet in the open sound. These barons abode ashore: Andrew Nicholson, Ogmund Krekedants, Erling Alfson, Andrew Pott, Ronald Urka, Thorlaug Bosi, and Paul Soor. All the fighting men with them on land were eight hundred or more. Of those, two hundred were on the height with Ogmund, but the rest were gathered together on the beach. Then the Scots drew nigh, numbering near fifteen hundred knights; their horses had all breast-plates, and many Spanish steeds were clad in mail. The Scots had also many soldiers on foot well weaponed, most of them with bows and spears.

Now the Northmen on the height drew back slowly toward the sea, thinking that the Scots might surround them. Andrew Nicholson then came up to the height, and bade Ogmund to back slowly to the beach, and not fly like routed men. The Scots thereupon attacked them fiercely with darts and stones. Many were the weapons showered on the Northmen, who defended themselves stoutly as they went. But when they came to the sea, all rushing swifter than they should, their fellows on the beach fancied they were routed; wherefore some leaped into their boats, and rowed in them from shore, and others leaped into the transport. The soldiers called out to them to stay, and some few men returned. Andrew

Pott leaped over two boats and into a third, and so from land. Many boats sunk down, and some men were drowned. After that the Northmen on shore turned about towards the water.

Here fell Haco of Steine, attendant of Haco the King. Then were the Norwegians driven south from the transport, and these were their leaders: Andrew Nicholson, Ogmund Krekedants, Thorlaug Bosi, and Paul Soor. Hard blows were dealt, and the foemen were ill-matched, for ten Scots fought against each Northman.

There was a young knight of the Scots, named Ferash, and rich both in birth and gear. He had a helmet all gold, and set with precious stones, and his armor was also gold. He rode up to the Northmen, but none followed. He rode up to the Northmen, and then back to his own host. Then Andrew Nicholson came close to the ranks of the Scots. He met that brave knight and struck at him so fiercely that he cut through the armor into his thigh, and reached even to the saddle. The Northman took off his costly belt. Then began hard blows. Many fell on both sides, but most of the Scots, as Sturlas sings:

> "Gathered in circle,
> With clangor of armor
> Our youth struck the mighty
> Donners of armlets;
> Limbs dead and bloody
> Glutted the death-birds.
> Who shall avenge now
> The mighty belt-wearer?"

While this fight was raging, there was so great a storm, that King Haco saw no hope of landing his host. Yet Ronald and Eilif of Naustadale rowed ashore with men and fought fiercely, together with those Northmen who had fled in their boats. Ronald was driven back to his ships, but Eilif stood firm. The Northmen now ranged themselves anew, and the Scots took the height. There were constant fights with stones and darts; but toward the end of day the Northmen rushed up against the Scots on the hill. The Scots then fled from the height, and betook themselves to their mountains. The Northmen then entered their boats, and rowed out to the fleet, and came safely through the storm. At morning they returned to land to look after those who had fallen. Among the dead were Haco of Steine and Thorgisl Gloppa, the king's housemen.

There fell also a good bondsman from Drontheim, called Karlhoved, and another from Fiorde, called Halkel. Besides these there perished three Light-Swains,* Thorstein Bat, John Ballhoved, and Halward Buniard. The Northmen could not tell how many of the Scots fell, for their dead bodies were taken up and carried to the woods. Haco ordered his dead men to be carried to Holy Church.

VII.

KING HACO SAILS NORTHWARD.

The fifth day after that the king took up his anchor, and guided his ship close under the Cumbras.

* *Kerti-sveinar*, Masters of the Lights.

That day came unto him the ships which had sailed up Skipa-Fjörd. The fast-day after it was good weather, and the king sent his vessels ashore, to burn the ships which had been wrecked; and that same day, a little after, the king sailed past Cumbra out to Melansey, and lay there several nights. Here came unto him the messengers he had sent to Ireland, and told him that the Irish Northmen would support his host till he freed them from the rule of the English king. Haco longed much to sail to Ireland, but the wind was not fair. He took counsel, and the whole host wished him not to sail. He said to them that he would depart for the Hebrides, for the host was short of food. Then did Haco the King order the corse of Ivar Holm to be carried into Bute, and·there it was buried.

After that the king sailed under Melansey, and lay some nights under Arran, and then to Sandey, and so to the Mull of Kintire, and came close under Gudey. Then sailed he out to Ila Sound, and lay there two nights. He laid levy on the island in three hundred head of cattle, but some was paid in meal and cheese. Then Haco the King sailed the first Sunday in winter, and met so much storm, with wrack, that scarce a ship bore its sails. Then the king took haven in Kiararey, and there messengers went between him and King John, but to little end. At this time the king was told that his men had harried much in Mull, and slain some men of Mull, and that two or three Northmen had fallen.

Next, King Haco sailed from the Calf of Mull, and lay there some nights. There he was left by King

Dugald and Allan his brother; and the king gave them those estates which King John had owned. Magnus, King of Man, and other Islesmen, had departed before. To Rudri he gave Bute, and Arran to Margad. To Dugald he gave the castle in Kintire, which Guthorm Backa-Rolf had taken in the summer. In this manner had Haco the King gained back all those lands which King Magnus Barefoot had wrested from the Scots and the Islesmen.

Haco the King sailed from the Calf of Mull to Rauney, and from Rauney northward. The wind blowing against him, he sailed into Wester-Fjörd, in Skye, and levied food of Islesmen. He next sailed past Cape Wrath, and at Dyrness the weather fell calm, and the king let the ships be steered into Gia-Fjörd. This was the Feast of the two Apostles, Simon and Jude, and the mass day was a Sunday. The king lay there for the night. On the mass day, after mass was sung, there came to him some Scots, whom the Northmen had taken. The king gave them liberty and sent them up the country, and made them promise to come back with cattle; but one was left behind in hostage. That same day nine men of Andrew Biusa's ship went ashore for water, and a little while after a cry was heard from the land. The crew rowed to shore from the fleet, and saw two men swimming, wounded sore, and took them aboard; but seven were slain on land, without arms, while their boat was aground. The Scots then fled to a wood, while the Northmen lifted their dead. On the Monday, King Haco sailed from Gia-Fjörd, and gave liberty to the Scottish hostage, and set him ashore. That night the king came to Orkney, and lay in a sound north from Asmundsvo; thence he sailed for Ronaldsvo and most of his fleet with him. As they sailed over Pentland Fjörd there rose a great whirlpool, into which fell a ship of Rygia-fylke, and all men there were drowned. John of Hestby drove through the straits, and came near being wrecked in the gulf; but with God's grace the ship was forced east to the open sea, and he hied to Norway.

While King Haco lay in Orkney most of his ships sailed to Norway, some with the king's leave, but many gave themselves leave. The king had said at first, when he came to the islands, that he would steer straight home; but the wind was in his teeth, and he thought to bide in the Orkneys during the winter. He named twenty ships to stay, and gave the rest leave to go. All his vassals remained, save Eilif of Naustdale, who sailed eastward home; but many of the best men in the land abode with the king. Then the king sent letters to Norway, concerning the things he should need. After All Saints' mass the king sailed his ships to Medalland Harbor, but he spent one day at Ronaldsha.

VIII.

KING HACO'S SICKNESS.

The Saturday ere Martinmas, King Haco rode out to Medalland's Harbor, and after mass he fell very sick. At night he was aboard his ship, but at morning he let mass be sung on land. Afterward he held a council where the ship should lie, and bade his men look well after their vessels. After that each skipper took charge of his own ship. Some were laid up in Medalland's Haven, and some in at Skalpeid.

Next, King Haco went to Skalpeid and rode to Kirkwall, and there abode in the bishop's palace with such men as dined at his board. Here the king and the bishop kept each his board in the hall for his own men, but the king dined in the room above. Andrew Plytt looked after the king's table, and gave to each of the followers his share. After all that was arranged, the divers skippers went where their ships were laid up. The barons in Kirkwall were Briniolf Johnson, Erling Alfson, Ronald Urka, Erling of Birkey, John Drotning, and Erlend Red. The other barons were in their districts.

King Haco had all the summer worked much and anxiously, and had slept little, and when he came to Kirkwall he lay sick in bed. When he had lain some nights the sickness lessened, and he was on foot three days. The first day he walked in his rooms, the second he heard mass in the bishop's chapel, and the third day he went to Magnus Kirk and around the shrine of the holy Earl Magnus. He then ordered a bath and was shaven. Then, some nights after, he sickened again and lay again in bed. In his sickness he had read to him the Bible and Latin books. But finding he grew sad in thinking on these things, he had read to him night and day books of the North—first the lives of holy men, and when these were ended, the tales of our kings from Halden the Swart, and so of all the Northern kings, each after each. Haco the King found his sickness still increase. He thought, therefore, of the pay due to his troops, and ordered a mark of fine silver to each court-man, and half a mark to each of the light-swains and other followers. He let all the silver plate of his board be weighed, and ordered it to be given forth, if the realm-silver was too little. King Haco was shriven the night before St. Lucia's mass. There were there Thorgisl, Bishop of Stavanger, Gilbert, Bishop of Hamar, Henry, Bishop of Orkney, Abbot Thorleif, and many other learned men, and before he was smeared all said farewell to the king and kissed him. He still spake clear, and his favorites asked him if he had any other son besides Prince Magnus, or any other heirs who might share in the state. But he vowed that he had no other son and no daughter but what all men knew.

Then were read the Sagas of the kings down to Suerer, and he ordered them to read the life of Suerer, and to read it night and day, as often as he was awake.

IX.

KING HACO'S DEATH AND FUNERAL.

The mass day of St. Lucia was a Thursday, and on the Saturday after the king's sickness grew so great that he lost speech, and at midnight Almighty God called King Haco out of this home's life. These barons beheld his death: Briniolf Johnson, Erling Alfson, John Drotning, Ronald Urka, and some serving men who had been near the king in his sickness. Directly after he died, bishops and learned men were sent for, and mass was sung. Then all the folk went forth, save Thorgisl the Bishop, Briniolf Johnson, and two other men, who watched the body, and did all the service due to so mighty a lord and prince as was Haco the King. On Saturday, the corpse was carried into the high chamber, and set on a bier. The body was clad in rich raiment, and a garland set on his head; and all bedight as became a crowned monarch. The light-swains stood with tapers, and the whole hall was lit. Then went all folk to see the body, and it was fair and blooming, and the face was fair in hue as in living men. There was great solace of the grief of all there to see their departed king so richly dight. Then was sung the high mass for the dead. The nobles kept wake by the corpse through the night. On Monday, the body was borne to Magnus Kirk, and royally laid out that night. On Tuesday, it was laid in a kist, and buried in the choir of St. Magnus Kirk, near the steps of the shrine of St. Magnus, the Earl. Afterward, the tomb was closed, and a pall spread over. Then was it settled that wake should be kept all winter over the grave. At Yule, the bishop and Andrew Plytt made feasts, as the king had ordered before he went, and good gifts were given to all the host.

Now, King Haco had given orders that his corse should be carried east to Norway, and he would be graved near his father and other kinsmen, and about the end of winter was launched that meikle ship which Haco the King had in the west. On Ash Wednesday, the corse of the king was taken out of the earth; this was on the third of the nones of March. The court-men then went with the corse to Skalpeid to the ship. The chief leaders of the ship were Thorgisl, the bishop, and Andrew Plytt. They sailed the first Saturday in Lent, and met hard weather, and anchored south in Silavog. Thence they sent letters to Prince Magnus, and told him the tidings. Afterward they sailed north to Bergen. They came to Silavog before the mass of St. Benedict. On mass-day, Prince Magnus met the corse. The ship was brought near the king's palace, and the corse was placed in the summer-hall. The morning after, it was borne out to Christ Kirk. There went with it Magnus the King, the two queens, and court-men and town folk. After that, the body was buried in the choir of Christ Kirk; and Magnus the King spake to the folk with many good words. There stood all the folk in great grief, as Sturlas sings:

> " Three nights came the mighty
> Warriors to Bergen,
> Ere in the earth-vale
> Lay the wise ruler,
> The pale weapon-breakers
> Stood gathered around him,
> Full weeping and joyless.
> (Meikle strife followed.)"

Haco the King was buried three nights before the mass of Mary; this was after the birth of our Lord Jesus Christ, one thousand two hundred and sixty-three years.

CHAPTER XV.

GLEN SLIGACHAN AND THE CUCHULLINS.

Sconser and Sligachan—Party and Guide—Dawn on the Cuchullins—Scuir-na-Gillean—A Rhapsody on Geology—Fire and Ice—The Path along the Glen—Hart-o'-Corry—Ben Blaven—A Monologue on Ossian—Schneider and the Red Deer—First Glimpse of the "Corry of the Water"—Lochan Dhu.

THE Cuchullin Hills are the Temple of Ossian, and the temple has two porches—Sligachan and Scavaig. Having now fairly halted on the threshold of one, we stood close to an enchanted world. Opposite our anchorage was the village of Sconser—a number of rude hovels scattered on the hillside, with many fine patches of green corn and potatoes, and bits of excellent pasture for the cows. A smack was at anchor close to us, skiffs were drawn up above high-water mark, and nets were drying everywhere on the beach; and we soon ascertained that the herring were "up the loch." Right above us, as we have said, rose Ben Glamaig, towering to a desolate and barren cone, seamed everywhere with the beds of streams, and covered with the gray sand and loose rocks deposited in seasons of flood. At times this red mountain is a worthy neighbor of the Cuchullins, but at others, notably when the sun is very bright and the air very clear, it appears sufficiently common-place. Commonplace is an adjective at no time applicable to Scuirna-Gillean or Blaven; these are magnificent in all weathers, no sunlight being able to rob them of the wildly beautiful outlines and lurid tints of the hypersthene.

Situated at the head of the loch is Sligachan Inn, the cleanest, snuggest, cheapest little place of the sort in all the Highlands of Scotland. Here, on the morning after our arrival, we procured ponies and a guide, and proceeded in ordinary tourist-fashion to make our way to the heart of the temple—to the melancholy lake of Corruisk, distant about nine miles from the head of Sligachan. Our party numbered five, including the guide. Two were mounted, while the Wanderer and Hamish Shaw trudged on foot. The guide (a gloomy Gael of thirteen, as sturdy as a whin-bush, and about as communicative) led the way, uttering ever and anon an eldritch whistle much like the doleful scream of the curlew. Our way lay up Glen Sligachan, along a footway discernable only by the experienced eye; and we had scarcely proceeded a quarter of a mile from the inn, when the Cuchullins, in all their grandeur and desolation, began to gather upon us—

"Taciti, soli, e sanza compagnia"—*

their wild outlines showing in strange contrast to the conical Red Hills, so called from the ruddy hues of the syenite and porphyry of which they are composed. Chief of the Red Hills is Glamaig; king of

* "Inferno," cant. xxiii.

the Cuchullins is Blaabhein, or Blaven. Down the round sides of Glamaig rolls the red *débris* of gravel and sand, washed into dark lines by innumerable watercourses, and giving to the lonely hill the aspect of a huge cone slowly moldering, rusting and decomposing, save where the deep heather gathers on its hollow flanks below. But Blaven, like all his brethren, preserves the one dark hue of hypersthene, while his sides are torn into craggy gulfs and lurid caves, and his hooked forehead cuts in sharp silhouette the gray and silent sky. The mountainous part of Skye consists of these two groups, so strangely contrasted in shape and color, so totally unlike in geological composition.* The range of the Cuchullins is almost completely detached from that of the Red Hills by the valley of Glen Sligachan.

Our start was made soon after dawn, and as we entered the great glen the mists of morning still brooded like white smoke over the hills on either side, while far away eastward the clouds parted above the mountain-tops, and revealed a glimpse of heaven, green as the delicate outer leaves of the water-lily. The rain had fallen heavily during the night, and the dead stillness of the air was broken only by the low murmur of the streams and new-born runlets. Passing by a glassy pool of Sligachan Burn, we saw a young salmon leap glittering like gold two feet into the air, giving us therewith his prophecy of a still and windless day; and while Schneider the wayward,

---

* See the admirable treatise on the "Geology of the Cuchullin Hills," by Professor Forbes, of St. Andrew's.

warm already in anticipation, plunged in for her morning bath, up rose the old cock-grouse from the margin of the pool, and fled, screaming his warning to the six or eight little "cheepers" which were following the old hen swiftly and furtively through the deep heather. The sun broke out on the burn, and it was full day. The damp rocks gleamed like silver, the heather glittered with innumerable gems. Not a member of the party but caught the glad contagion. The ponies pricked up their ears, and carried their riders more swiftly along the devious track. Schneider went raving mad with delight, and rushed around the party in dripping circles. The Wanderer leapt like a very hart for joy. Hamish Shaw murmured a Gaelic ditty of love and gladness; and the boy-guide answered with a blither scream.

To the Wanderer, however, the path was as familiar as to the guide, for he had trod it many a time, both alone and in the best of company; and, indeed, his present rapture was far more allied to physical delight in the glorious dawn than to thorough perception of the beautiful scenes opening up around him. Such scenery—the scenery whose appeal is to the soul—does not startle suddenly; its supreme effect is subtle and slow; the first emotion in perceiving it sometimes even is like disappointment. The Wanderer's mind, too, is like a well, profound, of course, but fed mysteriously; slow, very slow, to gather in thoughts from the numberless veins and pores of communication. He drank the dawn like an animal—like a ruminant cow, like a mountain-goat. He had scarcely a thought for the marvelous landscape.

There was no more speculation in his eyes than in those of the guide. Meantime his heart could only dance, his brain only spin, his eyes only gleam. He saw everything, but lightly, dazzlingly, through the gleam of the senses. The first sip of the mystic cup merely produced intoxication.

Then, slowly, minute by minute, the wild animal instinct cleared off, and the gray light of spiritual perception settled into the eyes. By this time, the mists on either side of the glen had changed into mere solitary vapors, dying a lingering death each in some lonely gorge screened from the sun; and the mountains shone darkly beautiful after their morning bath of rain. Prominent above all, on the northeast side of the glen, rose the serrated outlines of Scuir-na-Gillean, or the Hill of the Young Men, so named after certain shepherds who lost their lives while vainly endeavoring to gain the summit. The height of this mountain, perhaps the highest of the Cuchullins, does not exceed 3200 feet, but the ascent is very perilous. Rent into huge fissures by the throes of earthquake, titanic and livid, from foot to base one stretch of stone, without one blade of grass or green heather, it stretched its weirdly broken outline against a windless and cloudless sky. Few feet have trod its highest cliffs. In 1836, when Professor Forbes first visited the locality, the ascent was deemed impossible. "Talking of it," writes the Professor, "with an active forester in the service of Lord Macdonald, named Duncan Macintyre, whom I engaged to guide me to Corruisk from Sligachan, he told me that he had attempted it repeatedly without success, both by himself, and also with different strangers, who had engaged him for the purpose; but he indicated a way different from those which he had tried, which he thought might be more successful. I engaged him to accompany me; and the next day (June 7) we succeeded in gaining the top, the extreme roughness of the rocks (all hypersthene) rendering the ascent safe, where, with any other formation, it might have been exceedingly perilous. Indeed, I have never seen a rock so adapted for clambering. At this time I erected a cairn and temporary flag, which stood, I was informed, a whole year; but having no barometer, I could not ascertain the height, which I estimated at 3000 feet. In 1843 I was in Skye with a barometer, but had not an opportunity of revisiting the Cuchullins; but in May, 1845, I ascended the lower summit, nearly adjoining, marked Bruch-na-Fray in the map; and wishing to ascertain the difference of the height of Scuir-na-Gillean, I proposed to Macintyre to try to ascend it from the west side. It was no sooner proposed than attempted. It was impossible to otherwise than descend deep in the rugged ravine of Loat-o'-Corry, which separates the summits, and then face an ascent, which from a distance appeared almost perpendicular; but, aided by the quality of the rocks already mentioned, we gained the Scur-na-Gillean from the west side, although on reaching the top, and gazing back, it looked like a dizzy precipice."* The barometrical record and

* At the foot of one of the precipices the mangled body of a young tourist was discovered during the autumn of 1870. The dead man was one of two friends who started to make the ascent

geological observations made by the Professor, both here and elsewhere among the Cuchullins, are of the very highest interest. Everywhere among the mountains of Skye are to be traced the proofs of direct glacial action. Many phenomena can be described only as the effects of moving ice; and it would be quite impossible to find these phenomena in greater perfection even among the Alps.

We have no patience with those imaginative people who are so far fascinated by transcendental meteors as to class geology in the prose sisterhood of algebra and mathematics. The typical geologist, indeed, whom we meet prowling, hammer in hand, in the darkness of Glen Sannox, or rock-tapping on the sea-shore in the society of elderly virgins, or examining Agassiz' atlas through blue spectacles on board the Highland steamboat—this typical being, we repeat, is frequently duller company than the Free Church minister or the domine; but he is a mere fumbler about the footprints of the fair science, with never the courage to look straight into those beautiful blind eyes of hers, and discover that she has a soul. By what name shall we call her, if not by the divine name of Mnemosyne—the sphinx-like spirit that broods and remembers—a soul, a divinity, brooding blind in the solitude, and feeling with her fingers the raised letters of the stone-book which she holds in her lap, and wherein God has written the veritable

of Scuir-na-Gillean together; but one of whom, being taken slightly unwell on the way, returned to Sligachan Inn, leaving his comrade to proceed to the heights alone, and meet there his terrible doom.

"Legend of the World?" A prose science?—say rather a sublime Muse! Why, her throne is made of the mountains of the earth, and her speech is the earth-slip and the volcano, and her taper is the lightning, and her forehead touches a coronal of stars. Only the fool misapprehends her and blasphemes. Whoso looks into her face with reverent eyes is appalled by the light of God there, and sinks to his knees, crying, "I would seek unto God, and unto God would I commit my cause, who doeth great things and unsearchable, marvelous things without number."

In sober words, without fine writing or rapture, it must be said that the Cuchullins cannot long be contemplated apart from their geology. Turn your eyes again for a moment on Scuir-na-Gillean! Note those somber hues, those terrific shadows, that jagged outline traced as with a frenzied finger along the sky. It is a gentle autumn morning, and the film of white cloud resting on yonder topmost peak is moveless as the ghost of the moon in an April heaven. There is no sound save the melancholy murmur of water. A strange awe steals over you as you gaze; the soul broods in its own twilight. Then as the first feeling of almost animal perception fails, the mind awakens from its torpor, and with it comes a sudden illumination. Along those serrated peaks runs a fiery tongue of flame, the abysses blacken, the air is filled with a deep groan, and a thunder-cloud, driving past in a great wind, clutches at the mountain, and clinging there, belches flame, and beats the darkness into fire with wings of iron. From a rent above, the drifting

stars gaze, like affrighted eyes, dim as corpse-lights.
In a moment, this wonder passes; the sudden tension
of the mind fails, and with it the phantasm, and you
are again in the torpid condition, gazing dreamily at
the jagged outline of the Titan, dark and silent in the
brightness of the autumn morning. Again Mnemosyne waves her hand, and again the mind flashes
into picture.

> "O hoary hills, though ye look aged, ye
>   Are but the children of a latter time!
>   Methinks I see ye, in that hour sublime
>   When from the hissing caldron of the sea
>   Ye were upheaven, while so terribly
>   The clouds boiled, and the lightning scorched ye bare.
>   Wild, new-born, blind, Titans in agony,
>   Ye glared at heaven through folds of fiery hair. . . .
>   Then, in an instant, while ye trembled thus,
>   A Hand from heaven, white and luminous,
>   Passed o'er your brows, and hushed your firey breath.
>   Lo! one by one the dim stars gathered round;
>   The great deep glassed itself, and with no sound
>   A cold snow glimmering fell; and all was still as death."

You have now a glimpse of the ninth circle of the
Inferno. Surrounded by the region of the Cold
Clime, girt round on every side by unearthly forms of
ice and rock, you see below you vales of frozen water,
and unfathomable deeps, blue as the overhanging
heaven. Where fire once raved, snow now broods.
Dome, pyramid, and pinnacle tower around with
walls and crags of glittering ice. Winds contend
silently, and heap the snow with rapid breath. Here
and there gleams the vaporous lightning, innocent
as the Aurora. The glaciers slip, and ever change.
And down through the heart of all this desolation,

past the very spot where you stand, filling the gigantic hollow of Glen Sligachan, welling onward with one deep murmur, carrying with it mighty rocks and blasted pine-trees, rolls a majestic river, here burnished black as ebony in the rush of its own speed, there foaming over broken boulders and tottering crags, and everywhere gathering into its troubled bosom the drifting glacier and the melting snow.

The Wanderer at least saw all this plain enough as he passed along the weary glen in the rear of his party; and the fanciful retrospect, instead of dulling the scene, lends it a solemn consecration. Poor indeed would be the songs of all the Muses, compared with the tale of Mnemosyne, if she could only be brought to utter half she knows.

While the Wanderer was brooding, the riders and their guide were getting well ahead. The ponies were little shaggy rascals, with short, stumpy legs, twisted like sticks of blackthorn, knees stiff as rusty hinges, and never on any account to be coaxed into a trot; small eyes, where drowsiness and mischief met; their invariable pace was a walk, slow, but steady; and when left entirely to themselves, they could be relied on to pass safely where the most cautious foot-traveler stumbled. The little, phlegmatic fellows seldom erred. They planted their feet alike on the rolling stone and the slippery rock, choosing sometimes the most unlikely passages, and avoiding by instinct the peat-bog and the green morass. Only when the unskilled rider, in his human vanity, fancied to improve matters by using the rein and

guiding the beast into what looked the right way,
did rider and steed seem in danger of getting
into trouble. And what a road was that to travel!
More than once on the way did the Wanderer congratulate himself on being afoot. Only a lynx's eye
could have made out the pathway along the glen.
Everywhere huge boulders were strewn thick as
pebbles, intersected constantly by brawling burns,
and padded round with knots of ancient heather.
To the left the heather and rock clomb over many
thymy knolls, until it fringed the base of the Red
Hills, which rose above, round, unpicturesque, and
discolored with rain-washed sand. To the right,
also, ever stretched heather and rock, until they
mingled in imperceptible shadow into the deepgreen hypersthene of the Cuchullins. The sun now
shone bright, but only deepened the shadows on the
neighboring hills, and still not a sound broke the
melancholy silence. "In Glen Sligachan, as in
many other parts of Skye," writes Alexander Smith,
"the scenery curiously repels you, and drives you in
on yourself. You have a quickened sense of your
own individuality. The enormous bulks, their
gradual receding to invisible crests, their utter
movelessness, their austere silence, daunt you. You
are conscious of their presence, and you hardly
care to speak, lest you be overheard. You can't
laugh; you would not crack a joke for the world.
Glen Sligachan would be the place to do a little
self-examination in. There you would have a sense
of your own meannesses, selfishnesses, paltry evasions
of truth and duty, and find out what a shabby fellow

you at heart are; and, looking up to your silent father-confessors, you would find no mercy in their grim faces." Such, doubtless, is the effect of the scene on some men, but most surely on those who live in cities and read Thackeray. Glen Sligachan is, indeed, weird and silent, but in no true sense of the word repelling. The eye is satisfied at every step, the shadows and the silence only deepen the beauty, and the mood awakened is one, not of shapeless, shuddering awe, but of brooding, mystic joy.

Pause here, where your path is the dry bed of a torrent, and look yonder to the northeast. Between two hills opens the great gorge of Hart-o'-Corry, which is closed in again far away by a wall of livid stone. 'Tis broad day here, but gray twilight yonder. In the hollow of the corry broods a dense vapor, and above it, down the deep-green fissures of the hypersthene, trickle streams like threads of hoary silver, frozen motionless by distance; while higher, far above the rayless abyss, the sky is serene and hyacinthine blue. That black speck over the topmost peak, that little mark scarce bigger than the dot of an *i*, is an eagle; it hovers for many minutes motionless, and then melts imperceptibly away. From the side of Hart-o'-Corry, Scuir-na-Gillean shoots up its rugged columns; and, close to the mouth of the corry, the sharply defined sweep of the deep-green hypersthene, overlaying the pale yellow felspar, has an effect of rare beauty. Turning now, and looking up the glen toward Camasunary, you behold Ben Blaven closing in the view, and towering into the sky from precipice to precipice, its ashen gray flanks corroding everywhere into veins of mineral green, until it cuts the ether with a sharp, hooked forehead of solid stone.

> ' O wonderful mountain of Blaven!
> How oft since our parting hour
> You have roared with the wintry torrents,
> You have gloomed through the thunder-shower!
> O Blaven, rocky Blaven!
> How I long to be with you again,
> To see lashed gulf and gully
> Smoke white in the windy rain—
> To see in the scarlet sunrise
> The mist-wreaths perish with heat;
> The wet rock slide with a trickling gleam
> Right down to the cataract's feet;
> While toward the crimson islands,
> Where the sea-birds flutter and skirl,
> A cormorant flaps o'er a sleek ocean floor
> Of tremulous mother-of-pearl."*

Blaven stands alone, separated from the chain of Cuchullins proper, and with the arms of the Red Hills encircling him and offering tribute. It is seldom he deigns to put aside his crown of mist, but on this golden day he is unkinged. "The sunbeam pours its light stream before him; his hair meets the wind of his hills, his face is settled from war, the calm dew of the morning lies on the hill of roses, for the sun is faint on his side, and the lake is settled and blue in the vale."

It is thus, as we gaze, that the thin sound of the

* Alexander Smith.

voice of Cona breaks in upon our meditations; "O bard! I hear thy voice; it is pleasant as the gale of the spring that sighs on the hunter's ear, when he wakens from dreams of joy, and has heard the music of the spirits of the hill." In the dreamy wanderings of our mind we had almost forgotten Ossian, the true spirit of the mystic scene. O ye ghosts of the lonely Cromla! Ye souls of chiefs that are no more! ye are "like a beam that has shone, like a mist that has fled away." "The sons of song are gone to rest." But one voice remains, strange and sad, "like a blast that roars loudly on a sea-surrounded rock, after the winds are laid."

What the Cuchullins are to all other British mountains, Ossian is to all other British bards. He abides in his place, neither greater nor less, challenging comparison with no one, solitary, sad, wrapt in eternal twilight. Just in the same way as Glen Sligachan repelled Alexander Smith, the song of Ossian tires and wearies Brown and Robinson; fashionable once, it is now in disrepute; by Byron, Goethe, and Napoleon cherished as a solemn inspiration, and lately pooh-poohed as conventional and artificial by the Saturday Reviewer, it abides forgotten, like Blaven, till such time as humorous critics may care to patronize it again. It keeps its place, though, as surely as Scuir-na-Gillean and Blaven keep theirs. It is based on the rock, and will endure. Meantime, let us for once join issue with Mr. Arnold, and exclaim, "Woody Morven, and echoing Lora, and Selma with its silent halls—we all owe them a debt of gratitude;

and when we are unjust enough to forget it, may the Muse forget us!"*.

As to the question of authenticity, that need not be introduced at this time of day. Gibbon's sneer and Johnson's abuse prove nothing. In this, as in all matters, Gibbon was a skeptic, as worthy to be heard on Ossian as Voltaire on Shakespeare, or Gigadibs on Walt Whitman. In this, as in everything else, Johnson was a bully, a dear, lovable, short-sighted bully, as fit to listen to Fingal as to paint the scenery of the Cuchullins. The philological battle still rages; but few of those competent to judge now doubt that Macpherson did receive Gaelic MSS., that the originals of his translations were really found in the Highlands—that, in a word, Macpherson's Ossian is a bonafide attempt to render into English a traditionary poetic literature similar in origin and history to the Homeric poems.† Truly has it been said that "Ossian drew into himself every lyrical runnel, augmented himself in every way, drained centuries of their songs; and living an oral and gypsy life, handed down from generation to generation, without being committed to

* "On the Study of Celtic Literature." By Matthew Arnold.

† Since this paper was written and printed, the Rev. Mr Clark has published his two exhaustive volumes of Ossian, containing the Gaelic originals, Macpherson's translation, and a new literal version, with a capital preliminary dissertation and invaluable illustrative notes. Mr. Clark has the reputation of being the best Celtic scholar in the Highlands, and his work is a monument that will not perish as long as men care to study at the fountainhead a poetry which, be it ever so faulty, is one of the great literary influences of the world.

writing, and having their outlines determinately fixed, these songs become vested in a multitude, every reciter having more or less to do to them. For centuries the floating legendary material was reshaped, added to, and altered by the changing spirit and emotion of the Celt." What remains to us is a set of titanic fragments, which, like the scattered boulders and *blocs perchés* of Glen Sligachan, show where a mighty antique landscape once existed. The translation of Macpherson, made as it was by a scholar familiar with modern literature, has numberless touches showing that the chisel has been used to polish the original granite, but it is on the whole a marvelous bit of workmanship, strong, free, subtle, full of genius— better than any English translation of the Iliad, nearer to the true antique than Chapman's, or Pope's, or Derby's, or Blackie's versions of the Greek. In this translation, retranslated, Goethe read it, and Napoleon; and each stole something from it, if only a phrase. Veritably, at first sight, it has a barbarous look. The prose breathes heavily, in a series of gasps, each gasp a sentence. The sound is to a degree monotonous, like the voice of the wind; it rises and falls, that is all, breaks occasionally into a shriek, dies sometimes into a sob; but it is always a wind-like voice. Yet, just as hour after hour we have sat by the fireside hearkening to the wind itself, feeling the sadness of Nature creep into the soul and subdue it, so have we sat listening to the sad " sound of the voice of Cona." It is a wind, a wind passing among mountains. Only a sound, yet the soul follows it out into the darkness— where it blows the beard from the thistle on the ruin, where it mists the pictures in the moonlight mere, where it meets the shadows shivering in the desolate corry, where it dies away with a divine whisper on the fringe of the mystic sea. A wind only, but a voice crying, " I have seen the walls of Balcutha, but they were desolate. The fire had resounded in the halls, and the voice of the people is heard no more. The stream of Clutha was removed from its place by the fall of the walls. The thistle shook there its lonely head; the moss whistled to the wind. The fox looked out from the windows; the rank grass of the wall waved round his head." It is an eerie wail out of the solitude. We are blown hither and thither on it, through the mists of Morven, over the livid Cuchullins, through the terror of tempest, the dewy dimness of dawn—where the heroes are fighting, where a thousand shields clang—where rises the smoke of the ruined home, the moan of the desolate children—where the dead bleed, and "the hawks of heaven come from all their winds to feed on the foes of Auner"—where the sea rolls far distant, and the white foam is like the sails of ships—where the narrow house looks pleasant in the waste, and " the gray stone of the dead." But ever and anon we pause, listening, and know that we are hearkening to a sound only, to the lonely cry of the wind.

After all, it is unfair to call this monotonousness a demerit. Ossian's poems have much more in common with the Theogony than the Iliad and Odyssey. Ulysses and Thersites were comparatively modern products of the Greek Epos. In the Ossianic period humanity dwelt in the twilight which precedes the dawn of culture. The heroes are not only colossal, but shadowy—dim in a dim light—figures vaguer than any in the Eddas; you see the gleam of their eyes, the flash of their swords, you hear the solemn sound of their voices; but they never laugh, and if they uplift a festal cup, it is with solemn armsweep and hushed speech. The landscape where they move is this landscape of Glen Sligachan, with a frequent glimpse of woodier Morven, and a far-off glimmer of the Western Sea; all this shadowy, for the " morning is gray on Cromla," or the " pale light of the night is sad." "I sit by the mossy fountain; on the top of the hill of wind. One tree is rustling above me. Dark waves roll over the heath. The lake is troubled below. The deer descend from the hill. It is midday, but all is silent." This is a day picture, but there is little sunlight. It is in this atmosphere that some readers expect variety. They weary of the wind, and the gray stone on the waste, and the shadows of heroes. "Oh for one gleam of humor, of the quick spirit of life!" they cry. As well might they look for Falstaff in the Iliad, or for Browning's Broad Church Pope in Shakespeare! Blaven and his brethren are not mirth-breeding; nor is Ossian. Here in the waste, and there in the book, humanity fades far off; though coming from both, we drink with fresher breath the strong salt air of the free waves of the world.

In these days of metre-mongers, in these days when poetry is a tinkling cymbal or a pretty picture, when Art has got hold of her sister Muse and bedaubed her with unnatural color, we might well expect the public to be indifferent to Ossian. Not the least objection to the Gael, in the eyes of library-readers, is the peculiar gasping prose in which the translation is written; and it is an objection; yet it affords scope for passages of wonderful melody, just as does the prose of Plato, or of Shakespeare,* or the semi-Biblical line of Walt Whitman. "Before the left side of the car is seen the snorting horse! The thin-maned, high-headed, strong-hoofed, fleet-bounding son of the hill; his name is Dusronnal, among the stormy sons of the sword." Such a passage is prose as fully acceptable as a more literal translation, broken up into lines like the original:

> "By the other side of the chariot
> Is the arch-neck'd, snorting,
> Narrow-maned, high-mettled, strong-hoofed,
> Swift-footed, wide-nostriled steed of the mountains;
> Dusrongeal is the name of the horse."

Music in our own day having run to tune, in poetry as in everything else, we eschew unrhymed metres and poetical prose; yet it is as legitimate to call Beethoven a barbarian as to abuse Ossian and Whitman for their want of melody. And as to the charge that Ossian lacks *humor*, where in our other British poetry is humor so rife that we imperatively demand it from the Gael. Where is Milton's humor? or Shelley's? Where in contemporary poetry is there a grain of the divine salt of life, such as makes Chaucer prince of tale-tellers, and gladdens the

---

* Take Hamlet's speech about himself (commencing, " I have of late, but wherefore I know not," etc.) as an example of what Coleridge calls " the wonderfulness of prose."

15*

academic period of rare Ben, and makes Falstaff lovable, and Bardolph's red nose delicious, and preserves the slovenly-scribbled "Beggar's Opera" for all time. In sober truth, humor and worldly wisdom, and all we *blasé* moderns mean by variety, were scarcely created in the Ossianic period. Why, they are rare enough in the lonely Hebrides even now. Now, in the nineteenth century, the Celtic islander smiles as little as old Fingal or Cuchullin. His laugh is grim and deep; he is too far back in time to laugh lovingly. His loving mood is earnest, tearful, almost painful, sometimes full of a dim brightness, but never exuberant and joyful.

Yet we moderns, who love hoary old Jack for his sins, and stand tearfully at his bed of death,[*] and like all fat men and sinners better for his sake, we to whom life is the quaintest and drollest of all plays, as well as the deepest and divinest of all mysteries, may listen very profitably, ever and anon, to the monoto-

---

[*] "*Host.* Nay, sure, he's not in hell; he's in Arthur's bosom, if ever man went to Arthur's bosom. 'A made a finer end, and went away, an it had been any christom child; 'a parted even just between twelve and one, e'en at turning o' the tide; for after I saw him fumble with the sheets, and play with the flowers, and smile upon his fingers' ends, I knew there was but one way; for his nose was as sharp as a pen, and 'a babbled of green fields. 'How now, Sir John?' quoth I; 'what, man! be of good cheer.' So 'a cried out 'God, God, God!' three or four times; now I, to comfort him, bid him 'a should not think of God; I hoped there was no need to trouble himself with any such thoughts yet. So, 'a bade me lay more clothes on his feet. I put my hand into the bed, and felt them, and they were as cold as any stone; then I felt to his knees, and so upward and upward, and all was as cold as any stone."—*Henry V.*, ii. 3.

nous wail of Cona, may pass a brooding hour in the twilight shadow of this eerie poetry. The influence of Ossian upon us is quite specific; not religious at all, not merely ghostly, but solemn and sad and beautiful; with just enough life to preserve a thread of human interest; with too little life to awaken us from the mood of brooding, mystic feeling produced by the lonely landscape, and the dim dawn, and the changeful moon. Ossian dreams not of a Supreme Being, has no religious feeling, but he believes in gracious spirits "fair as the ghost of the hill, when it moves in a sunbeam at noon, over the silence of Morven." If there is no humor in his poems, there is a great deal of exquisitely human tenderness. Nothing can be more touching in its way than the death of Fellan: " Ossian, lay me in that hollow rock. Raise no stone above me, lest one should ask about my fame. I am fallen in the first of my fields, fallen without renown." Perfect in its way, too, is the imagery in the lament of Malvina over the death of Oscar: " I was a lovely tree in thy presence, Oscar! with all my branches round me. But thy breath came like a blast from the desert and laid my green head low. The spring returned with its showers, but no leaf of mine arose."

Sweetest and tenderest of all Ossian's songs, the song which fills the soul here in the gorges of Glen Sligachan, is "Berrathon," the "last sound of the voice of Cona." It is a wind indeed, strange and tender, deep and true. All the strife is hushed now; Malvina the beautiful is dead, and the old bard, knowing that his hour is drawing nigh, murmurs over a fair legend of the past. "Such were my deeds, son of Appin, when the arm of my youth was young. But I am alone at Lutha. My voice is like the last sound of the wind, when it forsakes the woods. But Ossian shall not be long alone; he sees the mist that shall receive his ghost; he beholds the mist that shall form his robe when he appears on his hills. The sons of feeble men shall behold me and admire the stature of the chiefs of old. They shall creep to their caves. . . . Lead, son of Appin, lead the aged to his woods. The wind begins to rise; the dark wave resounds. . . . Bring me the harp, son of Appin. Another song shall arise. My soul shall depart in the sound. . . . Bear the mournful sound away to Fingal's airy hall; bear it to Fingal's hall, that he may hear the voice of his son. . . . The blast of the north opens thy gates. O king! I behold thee sitting on mist, dimly gleaming in all thine arms. Thy form now is not the terror of the valiant. It is like a watery cloud, when we see the stars behind it with their weeping eyes. Thy shield is the aged moon; thy sword a vapor half kindled with fire. Dim and feeble is the chief who traveled in brightness before. . . . I hear the voice of Fingal. Long has it been absent from mine ear! 'Come, Ossian, come away!' he says. . . . 'Come, Ossian, come away!' he says. 'Come, fly with thy fathers on clouds.' I come, I come, thou king of men. The life of Ossian fails. I begin to vanish on Cona. My steps are not seen in Selma. Beside the stone of Mora I shall fall asleep. The winds whistling in my gray hair shall not awaken me. . . . Another race shall arise." If this be not a veritable voice then poesy is dumb indeed. The desolate cry of Lear is not more real.

Read these poems to-day on Glen Sligachan, or on the slopes of Blaven. Is not the solemn grayness everywhere? Is there a touch, a tint of the quiet landscape lost? Not that Ossian described Nature; that was left for the modern. He contrives, however, while using the simplest imagery, while never pausing to transcribe, to conjure up before us the very spirit of such scenes as this. Mere description, however powerful, is of little avail; and painting is not much better. Ossian's verse resembles Loch Corruisk more closely than Turner's picture, powerful and suggestive as that picture is.

While we are listening to the thin voice of Cona, and being betrayed into a monologue, our exploring party is getting well ahead; and turning off across a marshy hollow to the right, guide and ponies begin to clamber up the sides of a hill—one of the sandy Red Hills, the shoulder of which overlooks the lonely lake of which we are in quest. The dog Schneider has vanished in frantic pursuit of some imaginary game—no, there she is, dwarfed to the size of a mouse, creeping along a seemingly inaccessible crag. Shouts are of no avail; they only make the hills moan. But look! what is that little group far above her? Deer, by Jove!—red deer, browsing, actually browsing, in a hollow that seems as stony and innocent of all herbage as a doorstep, and looking in their unconcern about the size of sheep. The field-glass brings them aggravatingly close, and a noble group they are— harts as well as hinds. O Hamish, Hamish Shaw, what a place for a stalk! A stiff walk round yonder shoulder, half a mile to leeward; a covered approach for a mile behind that ridge; then a creep along the dry bed of a torrent, steadily, oh, how steadily! lest a rattle of small stones should spoil all; then a crawl on one's belly to the great boulder to leeward of them, and *then*, Hamish, a cool pulse, a steady aim, and the finest set of antlers there! To look on, gunless, hopeless, is almost more than flesh and blood can endure. Natural scenery, Ossian, mysticism, are forgotten in a moment. Ah, but they had the best of it—those old heroes of the chase, those seekers of perilous adventures by flood and field; and Fingal stalked his stag in that era like a genuine sportsman! Come along, Hamish Shaw; let us turn our faces away, lest we cry with longing. See, though, the dog is winding them—she sees—she charges them. They stand their ground coolly, only one big fellow begins to tickle the earth with his antlers. Schneider's pace grows slower and more reflective. She expected to scatter them like wind, and she is amazed at their stolidity. Obviously thinking discretion the better part of valor, she pauses, and gazes at them from a distance of twenty yards. They don't stir, but gaze at her with uplifted heads. At last, tired of the scrutiny, they turn slowly, very slowly, and walk, at a snail's pace, up the ravine; while Schneider, obviously staggered at the discovery that at least one kind of animal is quite a match for her, and won't scud out of her fiery path like a snipe or a rabbit, descends the hill dreamily—quite prepared to accept her thrashing in exchange for the half-hour's novel sport that she has had among the mountains.

How steadily the ponies make their way up this pathway, which is sometimes slippery as glass, sometimes crumbling like a ruin; they keep their feet with only an occasional stumble, and do not appear the least bit exhausted by their efforts. Parts of the way are precipitous to a degree, parts are formed by the unstable bed of a shallow burn. At last the topmost ridge is gained, the riders dismount, and the guide, stripping the ponies of their saddles and bridles, turns them out to crop a noontide meal on the mossy ground. Lunch is thereupon spread out on a rock, and before casting one glance around them, the Wanderer and the other human machines begin to feed and drink, winding up the jaded body to the point of rational enjoyment and spiritual perception.

The views from this hillside—the usual point sought by tourists from Sligachan—are inferior in beauty to many we have seen *en route*, but they are very grand. One glimpse, indeed, of the peaks of Scuir-na-Gillean, seen peeping jagged over an intervening chain of mountain, is beyond all parallel magnificent. The view of Loch Corruisk,* for which the tourists come, is simply disappointing. Only one corner of the loch is visible, lying below at a distance of about two miles, and gives not the faintest idea of its grandeur. The usual plan adopted by good walkers is to descend to the side of Corruisk, leaving the guide to await their return on the summit of the ridge.

* Anglicé, the "Corry of the Water."

But on the present occasion, the Wanderer has determined to pass the summer night here in the solitude, leaving the rest of the party to return alone—all save the faithful henchman, Hamish, on whose back is strapped a waterproof sleeping-bag, a box of apparatus for cooking breakfast, etc. Schneider, too, will remain, constant as ever to her liege lord and master. So, after a parting caulker with the men, and a good-night's kiss from the lady, the Wanderer whistles his dog and plunges down the hill at his favorite headlong rate, while Hamish, more heavily loaded, follows leisurely, with the swinging gait, slow but steady, peculiar to mariners of all sorts on land. A very short run brings the Wanderer to the shores of Lochan Dhu, a dark and desolate tarn, situated high up on the hillside, and surrounded by wild stretches of marsh, and rock, and bog. Standing here for a moment, he waves a last farewell to the party on the peak, who stand far above him, darkly silhouetted against the sky.

CHAPTER XVI.

CORRUISK; OR, THE CORRY OF THE WATER.

The Lone Water—The Region of Twilight—*Blocs Perches*—Hamish Shaw's Views—The Cave of the Ghost—The Dunvegan Pilot's Story—Echoes, Mists, and Shadows—Squalls in Loch Scavaig—A Highlander's Ideas of Beauty—Camping Out in the Corry—A Stormy Dawn—The Fishermen and the Strange Harbor—Loch Scavaig—The Spar Cave—Camasunary.

Out of the gloomy breast of Lochan Dhu issues a brawling burn, which plunges from shelf to shelf downward, here narrowing to a rush-fringed rapid, there broadening out into miniature meres that glitter golden in the sunlight and are full of tiny trout, and in more than one place overflowing incontinently, and breaking up into rivulets and scattered pools, interspersed with huge boulders, moss-grown stones, and clumps of vari-colored heather. With the burn for his guide, the Wanderer sped, more than once missing his leaps from stone to stone, and cooling his heated legs in the limpid water, and, indeed, rather courting the bath than otherwise, so pleasantly the water prattled and sparkled. The afternoon was well advanced now, and still not a cloud came to destroy the golden glory of the day. The sun had drunk all the dew of the heather, and the very bogs looked dry and brown. Below there was a glimpse of the Lone Water, glassy, calm, and black as ebony. A few steps downward, still downward, and the golden day was dimming into shadow. Coming suddenly on Loch Corruisk, the Wanderer seemed in a moment surrounded with twilight. He paused close to the corry, on a rocky knoll, with the hot sun in his eyes, but before him the shadows lay moveless—not a glimmer of sunlight touched the solemn mere—everywhere the place brooded in its own mystery, silent, beautiful, and dark.

To speak in the first place by the card, Corruisk, or the Corry of the Water, is a wild gorge, oval in shape, about three miles long and a mile broad, in the center of which a sheet of water stretches for about two miles, surrounded on every side by rocky precipices totally without vegetation, and towering in one sheer plane of livid rock, until they mingle with the wildly picturesque and jagged outlines of the topmost peak of the Cuchullins. Directly on entering its somber darkness, the student is inevitably reminded of the awful region of Malebolge:

> "Luogo è in Inferno detto Malebolge
> Tutto di pietra e di color ferrigno,
> Come la cerchia, che d'intorno 'l volge."

The mere is black as jet, its waters only broken and brightened by four small, grassy islands, on the edges of the largest of which that summer day the black-backed gulls were sitting, with the feathery gleam of their shadows faintly breaking the glassy blackness below them. These islands form the only bit of vegetable green in all the lonely prospect.

Close to the shores of the loch, and at the foot of the crags, there are dark-brown stretches of heath; but the heights above them are leafless as the columns of a cathedral.

Coming abruptly on the shores of this loneliest of lakes, the Wanderer had passed instantaneously from sunlight to twilight, from brightness to mystery, from the gladsome stir of the day to a silence unbroken by the movement of any created thing. Every feature of the scene was familiar to him—he had seen it in all weathers, under all aspects—yet his spirit was possessed as completely, as awe-stricken, as solemnized, as when he came thither out of the world's stir for the first time. The brooding desolation is there forever. There was no sign to show that it had ever been broken by a human foot since his last visit. He left it in twilight, and in twilight he found it. Since he had departed, scarce a sunbeam had broken the darkness of the dead mere; so close do the mountain pinnacles tower on all sides, that only when the sun is sheer above can the twilight be broken; and when it is borne in mind that the Cuchullins are the chosen lairs of all the winds, that their hollows are the dark breeding-places of all the monsters of storm, that scarce a day passes over them without mist and tears, one ceases to wonder at the unbroken darkness. A great cathedral is solemn; solemner still is such an island as Haskeir, when it sleeps silent amid the rainy grief of a dead still sea; but Corruisk is beyond all expression solemnest of all. Perpetual twilight, perfect silence, terribly brooding desolation. Though there are a thousand voices on all sides—the voices of winds, of wild waters, of shifting crags—they die away here into a heart-beat. See! down the torn cheeks of all those precipices tear headlong torrents white in foam, and each is crying, though you cannot hear it. Only one low murmur, deeper than silence, fills the dead air. The black water laps silently on the dark claystone shingle of the shore. The cloud passes silently, far away over the melancholy peaks.

Streams innumerable come from all directions to pour themselves into the abyss; and enormous fragments of stone lie everywhere, as if freshly fallen from the precipices, while many of these gigantic boulders, as McCulloch observes, are "poised in such a manner on the very edges of the precipitous rocks on which they have fallen, as to render it difficult to imagine how they could have rested in such places, though the presence of *snow* at the time of their fall may perhaps explain this difficulty." These, indeed, are the true *blocs perchés*, marking the course of the glacier which once invaded those wilds. "The interval between the borders of the lake and the side of Garsven is strewed with them; the whole, of whatever size, lying on the surface in a state of uniform freshness and integrity, unattended by a single plant or atom of soil, as if they had all but recently fallen in a single shower." The mode in which they lie is no less remarkable. The bottom of the valley is covered with rocky eminences, of which the summits are not only bare, but often very narrow, while their declivities are always steep, and often perpendicular. Upon these rocks the fragments lie just as on the more level ground. One, weighing about one hundred tons, has become a rocking stone ; another, of not less than fifty, stands on the narrow edge of a rock a hundred feet higher than that ground which must have first met it in the descent.

> " Mighty rocks,
> Which have from unimaginable years
> Sustained themselves with terror and with toil
> Over a gulf, and with the agony
> With which they cling seem slowly coming down—
> Even as a wretched soul hour after hour
> Clings to the mass of life—yet, clinging, lean;
> And, leaning, make more dark the dread abyss
> In which they fear to fall." *

Strangely beautiful as is the scene, it is a ruin. The vast fragments are the remains of a magnificent temple rising into pinnacles and minarets of ice, glittering with all the colors of the prism. Here the silent-footed glacier slipped, and the snow shifted under the footsteps of the wind, and there, perhaps, where the lonely lake lies, glittered a cold sheet of hyacinthine blue ; and no gray rain-cloud brooded on the temple's dome—only delicate spirits of the vapor, drinking soft radiance from the light of sun and star. Around this temple crawled the elk and bear, and swift-footed mountain deer. Summer after summer it abode in beauty, not stable like temples built by hands, but ever changing, full of the low murmur of its change, the melancholy sound of its own shifting walls and domes. Then more than once Fire swept out of the abyss, and clung like a snake about the temple, while Earthquake, like a chained monster, groaned below; wild elements came from all the

---

* Shelley's " Cenci."

winds to overthrow it; wall after wall fell, fragment after fragment dashed down. The fairy fretwork of snow melted, the fair carvings of ice were obliterated, pinnacle and minaret dissolved in the sun, like the baseless fragment of a vision. Dark twilight settled on the ruin, and Melancholy marked it for her own. The walls of livid rock remain, gray from the volcano, and torn into rugged rents, casting perpetual darkness downward, where the water, bubbling up from unseen abysses, has spread itself into a mirror. All ruins are sad, but this is sad utterly. All ruins are beautiful, but this is beautiful beyond expression. The solemn Spirit of Death comes more or less to all ruins, whenever the meditative mind conjures and wishes; but here it abides, at once overshadowing whosoever approaches by the still sense of doom. "Thus saith the Lord God, Behold, O Mount Seir, I am against thee, and I will make thee most desolate. When the whole earth rejoiceth, I will make thee desolate." The fiat has also been spoken here. The place has been solemnized to desolation.

In deep, unutterable awe does the human visitant explore with timid eye the mighty crags above him, the layers of volcanic stone, until he finds himself fascinated by the strange outlines of the peaks where they touch the sky, and detecting fancied resemblances to things that live. Yonder crouches, black and distinct against the light, a maned beast, like a lion, watching; its eyes invisible, but fixed, doubtless, on yours. Higher still is a dimmer outline, as of some huge bird, winged like the griffin. These two resemblances infect the whole scene instantaneously.

There are shapes everywhere—in the peaks, in the gorges, by the torrents—living shapes, or phantoms, frozen still to listen or to watch, and horrifying you with their deathly silence. Your heart leaps as if something were going to happen ; and you feel, if the stillness were suddenly broken, and these shapes were to spring into motion, you would shriek and faint.

How dark and fathomless look the abysses yonder, at the head of the loch ! A wild scarf of mist is folding itself round the peaks (betokening surely that the clear, still weather will not remain much longer unbroken), and faint, gray light travels along the wildly indented wall beneath. It is not two miles to the base of the crags, yet the distance seems interminable ; and shadows, shifting and deepening, weary the eye with mysteries and dimly-reflected vistas.

As one paces up the aisle of some vast temple, the Wanderer walked thither, threading his way among gigantic boulders, which in some wild hour have been torn loose and dashed down from the heights. He felt dwarfed to the utter significance of a pigmy, small as a mouse crawling on the pavement of the great cathedral at Cologne.

A voice broke in upon his musings.

" I've traveled far, and seen heaps o' places," says Hamish Shaw, whom the Wanderer had altogether forgotten ; "but I never saw the like of this. It's no' a canny place. Glen Sannox is wild, but this is awesome. Is it no' strange that the Lord should make a place like this, for no use to man or beast ? "

This was a question involving so many philosophical issues, that the Wanderer did not like to make any decided answer. Instead of replying, he asked Hamish if he had never been in the locality before.

"Ay, once, years, ago, ween I was but a lad. The herring were in Loch Scavaig, and the harbor out yonder was just a causeway o' fishing-boats, and there were fires on shore, and plenty o' folk to make it look cheery like. We were here a week, and didna see a soul ashore, but one day an old piper coming in his Sabbath claise frae a wedding far o'er the hills, and he was that fu'* that he had burstit his pipes, and lost his bonnet; and, with his gray hair blowing in his een, he looked like the Deil. We keepit him a nicht till he was sober; and when he waken'd he was that mad about his pipes, that he was for louping † into the sea. I mind fine o' him vanishing up the hills yonder, as white as death; and Lord kens if he ever reached hame, for it rained that night like to drown the world, and you couldna see the length o' your arm for reek." ‡

As he walked on in the track of the Wanderer, Shaw still pursued his own reminiscences aloud.

"For a' that there wasna a fisherman would hae willingly come this length alane—they were that fear'd o' the place, most o' a' in the gloaming. It's more fearsome without a house, or folk, or sae much as a sheep feeding; nothing but stanes and darkness. There were auld men among us that had strange tales and liked to fright the lads, though they were just as frightit themsel's. There's a cave up there called the Cave o' the Ghost, and the taisch§ o' a shepherd

---

* Drunk. † Jumping. ‡ Mist.
§ Spirit.

has been seen in it sitting cross-leggit, and branding a bluidy sheep. But the drollest thing e'er I heard o' Loch Corruisk was frae an auld pilot o' Dunvegan, whose folk had dwelt yonder on the far side o' Garsven. He minded fine, when he was a wean, his grandfather would gang awa' for days, and come back wi' his pouch full o' precious stanes the size o' seeds and the color o' blood. He would tell nae man how or where he found them; and though they tried to watch him, he was o'er cunning. More than once he came back wi' gold. He sent the gold and stanes south, and was weel paid for them. It was whispered about that he had sold himsel' to the Deil, at night, here by the loch; and he didna deny it. He came back one day sick, and took to his bed wi' the influenza fever; and he ravit till the priest came, and before he dee'd he cried till the priest that the gold and stanes had changed his heart wi' greed, and he was feared to face his God. One day he had wandered himsel', * and night came on him, and he creepit into a cave to sleep; and when the day came, he saw strange marks like writing all o'er the walls. When he keekit closer, he saw the stanes, and they were that loose he could free them wi' his gully,† and he filled his pouches, shaking a' the time wi' fear. But the strangest thing o' a' was this—he wasna the first man that had been there, for at the mouth o' the cave there was the coulter o' a plow, and twa old brogues rotten wi' dirt and rain."

"Did this description enable his relations to find the place?" asked the Wanderer, much interested.

* Lost his path.   † Claspknife.

"They search'd and search'd," answered Hamish, "but they couldna found it, and they gave it up in despair. After that his folk didna thrive; and the man that told me the tale was the only ane o' them left. I've heard tell that 'twas true the old man had sold himsel' to the Deil, and that the cave, and the strange writing, and a' that, were just magic to beguile his een; but it's strange. I'm o' the opinion that the cave might be found yet, for gold and stanes couldna come o' naething. If it hadna been for the auld man's greed, his folk might hae thriven."

"Do you think you would have kept the secret if you had been in his place?"

"I'm no' sae sure," answered Hamish, after a pause. "Ye see, 'twas a sair temptation, for a man's ain folk are whiles the hardest against him aboot siller. It was the safest way, but a bad way for ither folk. He should hae put the marks o' the place in writing, for use after his death."

Hamish's story, with its quaint touches of realism, only made the lonely scene more lone, adding as it did a touch of human eerieness to the associations connected with it. An appropriate abode, surely, for one of those evil spirits of whom we read in Teutonic romance, and who were prepared, in exchange for a little document signed with the party's blood, to load the lost mortal with gems and gold! This was a fleeting impression, only lasting a moment. Another glance at those dimly-lighted walls, that darkly-brooding water, those sublime peaks, now beginning to disappear in the fast-gathering white vapor—one more look around the lonely corry—served to show that it was too silent, too ethereally thoughtful, to be haunted by such vulgar spirits as those that figure in popular superstition. The popular ghost would be as out of place there as inside a church. To break for a moment the dead monotony, the Wanderer cast a stone into the water, and Schneider, barking furiously, plunged into the water. Hark! a thousand voices barked an answer! We shouted aloud, and the hills reverberated. The cries of men and the barking of dogs faded far off, like the ghostly voices of the Wild Huntsmen among the Harz Mountains. Echo cried to echo:

> " As multitudinous a harmony
> Of sounds as rang the heights of Latmos over,
> When, from the soft couch of her sleeping lover
> Upstarting, Cynthia skimmed the mountain dew
> In keen pursuit, and gave where'er she flew
> Impetuous motion to the stars above her!"

Truly, there were spirits among the peaks, but not such spirits as Defoe chronicled, and the Poughkeepsie Seer summons; nay, gentle ghosts, " with eyes as fair as starbeams among twilight trees;" phantoms of the delicate ether, not arrayed in vulgar horrors, but soft as the breath of Cytherea.

> " Mountain winds, and babbling springs,
> And mountain seas that are the voice
> Of these inexplicable things!"

The home of mystery is far removed from that of terror, and he who approaches it, as we did then, is held by the tenderest fibers of his soul, instead of being galvanized into gaping abjection. God's profoundest agents are as tender as they are powerful. Their breath, invisible as the wind, troubles the fount of divine tears which distills itself, drop by drop, in every human thing, however strong, however dark and cold.

We were now at the head of the loch. Sir Walter Scott, in the notes of his visit to Skye, describes the Cuchullins as rising "so perpendicularly from the water's edge that Borrowdale, or even Glencoe, is a jest to them;" but Sir Walter only surveyed the scene from the far end of the corry, where it opens on the sea.* So far from rising perpendicular from the

* Sir Walter's prose account of his visit to Corruisk is so interesting that we subjoin it in full: "The ground on which we walked was the margin of a lake, which seemed to have sustained the constant ravage of torrents from these rude neighbors. The shores consisted of huge strata of naked granite, here and there intermixed with bogs, and heaps of gravel and sand piled in the empty water-courses. Vegetation there was little or none; and the mountains rose so perpendicularly from the water edge that Borrowdale, or even Glencoe, is a jest to them. We proceeded a mile and a half up this deep, dark, and solitary lake, which was about two miles long, half a mile broad, and is, as we learned, of extreme depth. The murky vapors which enveloped the mountain ridges obliged us by assuming a thousand varied shapes, changing their drapery into all sorts of forms, and sometimes clearing off altogether. It is true, the mist made us pay the penalty by some heavy and downright showers, from the frequency of which a Highland boy, whom we brought from the farm, told us the lake was popularly called the Water-kettle. The proper name is Loch Corriskin, from the deep corrie, or hollow, in the mountains of Cuilin, which affords the basin for this wonderful sheet of water. It is as exquisite a savage scene as Loch Katrine is a scene of romantic beauty. After having penetrated so far as distinctly to observe the termination of the lake under an immense precipice, which rises abruptly from the water, we returned, and often stopped to admire the ravages which storms must have made in the recesses, where all human witnesses were driven to places of more shelter and security. Stones, or rather large masses and fragments of rocks, of a com-

water's edge, the mountains slope gradually upward, from stony layer to layer, and at their base is a plain of grass as green as emerald, through which a small river, after draining the silent dews of the hills, wanders to Corruisk. Where we stood, surrounded by the colossal fragments of ruin, on the rough rock of the solid hillside, the darkness deepened. Vapors were gathering above us, shutting out the hill-tops from our gaze. Out of every fissure and crevasse, from behind every fragment of stone, a white shape of mist stole, small or huge, and hovered like a living

posite kind, perfectly different from the strata of the lake, were scattered upon the bare, rocky beach in the strangest and most precarious situations, as if abandoned by the torrents which had borne them down from above. Some lay loose and tottering upon the ledges of the natural rock, with so little security that the slightest push moved them, though their weight might exceed many tons. These detached rocks, or stones, were chiefly what are called plum-pudding stones. The bare rocks, which formed the shore of the lake, seemed quite pathless and inaccessible, as a huge mountain, one of the detached ridges of the Cuilin hills, sinks in a profound and perpendicular precipice down to the water. On the left-hand side, which we traversed, rose a higher and equally inaccessible mountain, the top of which strongly resembled the shivered crata of an exhausted volcano. I never saw a spot in which there was less appearance of vegetation of any kind. The eye rested on nothing but barren and naked crags, and the rocks on which we walked by the side of the loch were as bare as the pavements of Cheapside. There are one or two small islets in the loch, which seem to bear juniper, or some such low, bushy shrub. Upon the whole, though I have seen many scenes of more extensive desolation, I never witnessed any in which it pressed me more deeply upon the eye and the heart than at Loch Corriskin; at the same time that its grandeur elevated and redeemed it from the wild and dreary character of utter barrenness."

thing. The invisible sun was now declining to the west, and the air growing chilly after the great heat of the day.

It was time now to seek a corner wherein we might pass the night in tolerable comfort. This was soon done. One huge stone stretched out its top like a roof, the rock beneath was dry and snug, and close at hand a little stream bubbled by, crystalline and cold. "Spread out the rugs, Hamish Shaw, light the spirit-lamp, and make all snug." It was as cosy as by the forecastle fire. Cold beef and bread went down gloriously, with cold caulkers from the spring; but we wound up, if you please, with a jorum of toddy as stiff as head could stand. Heat the water over the spirit-lamp, drop in the sugar, and you have a beverage fit for the gods. You, Hamish, take yours neat, and you are wise. Now, having lit our pipes, and stretched ourselves out for a siesta, do we envy the ease of any wight in Christendom?

"The nicht will be a good nicht," said Hamish; "but I'm thinking there'll be wind the morn,* and here, when it blows it rains. When I was here wi' the *Heatherbell*, at the time I was speaking o', I dinna mind o' a dry day—a day without showers. I ne'er saw the hills as clear as they were this forenoon. There's aye wind among the gullies yonder, and the squalls at Sligachan are naething to what ye hae here. I wouldna sail aboot Scavaig in a lug-sail skiff—no' if I had the sheet in my hand, and the sail nae bigger than a clout—in the finest day in summer. It

* *i. e.*, To-morrow morning.

strikes down on ye like the blows o' a hammer—right, left, ahint, before, straight down on your head, right up under your nose—coming from Lord kens where, though the sea be smooth as my cheek. I've seen the punt heeling o'er to the gunnel with neither mast nor sail. I mind o' seeing a brig carry away her topmast, and tear her foresail like a rag, on a day when we would hae been carrying just a reef in the mainsail o' the *Tern ;* and I've seen the day when the fishing-boats running out o' the wee harbor there would be taking their sails on and off, as the puffs came, twenty times in as many minutes. Many's the life's been lost off Skye wi' the damned wind frae these hills. They're for nae good to the beasts—the very deer are starved in them—and they catch every mist frae the Western Ocean, and soock the wind out o' its belly, and shoot it out again on Scavaig like a cannon-ball. Is it no' strange there should be such places, for nae use to man?"

"They are very beautiful to look at, Shaw," observed the Wanderer, "you can't deny that; and beautiful things have a use of their own, you know. Look up there, where the mists are dividing, and burning red round the edges of that peak, and tell me if you ever saw anything more splendid."

"I'll no' deny," says Shaw, glancing up with little enthusiasm, "I'll no' deny that it looks awesome; and it's hard for a common man like me to tell the taste o' learned men and gentry. They gang snooving aboot, and see bonnieness where the folk o' the place see naething but ugliness. But put it to yoursel'. Just supposing you had a twin brother, and your father had left your brother a green farm o' five hundred acres, and gien this place for a birthright to yoursel', what would ye hae said then? There's no' an acre o' green grass, nor a tree where a bird might build, nor a haufu' o' earth to plow or harrow! Ye're smiling, but ye wouldna smile if ye depended on this place for your drop o' milk and bit o' porridge. This may be awesome; but green, long grass, and trees, and the kye crying, and the birds singing, and the smell o' the farm-yard wherever you keek, that's the kind o' place for a man to spend his days in."

And here let us remark that the grim, sunburnt, hirsute Celt—our philosophic Hamish, as independent as Socrates of schools and dogmas—was right enough, with all his bigotry. Corruisk is well at times, but it lacks the greenness of the true, living world—and the intellectual mood it awakens is a purely cultivated mood, impossible to man in his natural state. The English gentleman, arriving from Kent or Sussex, *blasé* with English flats, surfeited of harvests, comes to such a scene as this to be galvanized; and the wild, weird prospect, the utter silence and desolation, speak to him with intensest spiritual power, because they are so unlike the monotonous paths he treads daily. The Celt, on the other hand, who is from boyhood familiar with the waste wilderness, tenanted only by the deer and the eagle, and with the enormous sheep-farm, stretching from hill to hill, comes upon a green spot, where leaves sprout, and birds sing, and flowers bud at the tree-roots, and at once realizes his dreams of earthly loveliness. Unlike the fair-weather tourist, who surveys the terrors of Nature for one inspired moment, the Highlander knows the meaning of storm, cold, poverty, and hunger; and when he pictures an Inferno, it is not one of insufferable flame, but rather Dante's last circle—a frozen realm.* What wonder, then, that such a man should find all the dreamy poetry of his nature awakened by the happy homestead bosomed in greenness, the waving fields of harvest hard by, the pleasant country road, with plump farm-women driving their pony-carts to market, the stream that waters the meadow-land and turns the mill—all the sights and sounds that indicate warmth, prosperity and rural joy. The basis of all heavens is physical comfort, and the Celt's dream of heaven is a dream of the light and the sunshine he seldom sees. " The valleys," says an old Gaelic chant, " were open and free to the ocean; trees loaded with leaves, which scarce moved to the light breeze, were scattered on the green slopes and rising grounds. The rude winds walked not on the mountains; no storm took its course through the sky. All was calm and bright; the pure sun of the autumn shone from its blue sky on the fields." We have wandered among the islands with all sorts of islanders, and ever found them moved most, like Hamish Shaw, by the tender oases of cultivated ground which are found here and there in the empty waste.

Let it not be imagined, however, that the wild scenery of the hills wherein they dwell, the fierce contentions of wind and rain and snow, exercise no fascination; they work subtly, secretly, weaving their

* The Celtic *Ifurin*, or the Isle of the Cold Clime.

solemn tints into the very tissue of life itself, solemnizing thought imperceptibly, troubling the spirit with mysterious emotion. More than most men the Celt distinguishes between loving and liking. He likes the green pasture; but he loves the bare mountains. He likes warmth, comfort, and prosperity; but he loves loneliness, dreaminess, and home. So familiar is he with the mountain peak and the driving mist, so constant is their influence upon him, that he scarcely perceives them; yet, transport him to flat lowlands, or into cities, and he pines for the desolate lake and the silent hillside. His love for them is unutterable, is the vital part of his existence. When he dreams, he sees the *fata morgana*, a cloud of delicious verdure suspended in the air; but it soon fades. He, like all men, yearns to the unknown and the unfamiliar; but such yearnings are not love.

So far as Hamish himself is concerned, what most moves him is the sea. It is his true home, and he loves it in all its moods. Days and nights, months and years, it has rocked him on its bosom. He does not watch it with an artist's eye; but no artist could linger over its looks more lovingly. It is no mere monster, repelling him like the somber Cuchullins. No; the mighty sea means health and life—the wondrous shoals of herring peopling the waters like locusts, the cod and ling hovering like shadows on the silent, deep seabank—the lobster in the tangled weed—all strange gifts from God, full of "use to man." He has a finer eye for the beauty of a boat than any artist ever drew. He knows the clouds as the shepherds know their sheep. The voices of seabirds are a speech to him. As he looks on the wondrous watery fields, he sees in them both a harvest and a grave. The shadow of mystery and death dwells everywhere on the perilous prospect. And if, with such dreamy imaginations, he unconsciously blends the same quiet, utilitarian feeling which the farmer has for his fields, and the huntsman for the prairie, why, perhaps it has only strengthened the emotions of joy he feels whenever he finds himself " at home " on the great waters.

After all, the solemn eerieness of the corry must have been appealing more or less subtly to Hamish's spirit, for erelong his chat drifted into the old channel of superstition; and as the rosy light of the sun grew dimmer on the peaks, and the hollow void blackened below, he now and then cast around him glances of troubled meaning. He talked again, as he has often talked before, of the Banshee, and the Taisch or second sight, and of witches and fays; not committing himself to believe in their existence, but assuredly not quite unbelieving. While Hamish soliloquized the Wanderer watched the dying sunlight, and dreamed —until the sound of his comrade's voice died away into an inarticulate murmur. It was such a scene as no tongue can describe, no pencil paint—the hills in their silentest hour, hushed like lambs around the feet of God. Not of wraiths, or corpse-lights, or any petty spirits that fret the common course of man, did the Wanderer think now; no dark vapors of the brain interposed to perplex him; but his soul turned, trembling like a star with its own lustrous yearning, to the Eternal Silences where broods the Almighty Father of the beautiful and wondrous world. In that moment, in that mood, without perfect religious confidence, yet with some faint feeling of awful communication with the unseen Intelligence, did he find his prayer shaping itself into sound and form—faint, perhaps, as imaging what he felt, yet in some measure consecrated for other ears by the holy spirit of the scene.

I.

Desolate ! How the peaks of ashen gray,
    The smoky mists that drift from hill to hill,
The waters dark, anticipate this day
    Death's sullen desolation. Oh, how still
The shadows come and vanish, with no will!
How still the melancholy waters lie ;
How still the vapors of the under sky,
    Mirrored below, drift onward, and fulfill
The mandate as they mingle ! Not a sound,
    Save that deep murmur of a torrent near,
Breaketh the silence. Hush ! the dark profound
    Groans, as some gray crag loosens and falls sheer
To the abyss. Wildly I look around.
    O Spirit of the Human, art Thou *here?*

II.

O Thou art beautiful ! and Thou dost bestow
    Thy beauty on this stillness. Still as sheep
    The hills lie under Thee ; the waters deep
Murmur for joy of Thee ; the voids below
Mirror Thy strange fair vapors as they flow ;
    And now, afar upon the ashen height,
    Thou sendest down a radiant look of light,
So that the still peaks glisten, and a glow,
Rose-colored, tints the little, snowy cloud
    That poises on the highest peak of all.
O Thou art beautiful !—the hills are bowed
    Beneath Thee ; on Thy name the soft winds call—
The monstrous ocean trumpets it aloud,
    The rain and snows intone it as they fall.

III.

Here by the sunless lake there is no air;
  Yet with how ceaseless motion, with how strange
  Flowing and fading, do the high mists range
The gloomy gorges of the mountains bare.
Some weary breathing never ceases there—
  The ashen peaks can feel it hour by hour;
  The purple depths are darkened by its power;
A soundless breath, a trouble all things share
That feel it come and go. See! onward swim
  The ghostly mists, from silent land to land,
From gulf to gulf; now the whole air grows dim—
  Like living men, darkling a space, they stand.
But lo! a sunbeam, like a cherubim,
  Scatters them onward like a flaming brand

IV.

I think this is the very stillest place
  On all God's earth, and yet no rest is here.
The vapors mirrored in the black loch's face
  Drift on like frantic shapes and disappear;
  A never-ceasing murmur in mine ear
Tells me of waters wild that flow.
  There is no rest at all afar or near
Only a sense of things that moan and go.
And lo! the still small life these limbs contain
  I feel flows on like those, restless and proud;
Before that breathing naught within my brain
  Pauses, but all drifts on like mist and cloud;
Only the bald peaks and the stones remain,
  Frozen before Thee, desolate and bowed.

V.

And whither, O ye vapors, do ye wend?
  Stirred by that weary breathing, whither away?
  And whither, O ye dreams that night and day
Drift o'er the troublous life, tremble, and blend
To broken lineaments of that far Friend,
  Whose strange breath's come and go ye feel so deep?

> O soul that has no rest and seekest sleep,
> Whither? and will thy wanderings ever end?
> All things that be are full of a quick pain;
> Onward we fleet, swift as the running rill;
> The vapors drift, the mists within the brain
> Float on obscuringly, and have no will;
> Only the bare peaks and the stones remain;
> These only—and a God, sublime and still.*

The light died off the peaks, the vapors darkened, and the cold chill of the night crept into the air. Then suddenly, without a ray of warning, the moon swept up out of the east—huge as a shield, yellow as a water-lily, more luminous than any gold. It wanted but the moon to complete the spell. The dim light scarcely penetrated into the corry, save where a deep streak of silver shadow broke the blackness of the lake. The walls of the hollow grew pitch dark, though the peaks were faintly lit. The vapors gathered in the hollow interstices of gloom. Now, where all had been stillness, mysterious noises grew—wild voices, whispers, murmurs, infinite ululations.

> " Vero è, che' u su la proda mi trovai
> Della valle d'abisso dolorosa,
> Che tuono accoglie d'infiniti guai!"

The moan of torrents was audible, the murmur of wind.

It is not our purpose to chronicle in detail the experiences of the night. Suffice it to say that for many a long hour we paced about the ghostly scene, and then, worn out and wearied, slipt ourselves into

---

* These sonnets have already appeared as a portion of "The Book of Orm: a Prelude to the Epic."

our coverings, and slept as snugly as worms in their cocoons under the overhanging eaves of the mighty rock. By this time the yellow moon, after burning her way through the gathering vapors and reddening to crimson fire at the edges, had disappeared altogether, taking with her all the stars; but the summer night still preserved a dim, dreary light in the very heart of shadows. How long the Wanderer first slept he knows not, but he awakened with a wild start, and found all the vials of heaven opening and pouring down on his devoted head. The darkness was full of a dull roar—the splashing of the heavy drops on solid stone, the moan of wind, the cry of torrents. "As a hundred hills on Morven; as the streams of a hundred hills; as clouds fly successive over heaven; or as the dark ocean assaults the shore of the desert; so roaring, so vast, so terrible, the armies mixed on Lena's echoing heath."*

* Or, as translated more literally by the Rev. Mr. Macpherson, of Inveraray:

"As a hundred winds in the oak of Morven;
As a hundred streams from the steep-sided mountain;
As clouds gathering thick and black;
As the great ocean pouring on the shore,
So broad, roaring, dark, and fierce,
Met the braves a-fire, on Lena.
The shout of the hosts on the bones of the mountains
Was a torrent in a night of storm
When bursts the clouds on gloomy Cona,
And a thousand ghosts are shrieking loud
On the viewless crooked wind of the cairns."
           OSSIAN'S POEMS. *Fingal*, book iii.

The Cuchullins were busy again at their old pastime of storm-brewing. It became expedient to draw closer under the shelter of the boulder out of the reach of the buckets of water dripping over the caves. This done, the Wanderer listened drowsily for a time to the wild sounds around him, and then, soothed by their monotony, slept again. Happy is the man who can sleep anywhere, on shipboard, in the saddle, up a tree, on the top of Ben Nevis, and under all circumstances, in all weathers. Something of this virtue had been imparted to the Wanderer by his wild life afloat; and he still carried the drowsy spell of the sea with him, mesmerizing body and mind to slumber anywhere at a moment's notice.

When he opened his eyes again, and with bodily sensations akin to those of a parboiled lobster gazed around him, it was daylight—a dim, doubtful, rainy light, but still the light of day. The corry was one mass of gray vapor, hiding everything to the utmost peaks, and a thin "smurr" of rain filled all the doubtful air above the loch. Hamish Shaw, wreathed up in the shape of the letter S, was breathing stentoriously, and to awaken him the Wanderer tickled his nose with a spike of heather; whereat he opened his eyes, smiled grimly, and at once, without a moment's hesitation, with all the quickness of instinct, delivered his criticism on the weather. "There'll be rain the day, and a breeze; the wind's awa' into the southwest." Then, without more preamble, he jumped up, rubbed his hands through his matted hair, and surveyed the scene about him.

"The sun had opened golden yellow
    From his case,
Though still the sky wore dark and drumly
    A scarred and frowning face;
Then troubled, tawny, dense, dun-bellied,
    Scowling, and sea-blue;
Every dye that's in the tartan
    O'er it grew.
Far away to the wild westward
    Grim it lowered,
Where rain-charged clouds on thick squalls wandering
    Loomed and towered."*

With a grim shake of the head, Hamish got out spirit-lamp, kitchener, etc., and proceeded to make breakfast. Meantime, the Wanderer threaded his way to the water's edge, and divesting himself of his hot, uncomfortable clothing, plunged in for a swim. A dozen strokes were enough; for the black deeps filled one with an eerie shudder, and the vapors hung cold and dreadful overhead. Dripping like a naiad, the Wanderer got into his clothes, and rushed about wildly to restore the circulation. A quarter of an hour afterward, he breakfasted royally on bread and cold meat, with a tumbler of spirits and water—in all of which he was gladly joined by the faithful Hamish. Breakfast over, the twain made their devious way down the corry, pausing ever and anon to contemplate the stormy scene behind them.

A high wind in sharp squalls was blowing mist and cloud from the sea; steadily and swiftly the vapor drifted along, with interstices dimly luminous, from the southwest; but directly they reached the unseen

* The "Birlinn." By Alastair Mac Mhaigstair Alastair.

heights, they seemed to pause altogether, and add to the motionless darkness. Below that darkness a gray reflected light—not light, but rather darkness visible— moved along the precipices of stone, save where mists streamed from the abyss, or the silver threads of cataracts flashed,

> "Motionless as ice,
> Frozen by distance."

Wild, unearthly noises, strange as the shriek of the water-kelpie, issued from the abysses. The black lake was broken into small, sharp waves, crested with foam of dazzling whiteness, contrasted with which the black furrows between seemed blacker and blacker; and over the waves here and there the gulls were screaming. The mighty rocks through which we wended diffused into the air a cold, white steam, while, smitten by the silver-glistering rain, their furrowed cheeks drip wildly; at the base of each glimmered a pool; and everywhere around them the swollen runlets leapt noisily to mingle with the mere. The corry, indeed, was silent no more; but the only sound within it was the murmur of its own weeping.

As we walked onward, looming gray in the mist, we suddenly became conscious of a figure standing at some little distance from us—the wild figure of a man clad in pilot trousers and a yellow oilskin coat, bareheaded, his matted locks hanging over his shoulders, his beard dripping with rain, his eyes with a look of frenzy glaring at us as we approached. Our first impulse was one of fear—there was something unearthly in this apparition; but we advanced rapidly, anxious to examine it more closely. To our astonishment the man, instead of inviting scrutiny, assumed a look of intense terror, and without a word of warning took to his heels. Anxious to reassure him, we followed as rapidly as possible, Hamish shouting loudly in Gaelic; but the sound of footsteps behind him and Hamish's voice, which the wind turned to a dismal moan, only made the man fly faster, never once casting a look backward, but scrambling along the perilous slopes as if all the fiends were at his heels, until the rainy mist blotted him altogether from our view. Hamish and the Wanderer looked at each other and laughed; it was rather a comical situation—man-chasing in the gorges of Corruisk.

"Who do you think he is?" said the Wanderer; "a man like ourselves, or a ghost?"

"Flesh and blood, sure enough," replied Hamish, with a sly twinkle in his eye. "I'm thinking there will be a boat o' some sort down in the harbor yonder, and this is one of the crew. Eh! but he seemed awfu' scared; nae doubt he thought us something uncanny, coming on him sae sudden in a place like this."

Wet and dripping, we reach the lower end of the loch, and after one glance backward at the corry, which seems buried in the deepest gloom of night, follow the course of the river, which runs foaming over a sheet of smooth rock into Loch Scavaig, that wonderful arm of the sea. The rocks here have the smoothed and swelling forms known as *roches moutonnées;* and, as Professor Forbes observes, "it would be quite impossible to find in the

Alps or elsewhere these phenomena (excepting only the high polish, which the rocks here do not admit of) in greater perfection than in the valley of Corruisk." The distance from the fresh-water loch to the salt water is little more than two hundred yards; and where the river joins the latter there is a dead-calm basin, enclosed seaward by promontories and islands, and perpetually sheltered from all the winds that blow. There is no snugger anchorage in the world than this. Shut in on every side by precipices that tower far above the mast, with no view but the bare loch landward or seaward, it is like a small mere, deep and green, in the hollow of the mountains. In the rocks at either side there are rings, to which any vessel at anchor in the basin may attach itself; for, though the place is sheltered from the full force of the wind, the squalls are terrifically sharp, and a warp is necessary, as there is no room to "swing."

And here, standing on the rock at the water's edge, we saw a small group of men, five in number, chief of whom was the fugitive from Corruisk. The latter, with excited gestures and flaming eyes, pointed to us as we approached, and all eyed us in grim and ominous silence. Fastened to the rock on which they stood was a skiff, one of those huge, shapeless fishing skiffs in which Highlanders delight, black and slimy with seaweed, with red nets heaped in the bottom, and a dog-fish—seemingly the only produce of a night's fishing—still gasping, with his liver cut out, in the bow. No sooner did Shaw get within earshot than he attacked the strangers with a sharp fire in Gaelic. After listening staggered for a moment, they opened on him like a pack of hounds in full cry; and it was soon apparent that the man we had met by the loch had taken us for a couple of ghosts prowling about in the dim, mysterious light of the early morning. The men were fishers from Loch Slapin, whither they were on the point of returning; and we proposed that they should row us round by the sea to Camasunary, nine miles' walk through the great glen from Sligachan Inn. A bargain being struck, we were soon dancing on the wild waters of Loch Scavaig, and taking our farewell view of the Cuchullins.

Landing at Camasunary, we plodded weary homeward, so full of wonders, so awed and abstracted with all we had seen, that we scarcely looked at the wild gorges through which we passed. The brain was quite full, and could receive no more. Tired to death, we at last reached the *Tern*, after a walk that seemed interminable. For many days after that it was impossible to recollect in detail any picture we had seen. All was confusion—darkness, rain, mist. When the vision cleared, and the perfect memory of Corruisk arose in the mind, it seemed only a vivid dream, strange and beautiful beyond all pictures seen with the waking eyes, a reminiscence from some forgotten life, a vision to be blent forever with the most secret apprehensions of the soul—sleep, death, oblivion, eternity, and the grave.

CHAPTER XVII.

EPILOGUE; THE "TERN'S" LAST FLIGHT.

IT was now growing late in the year, and we were yearning to return again to the moors of Lorne. Quitting Loch Sligachan, we ran through the Sound of Scalpa, past Broadford Bay and Pabbay Island, through the narrow passage of Kyle Akin, and so on through Kyle Rhea to Isle Ornsay, where we anchored. Page after page might be filled with the exquisite pictures seen on the way through these island channels. At Isle Ornsay we were detained for nearly a fortnight by a fearful gale of wind, and occupied the time in fishing for "cuddies" over the vessel's side, rowing about in the punt, and reading Björnson's great viking-drama in the tiny cabin. Beguiled by a treacherous peep of fine weather, we slipt out into the Sound of Sleat, intending to sail round Ardnamurchan; but the heavy sea soon compelled us to take shelter in Loch Nevis. After spending a black day at the last-named anchorage, we set sail again, and encountered a nasty wind from the southwest. The little *Tern* got as severe a buffeting on that occasion as a craft of the sort could well weather; and only by the skilled seamanship of Hamish Shaw did we manage to reach our old anchorage in Rum before the gale burst in all its fury. The weather was now thoroughly broken. We were detained several days in Loch Scresort, fearing to face the great seas of the Atlantic in passing round the Rhu. A good day came at last. We had as pleasant a sail through the open sea as could well be desired. On the night of the following day the *Tern* was at her moorings in Oban Bay, and we enjoyed, for the first time after many months, the luxury of a snug bed ashore, in the White House on the Hill.

Never had the seasons been more delightfully spent. We had enjoyed sport and adventure to the full, we had drunk into our veins the fresh sense of renewed physical life, and we had enriched the soul with a set of picturesque memories of inestimable brightness and beauty. Possibly no such novel experience could have been gained by rambling half round the civilized world in search of the beautiful. "How little do men know," we repeated, "of the wonders lying at their own thresholds!" Within two days' journey of the Great City lie these Hebrides, comparatively unknown, yet abounding in shapes of beauty and forms of life as fresh and new as those met with in the remotest islands of the Pacific. To the patient reader of our travels afloat and ashore we have only one advice to give in conclusion: "Go and do likewise; and, until you have explored the isles of the north in such a vessel as carried us so bravely and for so long, do not think that you have exhausted travel, or that Providence, even in the narrow limits of these British Islands of which you know so little, cannot supply your jaded humanity with a new sensation!"

THE END.

www.ingramcontent.com/pod-product-compliance
Lightning Source LLC
Chambersburg PA
CBHW030358230426
43664CB00007BB/652